American Musicians
Making History

American Musicians Making History

Donna B. Levene

TEACHER IDEAS PRESS
Portsmouth, NH

Teacher Ideas Press
A division of Reed Elsevier Inc.
361 Hanover Street
Portsmouth, NH 03801–3912
www.teacherideaspress.com

Offices and agents throughout the world

The author and publisher wish to thank those who have generously given permission to reprint borrowed material:

Sheet music cover of "Old Folks at Home." Written and composed by E. P. Christy. Published by Firth, Pond and Co., New York, 1851. Used by permission of Brown University Library.

Sheet music cover of "St. Louis Blues" by W. C. Handy. Published by Pace & Handy Music Co., 1918. Used by permission of Brown University Library.

Title page of *Our Singing Country: A Second Volume of American Ballads and Folk Songs*. Collected and compiled by John A. Lomax and Alan Lomax. Published by The Macmillan Company, 1941. Used by permission of The Alan Lomax Archive.

"Simple Gifts" is reprinted from *The Gift to be Simple: Songs, Dances and Rituals of the American Shakers* by Edward D. Andrew. Published by Dover Publications, 1962.

Sheet music covers of "Alexander's Ragtime Band" by Irving Berlin. New York: Ted Snyder, 1911; "Jazzin' the Cotton Town Blues." Words by Roger Lewis, Music by Harry Olsen. New York: M. Witmark & Sons, 1917; and "The Little Old Cabin in the Lane." Words and Music by Will S. Hayes. Boston: Oliver Ditons, 1871, are used by permission of the Rare Book, Manuscript, and Special Collections Library of Duke University.

Sheet music covers of " 'Get Off the Track!' A Song for Emancipation" by Jesse Hutchinson Junr. Boston: Published by the Author, 1844; and *Maple Leaf Rag*. Composed by Scott Joplin. Sedalia, MO: John Stark & Son, 1899, are used courtesy of the Lester S. Levy Collection of Sheet Music, Special Collections, Johns Hopkins University.

Library of Congress Cataloging-in-Publication Data
Levene, Donna B.
  American musicians making history / by Donna B. Levene.
    p. cm.
  ISBN 1-56308-950-5
  1. Music—United States—History and criticism. 2. Music—Instruction and study—United States. 3. Musicians—United States.
  I. Title.
  ML200 .L47 2003
  780'.71'073—dc21

2003013835

Editor: Suzanne Barchers
Production Coordinator: Angela Laughlin
Typesetter: Westchester Book Services
Cover design: Darci Mehall
Manufacturing: Steve Bernier

Printed in the United States of America on acid-free paper

08   07   06   05   04   VP   1   2   3   4   5

To my husband Barry for his calmness and perceptive suggestions and my American Memory partner, Eliza Hamrick, for her insightful advice on framing critical thinking questions.

Contents

Introduction

This is a book about American musicians making, influencing, and reflecting American history. If it had a theme song it would be Aaron Copland's *Fanfare for the Common Man*. This orchestral piece was written for the Cincinnati Symphony's 1942–43 season as one of eighteen fanfares commissioned to express patriotism for the war effort. Copland decided that since the common man was in the trenches, he deserved a fanfare. (Pollack, 2000, 360)

The common man is a consistent theme in the history of American music. Music begins with the common man, the folk, the people. Originally passed down orally from one Appalachian mother, or African-American slave, or stevedore, or cowboy, to another, American music has embodied the life and feelings of "everyman" throughout history. Folk music, spirituals, blues, and jazz began as spontaneous music of the people. In the publication of this music, American music became codified. Leonard Bernstein, the first American to lead a major American orchestra, said the following about folk songs during one of his *Young People's Concerts*, ". . . folksongs reflect the rhythms and accents and speeds of the way a particular people talks: in other words, their language—especially the language of their poetry—sort of grows into musical notes. And those speaking-rhythms and accents finally pass from folk-music into the art-music." (Bernstein, 1961)

The idea for this book came from my experience at an American Memory Fellows Institute sponsored by the Library of Congress. This weeklong workshop for pairs of social studies teachers and library media specialists focused on using the digitized primary sources in the Library of Congress American Memory collections to write American history lessons. These lessons were inquiry-based and asked students to analyze primary documents in order to form an idea about a particular aspect of American history. Along with documents, photographs, maps, and memorabilia, there are significant collections of sheet music, letters, papers, manuscripts, and sound recordings of American music. The collections of Aaron Copland, Leonard Bernstein, and Woody Guthrie alone would provide a student with a history of this music.

These sources contain fascinating information about how music fits into the story of America. Though I began with a list of musical forms and significant American musicians, my eventual choices for the book were determined by the extent of the online resources. In addition to the Library of Congress, many universities and institutions are digitizing their collections and making them available to a wider audience. The National Public Radio's site, *The NPR 100*, provided a virtual history of American music with its radio segments on the top 100 American musical compositions of the century. Their list reinforced my selections.

I tried to include relatively stable Internet sites and have cited mainly universities, archives, and organizations. Many musical pieces are available on the Internet as audio files, so I haven't listed many CDs in the resources sections. However, many earlier standards in jazz and folk music are being reissued and are readily available in CD format. There are jazz recordings that accompany the PBS series, *Jazz: A Film by Ken Burns*, and the Smithsonian has reissued many of the recordings from the pioneering Folkways label.

Although the online digitized sheet music and letters are the foundation of the lessons, in researching for details of the musicians' lives and music, I discovered that books still have more comprehensive information. The collections of the Denver Public Library, the Aurora Public Library, and the Overland High School Library Media Center, Aurora, Colorado, provided most of the print resources listed in the Research Resources of each lesson. Even though I tried to use books that were published within the last five years, I still needed to refer to the older editions that are available in the public library collections. The Internet has an array of booksellers online, both for current and out-of-print resources that are not available at local libraries. Using a combination of print and online resources, teachers and students should be able to find any of the resources listed and many more.

The lessons are divided into two parts: a teacher section that provides background information and resources to use in introducing the musician to the students, and a student section that provides questions to research, possible products that demonstrate learning, and an extensive list of resources from which to gather information. The student pages can be given to the students either in print format or as a document on a server as a starting point for inquiries.

These lessons can be used for studying music history, or for studying a period in American history through its music and musicians. Analyzing the music of a time period adds a dimension that will appeal to students who need motivation. It also adds an aural aspect that will enrich the classroom environment.

Each lesson on a musician is headed by a brief timeline of significant dates in his life. To show concurrent events in other realms of music, at least one event in another musician's life is interspersed. Since many of these musicians were active during the same period or borrowed from other periods, there is a section in each lesson that shows the connections between them.

In the chapters on musicians the Internet resources are divided into three sections: Biographical, Historical, and Musical. These divisions focus the student investigations and provide a natural breakdown for group projects. They also encourage collaboration between social studies teachers, music teachers, and library media specialists. The projects are varied to allow for diverse student interests and abilities.

Since standards vary from state to state, they are not listed for each lesson. However, the national Information Literacy Standards for Student Learning published by the American Association of School Librarians detail the process of searching for resources to answer a question. These standards are available at the AASL's web site: http://www.ala.org/aasl/ip_nine.html. McREL, or the Mid-continent Research for Education and Learning, lists standards at its web site: http://www.mcrel.org/standardsbenchmarks/index.asp. Music Standard 7 relates to all of the lessons: "Understands the relationship between music and history and culture." The United States history standards can be met by studying each era through its music.

The musicians in this book were not creating in a vacuum. Though the composing or performing of music was their prime motivation, their creative expressions were influenced by their precursors, the events taking place around them, and the responses and desires of their audiences. Yet, the music spoke to the heart and has endured as both a mirror of its times and of all times. Woody Guthrie summed up the purpose of a song in a 1941 letter to Pete Seeger, Millard Lampell, and Lee Hays, the members of the Almanac Singers:

> *Our job aint so much to go way back into history . . . Our job is the Here & Now. Today.*
> *This week. This month. This year. But we've got to try and include a Timeless Element in*
> *our songs. Something that will not tomorrow be gone with the wind. But something that*
> *tomorrow will be as true as it is today. (Guthrie, 1990, 55)*

Though the purpose of this book is to explore the past and music's impact on the history of the United States, an aspect of this search is the music itself. Hopefully students will discover the joy that went into composing and performing this music and will appreciate the musical heritage we all have in common.

SOURCES

Bernstein, Leonard. "Young People's Concerts Scripts: Folk Music in the Concert Hall, April 9, 1961." *The Leonard Bernstein Collection, ca. 1920–1989.*
URL: http://memory.loc.gov/ammem/lbhtml/lbhome.html

Guthrie, Woody. *Pastures of Plenty: A Self-Portrait.* Edited by Dave Marsh and Harold Leventhal. New York: HarperCollins, 1990.

Pollack, Howard. *Aaron Copland: The Life and Work of an Uncommom Man.* Urbana: Univ. of Illinois Press, 2000.

American Musicians
Making History

MINSTREL SONGS AND PARLOR SONGS

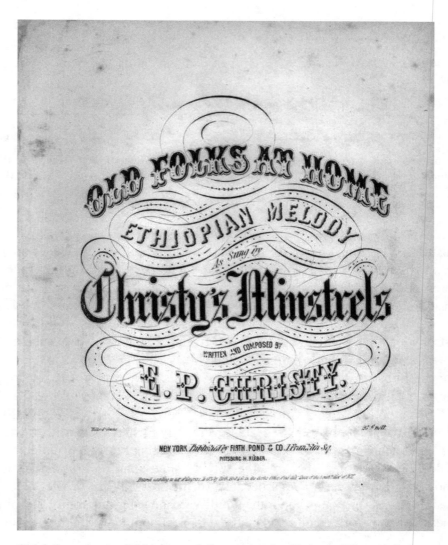

Old folks at home: Ethiopian melody as sung by Christy's Minstrels/written and composed by E. P. Christy. Originally published: New York: Firth, Pond & Co., c1851. *African-American Sheet Music, 1850–1920 (from Brown University).* http://memory.loc.gov/ammem/award97/rpbhtml/aasmhome.html

Chapter I
Stephen C. Foster, 1826–1864
Songwriter

1847	1852	1853	1878
Premier of "Oh! Susanna"	*Uncle Tom's Cabin* published	"My Old Kentucky Home" published	James A. Bland published "Carry Me Back to Old Virginny"

Stephen Foster first became known for his "Ethiopian" melodies that were popularized in the minstrel shows, which began with white entertainers who performed in blackface. Their songs and skits expressed the white performers' views of African-Americans and life on the plantation. In addition to their inherent racism, the songs often depicted African-Americans in a condescending way. Sales of "Oh! Susanna," "Camptown Races," and "Old Folks at Home," Foster's minstrel songs, far exceeded the revenue from his "parlor songs" such as "Jeanie with the Light Brown Hair" and "Gentle Annie." (Emerson, 1998, 174)

To promote the minstrel songs, Foster gave the rights of first performance to the Christy's Minstrels, one of the most popular minstrel shows of the time. He even allowed E. P. Christy to publish "Old Folks at Home" under Christy's name. (Crawford, 2001, 213) Initially Foster tried to distance himself from his minstrel songs, but eventually Foster wrote minstrel songs that portrayed African-Americans in a more sympathetic way and that didn't use dialect.

Though "Old Folks at Home" became the official state song of Florida, some performing groups will not program Foster's songs because of the racist lyrics. Foster also wrote parlor songs of love and separation, songs about the Civil War, and religious songs. Despite the "political incorrectness" of some of Foster's songs, they are still popular in the twenty-first century.

OBJECTIVES

Students will examine Stephen Foster's lyrics to determine the values of the culture of his time.

Students will examine Stephen Foster's songs to determine the views white people had about African-Americans during this time period.

Students will compare the racial messages of the songs of the mid- and late-nineteenth century with the literature of the same period.

Students will examine the musical elements of Foster's songs to explain their longevity in popularity.

INTRODUCING THE MUSICIAN

Sheet Music

Use the following web site to introduce students to the variety of musical styles of Stephen Foster. Using the analysis guide in Appendix A, have students compare the styles and relate them to the social norms of the time period.

> "Gallery: The Music of Stephen Foster." *Stephen Foster: American Experience.*
>   URL: http://www.pbs.org/wgbh/amex/foster/gallery/index.html

Quotations

- Singer Thomas Hampson on Foster's music:
  With his spontaneous eclecticism and unabashed heart-on-sleeve naiveté and romanticism, Stephen Collins Foster came to be the standard bearer of what poet Walt Whitman called heart singing—of the kind of music-making in which word elevates music and music buoys up the spirit. His poems are the narrations of an American dreamer, his melodies the voices of the heart. (Hampson)

- Writer and abolitionist Frederick Douglass on Foster's songs (told to Rochester (New York) Ladies' Anti-Slavery Society in 1855):
  It would seem almost absurd to say it, considering the use that has been made of them, that we have allies in the Ethiopian songs... "Lucy Neal," "Old Kentucky Home," and "Uncle Ned," can make the heart sad as well as merry, and can call forth a tear as well as a smile. They awaken the sympathies for the slave, in which anti-slavery principles take root and flourish. (Emerson, 1998, 107)

- Article in *Musical World*, January 29, 1853:
  Mr. Foster possesses more than ordinary abilities as a composer; and we hope he will soon realize enough from his Ethiopian melodies to enable him to afford to drop them and turn his attention to the production of a higher kind of music. Much of his music is now excellent, but being wedded to negro idioms it is, of course, discarded by many who would otherwise gladly welcome it to their pianos. We were glad to learn from Mr. F. that he intends to devote himself principally hereafter to the production of "White men's" music. (Emerson, 1998, 206)

- Stephen Foster on minstrel songs in letter to E. P. Christy, May 25, 1852:
  As I once intimated to you, I had the intention of omitting my name on my Ethiopian songs, owing to the prejudice against them by some, which might injure my reputation as a writer of another style of music, but I find that by my efforts I have done a great deal to build up a taste for the Ethiopian songs among refined people by making the words suitable to their taste, instead of the trashy and really offensive words which belong to some songs of that order. (Emerson, 1998, 183)

Connections to Other Musicians in This Book

- **Charles Ives** at his father's instigation would sing "Old Folks at Home" in one key while his father accompanied in another key. (Crawford, 2001, 503)

- **Ives** quoted Foster's "Old Folks at Home (Way Down Upon the Swanee River)" in his piece *Washington's Birthday*. (See Chapter 21)

- **Irving Berlin's** song "Alexander's Ragtime Band" asked "Do you want to hear 'The Swanee River' played in ragtime?" and used the same melodic phrase that Foster used in "Old Folks at Home."

- Foster wrote **Civil War songs**, including "We Are Coming, Father Abraam 300,000 More."

- **George Gershwin's** first hit was "Swanee." (Crawford, 2001, 573)

- Foster allowed E. P. Christy of **Christy's Minstrels** to claim authorship of "Old Folks at Home" in order to promote the song. (Crawford, 2001, 213)

- **Aaron Copland** used a melody from Foster's "Camptown Races" in his *Lincoln Portrait*. (Crawford, 2001, 594)

Periods in American History
Gold Rush, Antebellum, Civil War

Musical Highlights of Foster's Life: Teachers, Colleagues, Events

1826	Born in Lawrenceville, Pennsylvania
1846	Published "There's a Good Time Coming"
1847	"Oh! Susanna" premiered at Eagle Ice Cream Saloon
1848	"Old Uncle Ned" copyrighted
1849	Contracted with the New York music publishing company Firth, Pond, & Co. "Nelly Was a Lady" copyrighted
1850	"Nelly Bly" and "Gwine to Run All Night, or De Camptown Races" copyrighted
1851	Became collaborator with E. P. Christy of Christy's Minstrels "Old Folks at Home" published with Christy listed as composer
1852	Harriet Beecher Stowe publishes *Uncle Tom's Cabin* "Massa's in de Cold Ground" copyrighted
1853	"My Old Kentucky Home, Good Night" copyrighted
1854	"Jeanie with the Light Brown Hair" copyrighted Published *The Social Orchestra*, arrangements of popular, operatic, and classical pieces for a variety of instruments
1855	"Hard Times Come Again No More" and "Come Where My Love Lies Dreaming" copyrighted
1856	"Gentle Annie" copyrighted
1860	"The Glendy Burk" and "Old Black Joe" copyrighted
1862	Wrote song to poem "We Are Coming, Father Abraam 300,000 More" "That's What's the Matter" copyrighted
1864	Died in New York City "Beautiful Dreamer" copyrighted
1929	"My Old Kentucky Home" became the official state song of Kentucky
1935	"Old Folks at Home" became the official state song of Florida

Foster Student Pages

Inquiries

- How does Foster portray African-Americans in his lyrics?
- How do the sheet music covers of his minstrel songs depict African-Americans?
- What was the relationship between Foster and the Christy's Minstrels?
- What message does "Old Folks at Home" convey? What are the feelings of the singer? Do the lyrics provoke sympathy for African-Americans?
- How did Foster's songs change through time in their depictions of African-Americans?
- What is the historical significance of Foster's "Nelly Was a Lady"?
- What were Mark Twain's views of minstrelsy and the role of African-Americans?
- How did Harriet Beecher Stowe's book *Uncle Tom's Cabin* affect the songs of the period?
- What was Harriet Beecher Stowe's view of minstrelsy?
- On what did Foster base his song "My Old Kentucky Home, Good Night?"
- What was life like for a popular music composer of the mid 1800s? How were songs copyrighted, published, and promoted?
- What is a "parlor song," and who bought this music?
- What can the parlor songs tell us about the popular culture of the time?
- How did Foster's songs change as the Civil War began?
- Which poets influenced Foster's lyrics?

Products

- Compare Foster's early minstrel songs with the later ones. Analyze the lyrics and relate the intent of the composer. Compare the messages and whether they changed over time.
- Demonstrate representative examples of Foster's various types of songs in a multimedia presentation.
- Use examples of Foster's minstrel songs and his parlor songs to portray the sentiments of the people of his time.
- Examine Foster's Civil War songs and describe what they tell us about the war.
- Compare Foster's minstrel songs with the literature of the day, specifically that of Harriet Beecher Stowe and Mark Twain.

- Present the history of Foster's song "My Old Kentucky Home, Good Night," including its connection to Harriet Beecher Stowe's *Uncle Tom's Cabin*.

- Present the history of Foster's song "Nelly Bly." Discuss the origin of the name, the meaning of some of the lyrics, and the later use of the name "Nelly Bly" by a journalist.

- Present the history of the song "Oh! Susanna." Include its role in the Gold Rush.

- Describe the sheet music publishing practices in Foster's time, using his music as examples.

- Compare some of Foster's lyrics to poetry of the same period.

RESEARCH RESOURCES

Web Sites
Biographical:

"Lawrenceville: Life and Works of Stephen C. Foster." *Pittsburgh Bulletin*, 9 March 1896. *Carnegie Library of Pittsburgh.*
   URL: http://www.clpgh.org/exhibit/neighborhoods/lawrenceville/law_n103.html

This article advertises the book about Stephen Foster by his brother Morrison and presents biographical information about Foster from the book.

Root, Dr. Deane. "People & Events: Stephen Collins Foster, 1826–1864." *American Experience: Stephen Foster.*
   URL: http://www.pbs.org/wgbh/amex/foster/peopleevents/p_sfoster.html

Root debunks some of the myths about Foster and examines his role as a songwriter in the days prior to the Civil War.

"Stephen Collins Foster: Biographical Sketch." *Center for American Music, Stephen Foster Pages.*
   URL: http://www.pitt.edu/~amerimus/foster.htm

An extensive biography that describes Foster's personal and professional life. The article includes links to information on "Old Folks at Home" and alphabetical and chronological lists of Foster's songs.

"Stephen Foster Chronology." *Center for American Music, Stephen Foster Pages, University of Pittsburgh.*
   URL: http://www.pitt.edu/~amerimus/time.htm

"This chronology has been adapted from John Tasker Howard's biography, Stephen Foster America's Troubadour."

"Timeline." *American Experience: Stephen Foster.*
   URL: http://www.pbs.org/wgbh/amex/foster/timeline/index.html

This extensive timeline of Foster's life includes important historical events.

Historical:

"Blackface Minstrelsy." *American Experience: Stephen Foster.*
   URL: http://www.pbs.org/wgbh/amex/foster/sfeature/sf_minstrelsy.html

Excerpts of interviews with historians answer questions about minstrelsy such as,

- "How were minstrel shows racist?"

- "Although blackface minstrelsy was racist, did it have any benefit for African Americans?"

- "What's the connection between blackface minstrelsy and rock and roll?"

Foster, Stephen C. "That's What's the Matter." New York: Charles Magnus [186–] *An American Time Capsule: Three Centuries of Broadsides and Other Printed Ephemera.*
URL: http://memory.loc.gov/ammem/rbpehtml/pehome.html

This broadside contains the words to Foster's Civil War song, "That's What's the Matter." Search by author or title.

"People and Events." *American Experience: Stephen Foster.*
URL: http://www.pbs.org/wgbh/amex/foster/peopleevents/index.html

Among thirteen articles are included articles on the minstrels, Christy and Emmett, the poet Thomas Moore, Harriet Beecher Stowe's Uncle Tom's Cabin, *and African-American music.*

"Teacher's Guide: Suggestions for Active Learning." *American Experience: Stephen Foster.*
URL: http://www.pbs.org/wgbh/amex/foster/tguide/index.html

Includes activities with thought-provoking questions relating to the period of Foster's life in the categories of history, economics, geography, and civics.

Musical:

"American Memory Collections: All Collections." *American Memory: Historical Collections for the National Digital Library.*
URL: http://memory.loc.gov/ammem/mdbquery.html

Search for songs by Stephen Foster with the keywords foster stephen collins *(match this exact phrase).*

Berlin, Irving. "On Stephen Foster." *Today's Speeches, TheHistoryChannel.com.*
URL: www.historychannel.com/speeches/archive/speech_18.html

This page includes a paragraph about Stephen Foster and an audio file of Berlin talking about Foster's songs.

"Chronological List of the Works." *Center for American Music, Stephen Foster Pages, University of Pittsburgh.*
URL: http://www.pitt.edu/~amerimus/chrono.htm

In this chronological list of Stephen Foster's songs each song is linked to a copy of the lyrics.

"Foster the Songwriter." *American Experience: Stephen Foster.*
URL: http://www.pbs.org/wgbh/amex/foster/sfeature/sf_foster.html

As a Flash plug-in or text-only, this site provides examples of the progression of Foster's songs.

"Gallery: The Music of Stephen Foster." *American Experience: Stephen Foster.*
URL: http://www.pbs.org/wgbh/amex/foster/gallery/index.html

Links to the sheet music and audio clips of seven of Foster's songs.

Hampson, Thomas. "Stephen Collins Foster, 1826–1864." *I Hear America Singing.*
URL: http://www.wnet.org/ihas/composer/foster.html

Hampson describes the variety of songs that Foster composed and the poets that influenced him, as well as the musicians who were influenced by Foster. "Jeanie with the Light Brown Hair" and "Beautiful Dreamer" are available as audio files.

"The Learning Page: Collection Connections: Arts and Humanities." *America Singing: Nineteenth-Century Song Sheets.*
URL: http://memory.loc.gov/ammem/ndlpedu/collections/amsing/langarts.html

The section on Stephen Foster provides questions for analyzing Foster's lyrics for literary devices and for surmising his role in reflecting popular culture.

The Lester S. Levy Collection of Sheet Music.
URL: http://levysheetmusic.mse.jhu.edu/advancedsearch.html

To find Foster's Civil War songs search for foster *with the author tag, and* civil war *with the subject tag. Search individual titles using the title tag.*

"Minstrels and Musicals: Hard Times." *Lift Every Voice: Music in American Life. University of Virginia Library.*
　　URL: http://www.lib.virginia.edu/speccol/exhibits/music/minstrels.html

A brief history of minstrelsy with examples of Daniel Decatur Emmett's sheet music and Stephen Foster's sheet music.

"The Old Folks at Home." *Center for American Music, Stephen Foster Pages.*
　　URL: http://www.pitt.edu/~amerimus/ofah.htm

This page provides the history of the song and reactions to it throughout history.

"Transcript." *American Experience: Stephen Foster.*
　　URL: http://www.pbs.org/wgbh/amex/foster/filmmore/pt.html

This transcript of the American Experience PBS show on Stephen Foster contains discussions of Foster's music by historians and musicologists.

"Timeline: 1850–1859." *Historic American Sheet Music, Rare Book, Manuscript, and Special Collections Library, Duke University.*
　　URL: http://scriptorium.lib.duke.edu/sheetmusic/timeline-1850.html

In addition to topical events of the decade 1850–1859, eight sheet music songs are shown including "Old Folks at Home" and "My Old Kentucky Home, Good Night."

Books

Crawford, Richard. "Songs of the Minstrel Show." In *America's Musical Life: A History.* New York: W. W. Norton, 2001.

Crawford discusses Foster's minstrel songs and his relationship with Christy's Minstrels.

Emerson, Ken. *Doo-dah! Stephen Foster and the Rise of American Popular Culture.* New York: Da Capo Press, 1998.

Emerson examines the various types of songs that Foster wrote during his lifetime and examines them in the context of the popular culture of the time.

Foster, Stephen. *Stephen Foster Song Book: Original Sheet Music of 40 Songs.* Selected, with Introduction and Notes, by Richard Jackson. New York: Dover Publications, 1974.

These reproductions of the songs include the original covers. "Notes on the Music" at the end of the book provides publishing information and explanations of the subject matter.

Root, Deane L. "Foster, Stephen C(ollins)" In Vol. 9 of *The New Grove Dictionary of Music and Musicians.* 2nd ed. Edited by Stanley Sadie. London: Macmillan Publishers; New York: Grove's Dictionaries, 2001.

This extensive biographical article includes a section titled "Reputation and Influence," which describes the changes in acceptance of Foster's music through the years.

CDs

Foster, Stephen. *American Dreamer: Songs of Stephen Foster.* Thomas Hampson, Jay Ungar, Molly Mason, David Alpher, and others. Angel Classics. 1992.

Includes twenty-two songs by Foster, including "Jeanie with the Light Brown Hair," "Beautiful Dreamer," and a "Foster Favorites Medley."

Mark Twain's America. Various artists. Decca, Universal Classics Group. 2002. 289 470 513-2.

Includes Foster's songs "Beautiful Dreamer" and "Jeanie with the Light Brown Hair."

Songs of the Civil War and Stephen Foster Favorites. The Mormon Tabernacle Choir. Richard P. Condie, Director & Conductor. Sony Masterworks. 1992. MDK 48297.

Includes nine songs by Stephen Foster.

Chapter 2
Minstrelsy, 1830s–1890s

1848	1861	1871	1878
Foster's "Oh Susanna" is hit in Christy's Minstrel Show	Civil War begins	Fisk Jubilee Singers begin first singing tour	James A. Bland publishes "Carry Me Back to Old Virginny"

Minstrel shows were the most popular form of entertainment in the middle and late nineteenth century, both in the North and the South. (Southern, 1997, 92) Before the Civil War the performers were white musicians and comics in blackface. These performances portrayed African-Americans as ignorant and lazy, and included an idealized plantation scene. After the Civil War African-American entertainers were allowed to perform in minstrel troupes and even formed their own troupes. However, their performances were also in blackface, and to please the audiences they continued using the songs and routines that promoted derogatory images of African-Americans. Today, the most well-known composers of minstrel songs from that period are Stephen Foster and James A. Bland.

The plantations were left behind as "coon songs" of vaudeville became popular in the 1880s. These songs, often written by African-Americans, made fun of urban African-Americans. As Jasen states, "The minstrel songs strut; coon songs swagger." (Jasen, 1998, 23) Eventually African-Americans who began in minstrelsy started writing and producing musical shows for vaudeville and on Broadway. Many of these musicians were classically trained, and musical theater was their only avenue for success in the music field. Well-known African-American writers teamed with musicians to compose musical theater with African-American casts and themes.

OBJECTIVES

Students will examine the political and social climate to determine the reasons for the popularity of the minstrel show.

Students will understand the role of the African-American performer and songwriter in minstrel shows.

Students will trace the history of African-American songwriters and lyricists from the minstrel show to musical theater.

Students will understand the musical antecedents of the minstrel show songs and their successors.

INTRODUCING THE MUSICIANS

Video

> *I'll Make Me a World. A Century of African American Arts: Hour 1: Lift Every Voice (1900–1924).* PBS Video. 1999.
> *For information on the series and suggestions for use in the classroom go to the PBS web site: http://www.pbs.org/immaw/suggestedactivities.htm#Hour1. This episode includes footage of Bert Williams, the minstrel and vaudeville star who became the first African-American to perform in the Ziegfeld Follies. Historians discuss Williams's role as an African-American performing in blackface.*

Bert Williams began his career selling elixirs and performing in minstrel shows. He teamed up with George Walker and eventually they were booked into Koster & Bial's vaudeville house in New York City. They were known for their comedy version of the cakewalk, a stylized, strutting dance that, in its original form, was performed by plantation slaves in a contest in which the prize was a cake. Despite Williams's success, he always performed in blackface. He was well-regarded by other comedians of the day, including Eddie Cantor. This video can be used to introduce an African-American performer and musician who exemplified the dubious progress of the minstrel performers.

Sheet Music

Introduce the minstrel show by showing some of the sheet music covers. The following song describes some of the elements of the minstrel show:

> Leighton Bros., and Ren Shields. "I Want To See a Minstrel Show." M. Witmark & Sons, 1913.
> *Historic American Sheet Music, 1850–1920.*
> URL: http://scriptorium.lib.duke.edu/sheetmusic/a/a88/a8868/

Quotations

- Excerpt from poem "We Wear the Mask" by Paul Laurence Dunbar:
  We wear the mask that grins and lies,
  It hides our cheeks and shades our eyes—
  This debt we pay to human guile;
  With torn and bleeding hearts we smile,
  And mouth with myriad subtleties.
  > "We Wear the Mask." In *Lyrics of Lowly Life. Paul Laurence Dunbar Digital Text Collection: Poetry Index.*
  > URL: http://www.libraries.wright.edu/dunbar/poetry_index.html. Click on *W* and then on *Lyrics of Lowly Life.*

- W. C. Handy on minstrel shows:
  The minstrel show at that time was one of the greatest outlets for talented musicians and artists. Some of them were paying for education of brothers and sisters, some taking care

of aged parents, others supporting their own families, but all contributing to a greater degree of happiness in the entertainment world. (Handy, 1969, 62)

- Author David Jasen on "coon songs":
  The aspiring African-American songwriters of the coon song era were faced with essentially the same proposition as those of the Reconstruction era: They had to sell what people were buying . . . Some black writers and singers transcended the coon song, some subverted it, a few specialized in it. But the verbal slumming of the coon song was Square One, the point of professional departure, for them all. It embodied a set of perceptions that they all had to deal with because they were the same color as the cartoons on the sheet music. (Jasen, 1998, 25)

- Mark Twain comparing minstrels to the Fisk Jubilee Singers:
  The so-called "Negro minstrels" simply misrepresent the thing; I do not think they ever saw a plantation or ever heard a slave sing. I was reared in the South, and my father owned slaves, and I do not know when anything has so moved me as did the plaintive melodies of the Jubilee Singers. (Ward, 2000, 164–165)

- Composer Will Marion Cook in an article in *Theatre Arts*, Sept. 1947, on the opening of his musical revue, *Clorindy, or The Origin of the Cakewalk* in 1898:
  Negroes were at last on Broadway, and there to stay. Gone was the uff-dah of the minstrel! Gone the Massa Linkum stuff! We were artists and we were going a long, long way. (Southern, 1997, 304)

Connections to Other Musicians in This Book

- **Stephen Foster** wrote songs for Christy's Minstrels. (See Chapter 1)

- **W. C. Handy** was a member of Mahara's Minstrels. (Jasen, 1998, 228)

- Minstrel composer James A. Bland adapted the **Fisk Jubilee Singers** spiritual "What Kind of Shoes Are You Going to Wear?" in his popular song, "Oh, Dem Golden Slippers." (See Chapter 5)

- A lithograph of Williams and Walker and two women doing the cakewalk was on the cover of **Scott Joplin's** *Maple Leaf Rag.* (Jasen, 1998, 44)

- **Duke Ellington** cited Will Marion Cook as a mentor. (See Chapter 12)

Periods in American History

Antebellum, Civil War, Reconstruction, 1890s, Early Twentieth Century

Musical Highlights of Minstrels' Lives: Teachers, Colleagues, Events

1828	Thomas Dartmouth "Daddy" Rice introduced the "Jim Crow" character
1843	Virginia Minstrels formed as first minstrel company
1848	"Oh! Susanna" by Stephen Foster became a hit in Christy's Minstrels show
1851	Stephen Foster's "Old Folks at Home" published with E. P. Christy as composer
1852	*Uncle Tom's Cabin* by Harriet Beecher Stowe published
1865	Georgia Minstrels formed, becoming the first black minstrel troupe
1878	James A. Bland published "Carry Me Back to Old Virginny"

1879   Bland's "Oh, Dem Golden Slippers" became favorite tune for the minstrel show walkaround

1880   Bland published "In the Evening by the Moonlight"

1893   World's Columbian Exposition in Chicago

1896   Ernest Hogan published his "All Coons Look Alike to Me," the first song to include a "Negro 'rag' Accompaniment."

1896   Williams and Walker started their comedy version of the cakewalk

1896   American Tobacco Company produced a series of eight trading cards with photographs of Williams and Walker and two actresses doing the cakewalk to advertise Old Virginia Cheroots cigars

1898   Premiere of the musical revue *Clorindy, or The Origin of the Cakewalk*, with music by Will Marion Cook and lyrics by Paul Laurence Dunbar, on Broadway

1906   The musical *The Shoo-Fly Regiment* by Bob Cole, J. Rosamond Johnson, and James Weldon Johnson opened on Broadway

MINSTRELSY STUDENT PAGES

Inquiries

- How did minstrel shows depict African-Americans?

- What is the history of the minstrel character "Jim Crow"? Why was the term later applied to laws?

- What is the format of the minstrel show? Why was this format used?

- Why were minstrel shows so popular?

- Why did African-Americans perform in and produce minstrel shows that depicted African-Americans in a derogatory manner?

- Were there differences in the songs composed by African-American composers and white composers? If so, what were they?

- Where were minstrel shows performed and why?

- What political views were presented in the minstrel shows? Why were minstrel shows used as vehicles for political views?

- What is the origin of the cakewalk, and how was it used in minstrel shows?

- What instruments were used in the minstrel shows and why?

- Were the minstrel songs based on actual "plantation songs"?

- Were there negative reactions to the minstrel songs? If so, from whom?

- When were "coon songs" sung, and how were they different from earlier minstrel songs?

- How were minstrel shows depicted in the literature of the time?

- Why did the poet Paul Laurence Dunbar write poems in dialect? What was the reaction of African-Americans at the time, and what is the reaction now?

- How did songs and shows written and produced by African-Americans change as the musicians changed from minstrelsy, to vaudeville, to musical theater? What accounts for this change?

Products

- Examine the lyrics of several minstrel songs and determine what message they contain about life for African-Americans of the period. Compare those written by African-Americans with those written by whites.

- Analyze the poem "We Wear the Mask" by Paul Laurence Dunbar, poet and song lyric writer, and relate it to minstrelsy.

- Compare the sheet music covers of minstrel songs with those of spirituals of the same period. Explain the reasons for the differences. Include a comparison of James A. Bland's "Oh, Dem Golden Slippers" with the Fisk Jubilee Singers' "What Kind of Shoes Are You Going to Wear?".

- Describe the various theories of prominent African-Americans, such as W. E. B. Dubois and Booker T. Washington, concerning the best way for the African-American people to succeed in the majority white society. Relate these opinions to the role of African-American musicians in minstrel shows.

- Investigate the lives of the poet/lyricist Paul Laurence Dunbar, composers Will Marion Cook and J. Rosamond Johnson, and librettist James Weldon Johnson to determine their perspective of their roles as artistic leaders of their race.

- Produce a timeline of the period containing examples of minstrel show music and explain the changes in the songs. Correlate the music with events in African-American history and speculate about the connections.

- Explain which musical instruments were used in the shows and their relation to the instruments used on the plantation.

- Examine the political aspects of the minstrel show. Present sheet music that has a political message and relate it to the views of the times.

- Explain the role the minstrel show had in the evolution of African-American performers in American musical history.

- Investigate the influence of minstrelsy on Mark Twain's writing.

- Analyze the songs written by African-Americans in minstrelsy, vaudeville, and musical theater and compare the lyrics and themes. Demonstrate the changes in the sophistication of the product and the attitude of the musicians. Speculate about the reasons for these changes.

RESEARCH RESOURCES

Web Sites
Biographical:

"Bert Williams (1874–1922); George Walker (1873–1911); and Aida Overton Walker (1870–1914) vaudeville actors, c. 1908." *Harlem 1900 to 1940: The Schomburg Center for Research in Black Culture Exhibition.*
URL: http://www.si.umich.edu/CHICO/Harlem/text/williams_walker.html

A brief history of the Williams and Walker vaudeville team.

Kranz, Rachel C. "James Bland (b. 1854–d. 1911)" *Wilberforce University: Biographies.*
URL: http://www.wilberforce.edu/library/archives/history/biographies/bland.htm

This brief biography discusses Bland's songs and his involvement with the Georgia Minstrels.

"Negro Songwriters of America, *African Methodist Episcopal Church Review, Vol. 15, Num. 3, 1/1899.*" *The African-American Experience in Ohio, 1850–1920.*
URL: http://dbs.ohiohistory.org/africanam/det.cfm?ID=2449

A review of an article in the Boston Evening Transcript *by John Edward Bruce, a New York State Commissioner to the Tennessee Centennial Exposition, outlining the reasons for the Negro as "the coming musician of the United States."*

"Paul Laurence Dunbar Website." *University of Dayton.*
   URL: http://www.udayton.edu/~dunbar/

The web site includes a biography of Dunbar, links to some of his poems read by Herbert Woodward Martin, a description of the opera written by Martin with Dunbar's poems as the libretto, and pictures of both Dunbar and Martin.

"Stephen Collins Foster: Biographical sketch." *Center for American Music, Stephen Foster Pages.*
   URL: http://www.pitt.edu/~amerimus/foster.htm

An extensive biography that describes Foster's personal and professional life. The article includes links to information on "Old Folks at Home" and alphabetical and chronological lists of Foster's songs.

Historical:

"Bitter Times." *Remembering Jim Crow. Minnesota Public Radio. American RadioWorks.*
   URL: http://www.americanradioworks.org/features/remembering/bitter.html

Site includes two audio links about the history of the term "Jim Crow": "Who Was Jim Crow" by Leon Litwack and "Song: Jump Jim Crow" by Bob Ekstrand.

"Blackface Minstrelsy." *American Experience: Stephen Foster.*
   URL: http://www.pbs.org/wgbh/amex/foster/sfeature/sf_minstrelsy.html

Excerpts of interviews with historians answering questions about minstrelsy such as,

- "How were minstrel shows racist?"
- "Although blackface minstrelsy was racist, did it have any benefit for African Americans?"
- "What's the connection between blackface minstrelsy and rock and roll?"

"The Development of an African-American Musical Theatre 1865–1910." *African-American Sheet Music, 1850–1920; Selected from the collections of Brown University*
   URL: http://memory.loc.gov/ammem/award97/rpbhtml/aasmsprs1.html

Includes the following timeline links with historical information and sheet music:

1865–1880: Dan Lewis, Sam Lucas, and the Hyers Sisters

1880–1890: James A. Bland

1890–1900: Vaudeville and musical theater, including *Clorindy, or The Origin of the Cakewalk* by Will Marion Cook and Paul Laurence Dunbar

1900–1910: Musicals including *In Dahomey*

"Ethnic Groups and Popular Songs." *Music for the Nation.*
   URL: http://memory.loc.gov/ammem/smhtml/smessay4.html

A brief description of minstrel songs with links to composers and songs. Includes James A. Bland's "Oh, Dem Golden Slippers."

Hampson, Thomas. "Daniel Decatur Emmett & the American Minstrel (1815–1904)." *I Hear America Singing.*
   URL: http://www.pbs.org/wnet/ihas/icon/emmet.html

A brief description of the history of the minstrel show, and the role of composer and performer Dan Emmett.

"Jim Crow." *Africans in America: Brotherly Love.*
   URL: http://www.pbs.org/wgbh/aia/part3/3h489.html

A brief history of the evolution of the Jim Crow character.

"The Learning Page: Collection Connections: U.S. History." *"We'll Sing to Abe Our Song": Sheet*

Music about Lincoln, Emancipation, and the Civil War, from the Alfred Whital Stern Collection of Lincolniana.
URL: http://memory.loc.gov/ammem/ndlpedu/collections/lincoln/history.html

With links to minstrel songs, this historical connection lesson points out the political views represented in minstrel songs.

"Minstrel Music." *Charles H. Templeton Sheet Music Collection, Mississippi State University Libraries.*
URL: http://library.msstate.edu/ragtime/minstrelmusic/minstrelmusic.html

This article provides background on the history of minstrel music and the use of the banjo in its performance. It lists songs from the period that are still popular today and the influences in today's music. Includes twenty-four PDF versions of sheet music from the time period.

"Minstrels and Musicals: Hard Times." *Lift Every Voice: Music in American Life. University of Virginia Library.*
URL: http://www.lib.virginia.edu/speccol/exhibits/music/minstrels.html

A brief history of minstrelsy with examples of Daniel Decatur Emmett's sheet music and Stephen Foster's sheet music.

"Minstrels Degrade Negros [sic]. *Cleveland Gazette*, 02/19/1887." *The African-American Experience in Ohio, 1850–1920.*
URL: http://dbs.ohiohistory.org/africanam/det.cfm?ID=15255

An 1887 article denouncing minstrelsy for its effect on the image of the "Negro."

"Minstrels in London. *Cleveland Gazette*, 07/26/1884." *The African-American Experience in Ohio, 1850–1920.*
URL: http://dbs.ohiohistory.org/africanam/det.cfm?ID=14284

Describes the London reception of an American minstrel troupe and recounts the fortunes of the performers, including James Bland, who stayed in London after their last appearance.

Railton, Stephen. "Blackface Minstrelsy." *Mark Twain in His Times.*
URL: http://etext.lib.virginia.edu/railton/huckfinn/minstrl.html

Railton contends that some of the dialogue between Huck and Jim are based on the minstrel show dialogues between Mr. Interlocutor and Mr. Bones.

Walton, Lester A. "The Negro on the American Stage. *African Methodist Episcopal Church Review, Vol. 29, Num. 3, 1/1913.*" *The African-American Experience in Ohio, 1850–1920.*
URL: http://dbs.ohiohistory.org/africanam/page.cfm?ID=2361

The author discusses the history of African-Americans on the stage from the Jim Crow minstrelsy to Bert Williams's success in Ziegfeld's Follies of 1912.

Musical:

"About the Collection." *African-American Sheet Music, 1850–1920; Selected from the Collections of Brown University.*
URL: http://memory.loc.gov/ammem/award97/rpbhtml/aasmabout.html

These pages provide an overview of the songs in the collection.

"American Memory Collections: All Collections." *American Memory, Historical Collections for the National Digital Library.*
URL: http://memory.loc.gov/ammem/mdbquery.html

Search for composer's or singer's names (match this exact phrase). For example: bland james a; williams bert; foster stephen collins

"Foster the Songwriter." *American Experience: Stephen Foster.*
URL: http://www.pbs.org/wgbh/amex/foster/sfeature/sf_foster.html

Provides examples of the progression of Foster's songs, including some audio clips.

"Minstrel Music." *Charles H. Templeton Sheet Music Collection: Mississippi State University Libraries.*
     URL: http://library.msstate.edu/ragtime/minstrelmusic/minstrelmusic.html
     Includes twenty-four songs in PDF format.

Reublin, Richard A. and Robert L. Main. " 'Coon Songs': Minstrelsy, Racism and American Song." *Parlor Songs: Popular Sheet Music from the 1800s to the 1920s.*
     URL: http://www.parlorsongs.net/insearch/coonsongs/coonsongs.asp

     A detailed description of the origins and content of the "coon song," including MIDI files.

University of Colorado Digital Sheet Music Collection.
     URL: http://www-libraries.colorado.edu/mus/smp/index.html

     Digitized sheet music from the Colorado, Ingram, and Ragtime Collections. Browse the Ragtime Collection for songs by African-American composers, including "Darktown is Out Tonight" by Will Marion Cook.

Books

35 Song Hits by Great Black Songwriters: Bert Williams, Eubie Blake, Ernest Hogan and Others. Edited by David A. Jasen. Mineola, NY: Dover Publications, 1998.
     This anthology of facsimiles of the original sheet music includes "Carry Me Back to Old Virginny" and "All Coons Look Alike to Me."

Crawford, Richard. "Blacks, Whites, and the Minstrel Stage." In *America's Musical Life: A History.* New York: W. W. Norton, 2001.
     Crawford explores the reasons for the popularity of minstrel shows and how they changed as the Civil War approached.

Dunbar, Paul Laurence. *Jump Back, Honey: The Poems of Paul Laurence Dunbar.* New York: Jump at the Sun/Hyperion Books for Children, 1999.
     This collection of Dunbar's poems includes both the poems in standard English and in black dialect. The introduction by Ashley Bryan and Andrea Davis Pinkney sketches Dunbar's life and relates the response to his dialect poems.

Dunbar, Paul Laurence. "Musical Lyrics and Fragments." In *In His Own Voice: The Dramatic and Other Uncollected Works of Paul Laurence Dunbar.* Edited by Herbert Woodward Martin and Ronald Primeau. With a foreword by Henry Louis Gates, Jr. Athens, OH: Ohio Univ. Press, 2002.
     Includes song lyrics for songs from In Dahomey *and* Clorindy, or The Origin of the Cakewalk. *In the introduction the meanings of the lyrics and Dunbar's intent are explained (pp. 12–14).*

Ellis, Rex M. *With a Banjo on My Knee: A Musical Journey from Slavery to Freedom.* [New York]: Franklin Watts, 2001.
     In addition to recording the history of the banjo in African-American music, Ellis relates the cultural and political explanations for the popularity of minstrel shows and the reasons for participation by African-American performers and songwriters.

Giddins, Gary. "Louis Armstrong/Mills Brothers (Signifying)" In *Visions of Jazz: The First Century.* New York: Oxford Univ. Press, 1998.
     Giddins describes a recording by Armstrong and the Mills Brothers of the minstrel song "Carry Me Back to Old Virginny" and how Armstrong compensates for the racist lyrics.

Handy, W. C. *Father of the Blues: An Autobiography.* New York: Da Capo Press, 1969.
     Handy relates many stories about his days with the minstrel show, Mahara's Minstrels. Many of the incidents portray the discrimination and violence that were a part of many of their tours.

Henderson, Clayton W. "Minstrelsy." In Vol. 3 of *The New Grove Dictionary of American Music.* Edited by H. Wiley Hitchcock and Stanley Sadie. London: Macmillan Press; New York: Grove's Dictionaries of Music, 1986.
     A brief history of minstrelsy, describing its permutations through the years.

Jasen, David A. and Gene Jones. *Spreadin' Rhythm Around: Black Popular Songwriters, 1880–1930.* New York: Schirmer Books, 1998.
Jasen and Jones provide an extensive history of black songwriters and entertainers from the minstrel era through the blues and tin pan alley of the 1920s.

Pryor, Al. "Minstrels." In *The Long Road to Freedom: An Anthology of Black Music.* N.p.: Belafonte Enterprises, 2001.
A brief history of minstrelsy that includes the origin of the Jim Crow character.

Reef, Catherine. *Paul Laurence Dunbar: Portrait of a Poet.* Berkeley Heights, NJ: Enslow, 2000.
This biography explores Dunbar's writings and his role in promoting African-American literature. It details his relationships with Will Marion Cook and James Weldon Johnson. The book includes a chronology and a list of works.

Southern, Eileen. "Black Ethiopian Minstrelsy." In *The Music of Black Americans: A History.* 3rd ed. New York: W. W. Norton, 1997.
Southern describes the life of an African-American minstrel, the format of the show, and some of the popular performers, including James Bland.

Southern, Eileen. "Ethiopian Minstrelsy." In *The Music of Black Americans: A History.* 3rd ed. New York: W. W. Norton, 1997.
Describes some of the white minstrelsy troupes, the origin of Jim Crow, and the legacy of the derogatory stereotypes.

Ward, Andrew. *Dark Midnight When I Rise: The Story of the Jubilee Singers Who Introduced the World to the Music of Black America.* New York: Farrar, Straus, & Giroux, 2000.
The history of the Fisk Jubilee Singers offers a contrast to the minstrel shows of the same period.

SONGS OF ABOLITION, SUFFRAGE, TEMPERANCE, AND WAR

"Get Off The Track!" A Song for Emancipation. Composer, Lyricist, Arranger: by Jesse Hutchinson Junr. Publication: Boston: Published by the Author, 1844. *The Lester S. Levy Collection of Sheet Music.* http:// levysheetmusic.mse.jhu.edu/ index. html

Chapter 3
The Hutchinson Family
Antidote to Minstrelsy

1841	1844	1847	1864
First concert of Hutchinson Family quartet	Abolitionist song "Get Off the Track"	Suffrage song "Song of the Shirt"	Civil War song "Tenting on the Old Campground"

In contrast to the message of the minstrel shows, and Hutchinson Family singers sang songs of social reform that addressed abolition, suffrage, and temperance. The three brothers, Judson, John, and Asa, and a sister, Abby, toured New England and various cities in the northeast during the 1840s. In the 1850s some of the family considered homesteading in Kansas in order to vote for a slave-free state. Instead they founded the town of Hutchinson in Minnesota.

As the original members of the group married, and their families grew, they formed separate singing groups: the Tribe of John, consisting of John, his wife Fanny, and children Henry and Viola, and the Tribe of Asa, consisting of Asa, his wife Lizzie, and children Abby, Fred, and Dennett. They were active in singing for Abraham Lincoln's campaign and sang for the troops during the Civil War. After the war John, Henry, and Viola traveled in Kansas with the suffragists, Elizabeth Cady Stanton and Susan B. Anthony, campaigning for woman's suffrage.

Because of their interest in social issues, the Hutchinsons were friends or acquaintances of many of the social reformers and literary figures of the time, including Frederick Douglass, Elizabeth Cady Stanton, Susan B. Anthony, Julia Ward Howe, Henry Ward Beecher, Harriet Beecher Stowe, and John Greenleaf Whittier. John Hutchinson, the last of the original quartet to die, lived through the administrations of twenty presidents. (Brink, 1947, 290)

OBJECTIVES

Students will investigate the role and effectiveness of song in pursuing social reform in the nineteenth century.

Students will compare how ideas were communicated during the nineteenth and the twentieth centuries.

INTRODUCING THE MUSICIANS

Sheet Music

Use the following sheet music to introduce the Hutchinson Family and their songs. "The Old Granite State" was their theme song, since it introduced them to the audience. "Get Off the Track!" was one of their well-known abolition songs. "Song of the Shirt" was a suffrage song.

"The Old Granite State." Composed, Arranged, and Sung by The Hutchinson Family. Publication: Boston: Oliver Ditson, Washington St., 1843.
Search by title in The Lester S. Levy Collection of Sheet Music.
URL: http://levysheetmusic.mse.jhu.edu/index.html

"Get Off The Track!" A Song for Emancipation. Composer, Lyricist, Arranger: by Jesse Hutchinson Junr. Publication: Boston: Published by the Author, 1844.
Search by title in The Lester S. Levy Collection of Sheet Music.
URL: http://levysheetmusic.mse.jhu.edu/index.html

"The Song of the Shirt." Composed and Sung by the Hutchinson Family. Words by the Late Thomas Hood. Arranged by S. O. Dyer. S. O. Dyer Hutchinson Family Publication: New York: C. Holt, Jr., Music Publishing Warehouse, 156 Fulton St., 1847.
Search by title in The Lester S. Levy Collection of Sheet Music.
URL: http://levysheetmusic.mse.jhu.edu/index.html

Quotations

- Writer Harriet Martineau in *People's Journal*, June 29, 1846:
How is it possible to give an idea of the soul-breathing music of the Hutchinsons to those who have not heard it? One might as well attempt to convey in words the colors of the sky or the strain of the nightingale as such utterance of the heart as theirs. (Brink, 1947, 126)

- P. T. Barnum, circus manager and friend of the Hutchinsons:
To endorse the Hutchinsons as the best of entertainers and philanthropists is as superfluous as a certificate to the sun for its warmth and brightness. (Brink, 1947, 72)

- Suffragist Elizabeth Cady Stanton:
The first time I saw "charming little Abby," as she was familiarly called, was on the platform with her four stalwart brothers in old Fanueil Hall. I was in a crowded anti-slavery meeting presided over by a howling mob. Neither the fiery eloquence of Garrison, nor the persuasive, silvery tones of Phillips could command a moment's hearing, but the Hutchinsons' sweet songs of freedom were listened to in breathless silence. (Brink, 1947, 132)

- Author Carol Brink in "Author's Note" in her book on the Hutchinson Family:
. . . the Hutchinsons have meaning for us because they so perfectly represent their times. There was scarcely a cause or fad or movement of the nineteenth century with which the Hutchinsons were not in some way connected. They vibrated to every popular breeze. So, in a measure, it seemed to me that to know the Hutchinsons was to know their century, its noble ideals as well as its follies and vanities. (Brink, 1947, iv)

Connections to Other Musicians in This Book

- The Hutchinsons used **Stephen Foster's** tune for "Nelly Bly" for a campaign song for Lincoln. (See Chapter 1: Emerson, 1998, 158)

- The Hutchinson brothers sang at Irvine Hall in St. Paul, Minnesota during the same time as **Dan Emmett's** minstrel company. (Brink, 1947, 192)

Periods in American History
Antebellum, Civil War

Musical Highlights of the Hutchinson Family's Life: Teachers, Colleagues, Events

1843 Sang at an anti-slavery rally at Boston's Faneuil Hall

1844 Published "Get Off the Track!"
Sang for President Tyler

1845 Singing tour of England

1846 Met Charles Dickens
Sang songs against the Mexican War
Met suffragist Lucretia Mott

1855 The brothers, John, Asa, and Judson, started for Kansas to found an antislavery town
Founded the town of Hutchinson in Minnesota

1858 Divided into two singing groups, the Tribe of John and the Tribe of Asa

1860 Wrote songs for Lincoln's campaign for presidency

1862 Quartet of John Hutchinson, his children, Henry and Viola, and Frank Martin sang for Lincoln at the White House
Sang for First New Jersey Regiment at Fairfax Seminary near Washington, D.C.

1863 Tribe of Asa sang Walter Kittredge's "Tenting on the Old Campground" at a concert at the family home at High Rock

1864 Asa shared in royalties in publication of "Tenting on the Old Campground"

1867 John, Henry, and Viola traveled with suffragists Stanton and Anthony to obtain the woman's vote in Kansas. They didn't succeed.

1876 Hutchinsons sang for the July 4th Centennial Convention in Philadelphia
Same day sang on the woman's suffrage program at the Women's Convention

1893 John and grandchildren sang at the World's Columbian Exposition in Chicago

HUTCHINSON FAMILY STUDENT PAGES

Inquiries

- How did music play a role in advocating political issues during the Antebellum and Civil War eras? Why is music a good medium for influencing public opinion?

- What were the means by which music reached the people? What was the procedure for setting up concerts? Where were these concerts performed and why?

- How did social reformers of the time period present their views to the people? How does this differ from the means of communication in the twentieth century?

- For which major events or gatherings did the Hutchinsons perform?

- What role did the Hutchinsons play in advocating for abolition, suffrage, and temperance?

- Why were the Hutchinsons temporarily refused access to the Union troops? What in their message was considered inflammatory?

- What incident may have affected the removal of General McClellan from his position of commander of the Union army?

- How did the Hutchinsons compose their songs? How does this compare to composers today?

Products

- Compare the issue of slavery as addressed in the minstrel shows and in the performances of the Hutchinson Family. Provide reasons for the differences.

- Produce a multimedia presentation of the abolition songs, suffrage songs, or Civil War songs. Explain their messages and use them to describe the history of the various movements of the nineteenth century.

- Chart the various avenues of performance for musical groups during this time period.

- Compare the uses of music for promoting social reforms during the nineteenth century to its use in the twentieth century.

- Compile a list of the important figures in abolition and suffrage who were contemporaries and acquaintances of the Hutchinsons. Provide dates and circumstances of common events that they attended.

RESEARCH RESOURCES

Web Sites
Historical:

> Allen, Robert Willis. "A Selection from Chapter 4 of *Marching On*"
>   URL: http://johnbrownsbody.net/Book_extract.htm
>
> *In Willis's account of the execution of John Brown, he relates the response of the Hutchinson Family, who were performing in Barre, Massachusetts, and devoted part of their concert to a discussion of John Brown and slavery.*
>
> Douglass, Frederick. *Life and Times of Frederick Douglass his Early Life as a Slave, his Escape from Bondage, and his Complete History to the Present Time.* Electronic Edition. *Documenting the American South, University of North Carolina at Chapel Hill Libraries.*
>   URL: http://docsouth.unc.edu/douglasslife/douglass.html
>
> *Use the browser's Find feature to discover Douglass's referrals to the Hutchinson Family.*
>
> "The Hutchinsons' last concert. Friday evening, January 19, 1844 at the Musical fund hall, Locust street." *An American Time Capsule: Three Centuries of Broadsides and Other Printed Ephemera*
>   URL: http://memory.loc.gov/ammem/rbpehtml/pehome.html
>
> *This advertisement for a program to be given by the Hutchinson Family lists the songs they will sing. Some of the verses and music are included. Of interest is Longfellow's poem "Excelsior." Search Descriptive Information using the keywords* hutchinson family *(match this exact phrase).*
>
> "Music at the White House, the 1840s." *The White House Historical Association.*
>   URL: http://www.whitehousehistory.org/04_history/subs_timeline/e_music/frame_e_1840.html
>
> *A picture and brief description of the Hutchinson Family, noting their performance for President John Tyler.*

Musical:

> "American Memory Collection: All Collections." *American Memory: Historical Collections for the National Digital Library.*
>   URL: http://memory.loc.gov/ammem/mdbquery.html
>
> *Search the American Memory Collection using the keywords* hutchinson family *(match this exact phrase).*
>
> "The Anti-Slavery Harp: A Collection of Songs for Anti-slavery Meetings." Compiled by William Wells Brown. Boston: Bela Marsh, 1848. *African American Odyssey.*
>   URL: http://memory.loc.gov/ammem/aaohtml/exhibit/aointro.html
>
> *Abolition song lyrics set to familiar tunes. Click on* Abolition *and scroll to "Abolitionist Songsters" or search by song title with "Search" link.*
>
> Clark, George W. "The Liberty Minstrel." New York: Leavitt & Alden [et al.], 1844. *African American Odyssey.*
>   URL: http://memory.loc.gov/ammem/aaohtml/exhibit/aointro.html
>
> *Clark wrote the music and words to most of these antislavery songs, but in some cases he used existing melodies. Click on* Abolition *and scroll to "Abolitionist Songster" or search by song title with "Search" link.*
>
> *The Lester S. Levy Collection of Sheet Music.*
>   URL: http://levysheetmusic.mse.jhu.edu/index.html
>
> *This collection includes many songs written and performed by the Hutchinson Family Singers, including the emancipation song, "Get Off the Track!" Search the collection by* hutchinson family *or by song title.*

"Protest Songs: Solidarity Forever." *Lift Every Voice: Music in American Life. University of Virginia Library.*
    URL: http://www.lib.virginia.edu/speccol/exhibits/music/protest.html
    Included in examples of protest songs is "The Ghost of Uncle Tom" sung by the Hutchinson Family.

"Timeline1850–1859." *Historic American Sheet Music, Rare Book, Manuscript, and Special Collections Library, Duke University.*
    URL: http://scriptorium.lib.duke.edu/sheetmusic/timeline1850.html
    Includes "Slavery Is a Hard Foe to Battle" sung by the Hutchinson family.

Books

Brink, Carol. *Harps in the Wind: The Story of the Singing Hutchinsons.* New York: Macmillan, 1947.
    In researching this book Brink talked to descendants of the Hutchinson Family singers and examined the diaries, scrapbooks, and photographs.

Crawford, Richard. "The Hutchinson Family and Songs of Social Reform." In *America's Musical Life: A History.* New York: W. W. Norton, 2001.
    Crawford describes the antislavery songs of the Hutchinsons, particularly "Get Off the Track!"

Silverman, Jerry. "Lincoln and Liberty." In *Songs and Stories of the Civil War.* Brookfield, CT: Twenty-First Century Books, 2002.
    In this chapter Silverman provides the history of this song. Jesse Hutchinson wrote the lyrics to this Lincoln campaign song and put them to the melody, "Old Rosin, the Beau."

Silverman, Jerry. "Tenting on the Old Camp Ground." In *Songs and Stories of the Civil War.* Brookfield, CT: Twenty-First Century Books, 2002.
    Silverman explains that this song was written by Walter Kittredge who had sung with the Hutchinsons. When Kittredge couldn't get the song published, Asa Hutchinson and his group promoted it in their concerts, and it was then published by Oliver Ditson.

CDs

Homespun America: Music for Brass Band, Social Orchestra & Choral Groups from the Mid-19th Century. Eastman Wind Ensemble and Chorale. The American Composers Series. Vox Box, 1995. CDX 5088. 2 compact discs.
    Includes ten songs by the Hutchinsons, including "Get Off the Track," "Excelsior," and "Old Granite State."

Glory hally, hallelujah! or The John Brown song! Hip, hip, hip hurrah!! Published by Horace Partridge, No. 27 Hanover Street, Boston. [n.d.] *American Singing: Nineteenth-Century Song Sheets.* http://memory.loc.gov/ammem/amsshtml/amsshome.html. From the American Memory Collection of the Library of Congress.

Chapter 4
Civil War Music, 1861–1865

1859	circa 1860	1862	1863
First performance of Dan Emmett's "Dixie's Land"	"John Brown's Body" sung in memory of abolitionist	Julia Ward Howe's "Battle Hymn of the Republic"	"Tenting on the Old Campground" by Kittredge

Songs, as rallying cries, as mourning for the dead, and as remembrances of home, were sung by soldiers and civilians alike during the Civil War. Often the lyrics of the songs were changed from Union to Confederate sympathies and vice versa. Many times if the song was very popular, other songs would be written to reply to the previous song or to present another view. For instance, after Abraham Lincoln called for men to enlist in the Union army, James Sloan Gibbons published the poem, "We Are Coming Father Abraham," which spawned a variety of songs. ("Learning Page...U.S. History." *We'll Sing to Abe...*) In addition to general songs about the war, many songs were published that recounted individual battles. They provide a vivid picture of the emotions and viewpoints during this conflict.

After Lincoln's Emancipation Proclamation, African-Americans enlisting in the army became an inflammatory issue. Songs supporting both sides of the issue were heard. In addition to the popular songs of the day, the freedmen of the black regiments sang their own songs that they had learned on the plantations. The spirituals told of a better life and the promise of freedom.

Thomas Wentworth Higginson (1823–1911) was the colonel of the black regiment, First South Carolina Volunteers, stationed in Port Royal, South Carolina. As an abolitionist he supported John Brown in his raid and was involved in recruiting people to settle in Kansas in order to vote for an slave-free state. These actions made him an ideal leader for the black regiment. He kept a diary and wrote many letters during the two years he commanded the troops. In these documents he praised the camp conduct of the men and was especially intrigued with their songs and dances. In 1870 he published *Army Life in a Black Regiment*, which outlined his experiences. His diaries, letters, and book provide a first-hand account of the spirituals and ring shouts of the African-American soldiers.

OBJECTIVES

Students will demonstrate the role music plays during a war.

Students will compare the views of the North and South factions of the Civil War period by studying their songs.

Students will understand the role of the black regiments in the Civil War.

Students will understand the types of music sung by the black soldiers and their uses in their camp life.

INTRODUCING THE MUSIC

Using the American Memory Collections and other web sites of sheet music listed below, instruct the students to search for a Civil War song, examine it using the analysis guide in Appendix C, and report what they learned to the class. Discuss the use of songs during wartime and their purpose. Compare the use of song during the Civil War with the use during recent wars.

Connections to Other Musicians in this Book

- **Stephen Foster** wrote Civil War songs.

- The **Hutchinson Family Singers** sang Civil War songs.

- The **Fisk Jubilee Singers** sang the spirituals that Higginson heard from the members of the First South Carolina Volunteers.

Period in American History

Civil War: 1861–1865

CIVIL WAR SONGS STUDENT PAGES

Inquiries

- What types of songs were sung during the Civil War? What purpose did they serve?

- What were the differences between the songs of the Union and Confederate soldiers? Why were they different?

- How did songs differ in their purpose from speeches or pamphlets?

- How did the songs about war change as the war progressed?

- What songs were sung by the black regiments? How were these different from the white troops' songs? What factors account for this difference?

- What is the relationship between "John Brown's Body" and "The Battle Hymn of the Republic"?

- How were the soldiers of the First South Carolina Volunteers trained? Was the training different than that of the white troops? Why would it be different?

- What do Higginson's accounts of the regiment members' stories and songs relate about the African-Americans during this time?

- What role did music play in the life of a black soldier?

- What did the abolitionists do to campaign for antislavery? How effective were these methods?

- What was the "unofficial theme song of black soldiers"? (Southern, 1997) Why?

- What songs were connected to Emancipation? What were the common themes?

- What songs described the black volunteer regiments? What sentiments did they reflect?

- How did the minstrelsy songs reflect the war?

Products

- Examine the lyrics of the Union and Confederate songs to determine their interchangeability and the differences or similarities of opinion they portray. Present these examples.

- Analyze the lyrics of some Civil War songs to determine the audience and sentiments about war. Discuss how the portrayal of war changed as the war progressed.

- Find examples in the American Memory sheet music collections of the songs described in Silverman's *Songs and Stories of the Civil War*. Using these resources describe the songs and their use in the war.

- Write a history of the variants of the song "John Brown's Body" that includes the history of the music and lyrics and the song's use by various regiments in the Civil War.

- Prepare a multimedia presentation of music that was sung by black soldiers. Explain the significance and purpose of each song.

- Compare the spirituals sung by the black regiment to those sung by the Fisk Jubilee Singers.

- Using song lyrics and compact discs, analyze the songs about the black volunteer regiments and report how the songs reflected people's views of the regiments.

- Prepare a report about a Civil War battle, including a song that commemorates it.

RESEARCH RESOURCES

Web Sites
Musical:

Allen, Robert Willis. "Various Versions of the John Brown Song Spanning More Than a Century." *John Brown's Ghost Haunts the Internet!!!*
URL: http://johnbrownsbody.net/JBBSong.htm

Willis has compiled various version of the lyrics for "John Brown's Body."

"American Memory Collections: All Collections." *American Memory: Historical Collections for the National Digital Library.*
URL: http://memory.loc.gov/ammem/mdbquery.html

Search the American Memory Collections web site above or the individual music collections listed below for Civil War music. Use keywords like civil war songs, freedmen songs, *and* civil war battle songs *(match all of these words). For songs about the black volunteer regiments that are on the* Long Road to Freedom *compact disc, use the keywords* colored volunteer *and* song first arkansas.

- *African-American Sheet Music, 1850–1920 (from Brown University).*
URL: http://memory.loc.gov/ammem/award97/rpbhtml/aasmhome.html

- *America Singing: Nineteenth-Century Song Sheets.*
URL: http://memory.loc.gov/ammem/amsshtml/amsshome.html

- *Historic American Sheet Music: 1850–1920.*
URL: http://memory.loc.gov/ammem/award97/ncdhtml/hasmhome.html

- *"We'll Sing to Abe Our Song!": Sheet Music about Lincoln, Emancipation, and the Civil War from the Alfred Whital Stern Collection of Lincolniana.*
URL: http://memory.loc.gov/ammem/scsmhtml/scsmhome.html

Higginson, Thomas Wentworth. "Negro Spirituals, from *The Atlantic Monthly*, June 1867." *University of Virginia.*
URL: http://xroads.virginia.edu/~hyper/TWH/Higg.html

Higginson, a Unitarian pastor and abolitionist, volunteered to be colonel of the first regiment of African-Americans, the First South Carolina Volunteers. In this article he describes the spirituals and their lyrics that were sung by the men.

"The Learning Page: Collection Connections: Critical Thinking." *America Singing: Nineteenth-Century Song Sheets.*

URL: http://memory.loc.gov/ammem/ndlpedu/collections/amsing/thinking.html

This learning page provides questions and song sheet links to address the topics of emancipation and the black regiments, John Brown, and the minstrel view of African-Americans.

"The Learning Page: Collection Connections: Critical Thinking." *"We'll Sing to Abe Our Song": Sheet Music about Lincoln, Emancipation, and the Civil War, from the Alfred Whital Stern Collection of Lincolniana.*
URL: http://memory.loc.gov/ammem/ndlpedu/collections/lincoln/thinking.html

In the section Historical Issue-Analysis and Decision-Making: The Emancipation Proclamation, *songs are listed that react to the call for the enlistment of African-American soldiers.*

"The Learning Page: Collection Connections: U.S. History." *America Singing: Nineteenth-Century Song Sheets.*
URL: http://memory.loc.gov/ammem/ndlpedu/collections/amsing/history.html

This learning page includes a section on the Civil War and the use of song sheets in promoting the viewpoints of either the Union or Confederacy.

"The Learning Page: Collection Connections: U.S. History." *"We'll Sing to Abe Our Song": Sheet Music about Lincoln, Emancipation, and the Civil War, from the Alfred Whital Stern Collection of Lincolniana.*
URL: http://memory.loc.gov/ammem/ndlpedu/collections/lincoln/history.html

This learning page for the collection includes examples of songs under the topics: Union Draft Songs, Regional Tensions: The Depiction of the South, The Emancipation Proclamation, and Minstrel Songs.

The Lester S. Levy Collection of Sheet Music.
URL: http://levysheetmusic.mse.jhu.edu/index.html

Search civil war *with the subject tag.*

"The New Jim Crow Song about the Darkies and the War." c1862.
America Singing: Nineteenth-Century Song Sheets.
URL: http://memory.loc.gov/ammem/amsshtml/amsshome.html

Although it uses the minstrel song refrain, "So I wheel about, I turn about, I do just so, And every time I wheel about, I jump Jim Crow," this song sheet is an abolition song. Search in the Title index.

Books

Evans, Mari. "War." In *The Long Road to Freedom: An Anthology of Black Music.* N.p.: Belafonte Enterprises, 2001.
Evans describes the songs of the Civil War that pertained to the black volunteer regiments. These include "The Colored Volunteer," "We Look Like Men of War," "Song of the First Arkansas Volunteers—Glory Hallelujah," and "Free at Las'." She includes a lengthy description of the first black regiment in the North, the 54th Massachusetts Volunteer Regiment.

Higginson, Thomas Wentworth. *The Complete Civil War Journal and Selected Letters.* Edited by Christopher Looby. Chicago: The Univ. of Chicago Press, 2000.
Higginson's diaries and letters provide a fascinating account of life in a Civil War camp, with special attention to the music of the African-American troops.

Higginson, Thomas Wentworth. "Colonel of the First Black Regiment." In *The Magnificent Activist: The Writings of Thomas Wentworth Higginson (1823–1911).* Edited by Howard N. Meyer. [New York]: Da Capo Press, 2000.
Meyer includes six of Higginson's writings on the men of his regiment and the spirituals.

Silverman, Jerry. *Songs and Stories of the Civil War.* Brookfield, CT: Twenty-First Century Books, 2002.
Silverman includes the stories and music to twelve Civil War songs. Also included are suggested recordings.

Southern, Eileen. "The War Years and Emancipation." In *The Music of Black Americans: A History.* 3rd ed. New York: W. W. Norton, 1997.
Southern discusses Higginson's role in notating the songs of African-Americans in his black regiment. She also provides information on the popular songs for blacks in the Union army and the contraband camps.

CDs

Howe, Julia Ward. "Battle Hymn of the Republic." In *This Land is Your Land: Songs of Freedom.* Various artists. Vanguard Records, 2002. 79710-2.
This song is sung by Odetta.

"The Long Road to Freedom: The War." On disc 2 of *The Long Road To Freedom: An Anthology of Black Music.* Belafonte Enterprises; Buddha Records, 2001.
This section of the compact disc includes four songs: "The Colored Volunteer," "We Look Like Men of War," "Song of the First Arkansas Volunteers—Glory Hallelujah," and "Free at Las'."

Root, George F. "Rally 'Round the Flag." In *This Land is Your Land: Songs of Freedom.* Various artists. Vanguard Records, 2002. 79710-2.
This song is sung by the Weavers.

Songs of the Civil War. Various artists. CMH Records. 2001. CD 8060.
Includes "When Johnny Comes Marching Home," "Home Sweet Home," "Darling Nellie Gray," "Maryland, My Maryland," and "Battle Hymn of the Republic." The instruments include banjo, clarinet, flute, penny whistle, fiddle, mandolin, guitar, snare, washboards, bass, hambone, and effing.

Songs of the Civil War & Stephen Foster Favorites. Mormon Tabernacle Choir. Richard P. Condie, Director & Conductor. Sony Music. 1992. MDK 48297.
Includes the Civil War songs "Tramp, Tramp, Tramp," "The Bonnie Blue Flag," "The Battle Hymn of the Republic," and "Tenting on the Old Camp Ground," among others.

SPIRITUALS

"I'm Going To Sing All the Way." As sung by the Jubilee Singers. 1880. *Music for a Nation: American Sheet Music, 1870–1885*. http://memory.loc.gov/ammem/smhtml/smhome.html. From the American Memory Collections of the Library of Congress.

Chapter 5
Fisk Jubilee Singers
Performing Choir from Fisk University

1871	1878	1879
Fisk Jubilee Singers first singing tour	"Carry Me Back to Old Virginny" published by James A. Bland	Bland's "Oh, Dem Golden Slippers" is favorite walkaround tune in minstrel shows

Fisk University in Nashville, Tennessee was founded in 1866 by the Freedmen's Bureau of the federal government as a school for former slaves. The Fisk choir, led by George White, began touring the North in 1871 in an effort to raise money for the school. The Fisk Jubilee Singers was the first African-American singing group to include black spirituals or jubilee songs in their concerts. White American audiences were not familiar with songs of the southern slaves. Minstrel songs, which were often stereotypical and derogatory to African-Americans, were more widespread and popular.

The Fisk Jubilee Singers began getting national recognition after appearing at the World Peace Jubilee in Boston in 1872. An earlier endorsement by the prominent New York minister Reverend Henry Ward Beecher had already advanced their reputation. (Southern, 1997, 229) The singers went on to tour in Europe and sang at the White House for President Grant. ("Timeline")

As the spirituals became popular, various editions were published. Henry Thacker Burleigh, an African-American composer, arranger, and concert artist, arranged many of them as art songs. As a student of Antonin Dvořák, Burleigh was influential in introducing these songs to the Czech composer. Dvořák, as director of the National Conservatory of Music in New York, enthusiastically promoted African-American and Native American music and included folk song themes in his Symphony no. 9 in E Minor, *From the New World*.

Burleigh's introduction to his series, *Negro Spirituals, Arranged for Solo Voice*, presents his explanation of spirituals and how they should be sung. (See **Sheet Music** below.)

Black spirituals combine elements of African songs and hymns sung at camp meetings and in white southern Churches. The call and response of African music is similar to the "lining-out" in hymns. (Lining-out is a method of singing hymns or psalms in which the leader sings one line, and the congregation repeats it.) (Crawford, 2001, 25) The black spirituals, however, show more variation in rhythm. The Fisk Jubilee Singers were classically trained, so their versions of the spirituals were more in the art song tradition than the oral one. However, their concerts and sheet music expanded the audience for a song form that had been limited by its oral tradition.

OBJECTIVES

Students will understand the musical characteristics of spirituals and the musical influences that formed them.

Students will determine the effect that spirituals had on white Americans' perception of African-Americans.

Students will analyze the religious and secular music of the time period to gain a better understanding of the views of Americans.

Students will distinguish between oral and published versions of songs and their characteristics.

Students will understand the life of African-Americans during Reconstruction and the role of the Freedmen's Bureau.

INTRODUCING THE MUSICIANS

Picture Book

Before reading the book to the students, ask them what they think life was like for African-Americans after the Civil War. Were the slaves' lives different after they gained their freedom? Ask if the students think the former slaves could read. Do they know about spirituals? If teaching this during a unit on the Civil War or Reconstruction, discuss the hardships of slavery years and the reality of Reconstruction. Do they know the term *jubilee*? Ask them to listen for the reason for the name "Jubilee Singers."

As you read the following book ask the students to be thinking of questions they still have about the time period or the songs. Ask the students for their reaction to the Fisk Jubilee Singers singing the popular songs of the day rather than their own songs. Ask the students to listen for terms describing the songs. List these words and other possible keywords for use in searching for further information.

> Hopkinson, Deborah. *A Band of Angels*. New York: Atheneum Books for Young Readers, 1999.
> *"Aunt Beth," a character based on Beth Howse, a reference librarian at Fisk University, relates the story of the Fisk Jubilee Singers from the viewpoint of Ella Sheppard Moore, Howse's ancestor. To raise money for the school, the Jubilee Singers toured the North during the last half of the nineteenth century, singing "jubilee" songs or spirituals.*

Songs Listed in *A Band of Angels*:

Annie Laurie	Nobody Knows the Trouble I See, Lord!
Go Down, Moses	Roll, Jordan, Roll
The Gospel Train	Room Enough
Home Sweet Home	Steal Away
I'm So Glad	Swing Low, Sweet Chariot
Many Thousand Gone	This Old Time Religion

Sheet Music

Show students the following sheet music covers and ask them to describe how the graphics, layout, and lyrics influence a person's view of African-Americans. Point out Burleigh's introduction to the music.

> Danks, H. P. "My Ole Home in Alabama 'fo' de War." 1875. *Historic American Sheet Music, 1850–1920.*
> URL: http://scriptorium.lib.duke.edu:80/sheetmusic/b/b06/b0658/

> "Go down, Moses; Let my people go! Negro spirituals." Arranged by H. T. Burleigh. 1917. *Historic American Sheet Music, 1850–1920.*
> URL: http://scriptorium.lib.duke.edu/sheetmusic/n/n07/n0708/

> "The Gospel Train." Arr. By D. C. A. 1881. *Music for the Nation: American Sheet Music, 1870–1885.*
> URL: http://memory.loc.gov/ammem/smhtml/smhome.html

> *Search with keywords* jubilee singers *(match this exact phrase) or song title.*

> Hays, Will S. "I'm Agwine Down South." 1874. *Historic American Sheet Music, 1850-1920.*
> URL: http://scriptorium.lib.duke.edu:80/sheetmusic/b/b06/b0624/

> Rutledge, John T. "I'm Going Back to Alabam' to Die; Plantation Melody." 1878. *Historic American Sheet Music, 1850–1920.*
> URL: http://scriptorium.lib.duke.edu:80/sheetmusic/b/b06/b0629/

Quotations

- W. E. B. Du Bois on "Sorrow Songs:"
  Throughout the Sorrow Songs there breathes a hope—a faith in the ultimate justice of things . . . that sometime, somewhere, men will judge by their souls and not by their skins. (Du Bois, 1903)

- Poet and abolitionist John Greenleaf Whittier signed the Fisk Jubilee Singers autograph book with this verse:
  Voice of a ransomed race: sing on,
  Till Freedom's every right is won,
  And slavery's every wrong undone. (Ward, 2000, 385)

- Antonin Dvořák, Czech composer, on African-American folk music:
  I am now satisfied that the future music of this country must be founded upon what are called the negro melodies . . . These are the folk-songs of America, and your composers must turn to them. (Southern, 1997, 267)

- J. B. T. Marsh's account (*The Story of the Jubilee Singers, With Their Songs, 1876*) of Fisk Jubilee Singers' reception at the World Peace Jubilee:
  Every word . . . rang through the great Coliseum as if sounded out of a trumpet. The great audience was carried away with a whirlwind of delight . . . men threw their hats in the air and the Coliseum rang with cheers and shouts of, "The Jubilees! The Jubilees forever!" (Southern, 1997, 229)

- Mark Twain wrote the following in a letter to Thomas Hood, March 10, 1872 after hearing the Fisk Jubilee Singers in Hartford, Connecticut:
  I think these gentlemen and ladies make eloquent music–and what is as much to the point, they reproduce the true melody of the plantation, and are the only persons I ever heard accomplish this on the public platform . . . I do not know when anything has so moved me as did the plaintive melodies of the Jubilee Singers. It was the first time for

twenty-five or thirty years, that I had heard such songs, or heard them sung in the gen-uine old way–and it is a way, I think, that white people cannot imitate–and never can, for that matter, for one must have been a slave himself in order to feel what that life was and so convey the pathos of it in the music. (Ward, 2000, 164–165)

Video

Introduce the Fisk Jubilee Singers by showing portions of this video.

> *Jubilee Singers: Sacrifice and Glory. American Experience.* PBS Home Video.
> *This story of the original Fisk Jubilee Singers includes songs sung by the current Jubilee Singers. The transcript of the program and a teacher's guide are available at the web site:*
> http://www.pbs.org/wgbh/amex/singers/index.html

Connections to Other Musicians in This Book

- **Bernstein** composed *Concerto for Orchestra ("Jubilee Games")*. See http://www.classicalnotes.net/features/bernstein.html for description of the meaning of the year of jubilee.

- **Gershwin** wrote his songs in *Porgy and Bess* in the style of spirituals. (See Chapter 10)

- Minstrel composer **James A. Bland** adapted the spiritual "What Kind of Shoes Are You Going To Wear?" in his popular song, "Oh, Dem Golden Slippers." (*Music for the Nation,* http://memory.loc.gov/ammem/smhtml/audiodir.html 7901966)

- Colonel Higginson heard the members of the **First South Carolina Volunteers** sing spirituals. (Higginson, "Negro Spirituals...")

- **John and Ruby Lomax** recorded spirituals in their 1939 trip recording trip in the south. (*The John and Ruby Lomax...*)

Period in American History

Reconstruction: 1863–1877

Musical Highlights of the Fisk Jubilee Singers: Teachers, Colleagues, Events

1866	Fisk Free Colored School dedicated
1871	First singing tour, following sites on the Underground Railroad Sang at Plymouth Church in Brooklyn; Henry Ward Beecher, minister
1872	Performed at church of Henry Ward Beecher in New York City Sang for President Ulysses S. Grant in Washington, D.C. Sang "The Battle Hymn of the Republic" at the World's Peace Jubilee in Boston
1873	Tour of Great Britain, including a performance in London for Queen Victoria
1875	Third tour of northeastern United States and tour of Great Britain Met with abolitionist Frederick Douglass at his home in Washington, D.C. Met with abolitionists William Lloyd Garrison and Wendell Phillips
1876	Dedication of the Fisk Jubilee Hall Tour of Switzerland and Holland
1877–1878	Tour of England and Germany

FISK JUBILEE SINGERS STUDENT PAGES

Inquiries

- What are the distinct musical elements of spirituals, and how do they relate to the elements in African music?

- What African and American musical forms influenced the spirituals?

- What were the differences between the published versions of the spirituals and the songs from the oral tradition?

- What was the role of the Freedman's Bureau in the Reconstruction? How did this affect the music of the period?

- What are the themes addressed in the lyrics of the spirituals?

- How do these songs differ from the minstrel songs of the same period in the depiction of the aspirations of African-Americans?

- What role did the Fisk Jubilee Singers play in bringing the music of spirituals into mainstream American musical traditions? Why were they able to accomplish this?

- How did the Fisk Jubilee Singers' efforts differ from those of H. T. Burleigh? What purpose did each serve?

Products

- Read the contemporary accounts about the Jubilee Singers or accounts by noted African-Americans of a later period. Using the following questions as a basis, analyze the effect of the spirituals on the audiences and the role of the Jubilee Singers in changing whites' perception of African-Americans.

Write a newspaper article reviewing an imaginary Fisk Jubilee concert, incorporating possible songs and descriptions of their singing.

1. Why does du Bois call the spirituals "sorrow songs"? How did George White's background lead to his founding of the Jubilee Singers? See Du Bois, W. E. B. *The Souls of Black Folk.* Chapter XIV: The Sorrow Songs. 1903, http://www.bartleby.com/114/14.html. Du Bois relates the history of the Fisk Jubilee Singers and the importance of the sorrow songs.

2. What can you tell about the Singers' selection of songs and how they were received by the audience? See "Fisk Jubilee Singers." *Cleveland Gazette.* Dec. 18, 1897. *The African-American Experience in Ohio, 1850–1920,* http://memory.loc.gov/ammem/award97/ohshtml/aaeohome.html. Search term: *jubilee singers* (match this exact phrase).

3. What did General Grant say about the Jubilee Singers? What did he mean when he uses the words, "sorrows of centuries of slavery" and "distilled its sadness into voices?"

See "Jubilee Singers." *The American Missionary*. Oct. 1880. *The Nineteenth Century in Print, the Making of American in Periodicals*, http://memory.loc.gov/ammem/ndlpcoop/moahtml/snchome.html. Search term: *jubilee singers* (match this exact phrase).

- Examine the online sheet music and answer the questions on the spirituals Analysis Guide (see Appendix B). Note any common musical elements in the spirituals. Compare the differences between the published versions.

- Examine the lyrics of the spirituals and describe the hopes and aspirations of African-Americans that are implicit in them. Compare these with other songs that relate to African-Americans that were published during this period.

- Investigate the terms *call and response* and *lining out*. Explain them and provide examples in the published spirituals.

- Prepare a demonstration of the musical concepts *call and response*, *lining out*, *pentatonic scale*, and *syncopation*.

- Compare the dates of publication of the pieces examined and decide which were published while the Fisk Jubilee Singers were touring. Discuss how a performance of an oral folk song might differ from a piece that is published and arranged. Read pages v and vi of *Slave Songs of the United States* (See **Books**) for a description of the singing.

- Perform a group of jubilee songs. Develop a presentation of recitations or oral reports that contains information about the Jubilee Singers and students' personal reactions to the music and its significance.

- Compare the sheet music covers of the Fisk Jubilee spirituals with other songs of the period by or about African-Americans.

RESEARCH RESOURCES

Web Sites
Biographical:

Ain't-A-That Good News? The Fisk Jubilee Singers in Concert.
URL: http://www.lpb.org/programs/goodnews/

This Louisiana Public Broadcasting web site introduces the Fisk Jubilee Singers with a brief slide show of the history of African-American music. Also on the web site is the history of Fisk University and history and biographical information on the original Fisk Jubilee Singers.

Austin, Ben S. *The Fisk University Jubilee Singers.*
URL: http://www.mtsu.edu/~baustin/jubilee.html

Includes a painting of the Fisk Jubilee Singers, a suggestion of a recording, and a brief history of the group.

Hampson, Thomas. "Henry Thacker Burleigh (1866–1949)." *I Hear America Singing.*
URL: http://www.thirteen.org/ihas/composer/burleigh.html

A short biography of Burleigh.

Jones, Randye L. "Biographies: H. T. Burleigh (1866–1949)." *Afrocentric Voices in 'Classical Music.'*
URL: http://www.afrovoices.com/burleigh.html

A lengthy biography that covers Burleigh's musical career and personal life. It includes descriptions of Burleigh's published pieces and his association with the composer Antonin Dvořák.

Historical:

The African-American Experience in Ohio, 1850–1920.
URL: http://memory.loc.gov/ammem/award97/ohshtml/

Search the keywords jubilee singers *(match this exact phrase). Includes two newspaper articles and a recollection by Frederick Douglass.*

Du Bois, W. E. B. *The Souls of Black Folk. Chapter XIV: The Sorrow Songs.* 1903.
URL: http://www.bartleby.com/114/14.html

Du Bois explains the sorrow songs and the role of George L. White and the Fisk Jubilee Singers in introducing them to the general public.

Early, Gerald. "Slavery." *Jazz, A Film by Ken Burns: Jazz in Time."*
URL: http://www.pbs.org/jazz/time/time_slavery.htm

Early explains the musical elements of spirituals and their arrangements for chorus by African-American composers such as Harry T. Burleigh and Samuel Coleridge Taylor.

"Ella Sheppard, Soprano." *American Experience: Jubilee Singers, Sacrifice and Glory.*
URL: http://www.pbs.org/wgbh/amex/singers/peopleevents/pande04.html

Biographical information on Ella Sheppard, soprano, accompanist, and Assistant Director of the Fisk Jubilee Singers.

"Hymns: Nobody Knows the Trouble I See." *Lift Every Voice: Music in American Life. University of Virginia Library.*
URL: http://www.lib.virginia.edu/speccol/exhibits/music/hymns_trouble.html

This site describes the origins and performance of spirituals and includes photos of the ring shout and the Fisk Jubilee Singers.

The Nineteenth Century in Print, the Making of American in Periodicals.
URL: http://memory.loc.gov/ammem/ndlpcoop/moahtml/snchome.html

Search the keywords jubilee singers *(match this exact phrase).*

Articles from The American Missionary *describing Fisk Jubilee Singers concerts.*

"An Old Scholar." *Harper's Weekly.* 21 May 1870. *HarpWeek.*
URL: http://blackhistory.harpweek.com/5CultureAndSociety/CultureLevelOne.htm

Click on title "An Old Scholar." A cartoon from Danville (Va.) Times *that shows the importance of education to African-Americans in the Reconstruction Period.*

"Timeline of the Jubilee Singers." *American Experience: Jubilee Singers, Sacrifice and Glory.*
URL: http://www.pbs.org/wgbh/amex/singers/timeline/index.html

A timeline from 1863–1879 that includes dates of the Fisk Jubilee Singers tours and important historical events.

Toward Racial Equality: Harper's Weekly Reports on Black America, 1857–1874; Reconstruction Timeline.
URL: http://blackhistory.harpweek.com/4Reconstruction/ReconLevelOne.htm

A timeline of the political events from 1863–1877.

Traveling Culture: Circuit Chautauqua in the Twentieth Century.
URL: http://memory.loc.gov/ammem/award98/iauhtml/tcchome.html

Includes many programs from the various Jubilee Singers through the years. Of special interest is an 1880 program in which the Fisk Jubilee Singers perform with Ole Bull, Ralph Waldo Emerson, and Oliver Wendell Holmes. Search keywords jubilee singers *(match this exact phrase).*

"Uncle Tom and His Grandchild." *Harper's Weekly.* 3 Nov. 1866. *HarpWeek.*
URL: http://blackhistory.harpweek.com/5CultureAndSociety/CultureLevelOne.htm

Click on Uncle Tom and His Grandchild *for another Reconstruction period cartoon emphasizing the importance of education to African-Americans.*

Musical:

Allen, William Francis, Charles Pickard Ware and Lucy McKim Garrison. *Slave Songs of the United States.* New York: A. Simpson, 1867. Electronic Edition.
URL: http://docsouth.unc.edu/church/allen/allen.html

African-American songs collected on Port Royal Islands, especially Coffin's Point, St. Helena Island. Includes melodies for 136 songs. Pages v and vi describe the singing.

"Ethnic Groups and Popular Songs." *Music for the Nation: American Sheet Music, 1870–1885.*
URL: http://memory.loc.gov/ammem/smhtml/smessay4.html

One of the paragraphs describes the use of spirituals in minstrel shows.

Higginson, Thomas Wentworth. "Negro Spirituals, from *The Atlantic Monthly*, June 1867." *University of Virginia.*
URL: http://xroads.virginia.edu/~hyper/TWH/Higg.html

Higginson, a Unitarian pastor and abolitionist, volunteered to be colonel of the first regiment of African-Americans in the Civil War, the First South Carolina Volunteers. In this article he describes the spirituals sung by the men in the company and includes many of the lyrics. The web site, which was "Prepared for the American Hypertext Workshop at the University of Virginia 1996 by John M. Picker," also includes a biography of Higginson, an index to the spiritual titles, pictures of Higginson and the Fisk Jubilee Singers, audio files of three songs sung by singers from Johns Island, South Carolina, and a bibliography.

Higginson, T. W. "Negro Spirituals." *Atlantic Monthly*, June 1867. *Making of America, Cornell University Library.*
URL: http://cdl.library.cornell.edu/moa/browse.journals/atla.html

Search for the article by title or Higginson, T. W. *Same as above.*

Historic American Sheet Music: 1850–1920. Selected from the Collections of Duke University.
URL: http://memory.loc.gov/ammem/award97/ncdhtml/hasmhome.html

Search by keywords burleigh *or individual titles of spirituals.*

The John and Ruby Lomax 1939 Southern States Recording Trip.
URL: http://memory.loc.gov/ammem/lohtml/lohome.html

Includes recordings of spirituals from the 1939 recording trip taken by the Lomaxes for the Archive of American Folk Song of the Library of Congress.

"Jubilee Songs." *American Experience: Jubilee Singers, Sacrifice and Glory.*
URL: http://www.pbs.org/wgbh/amex/singers/sfeature/songs.html

Lyrics and audio of "Steal Away" and "Swing Low Sweet Chariot" and other songs performed by the current Jubilee Singers.

Music for the Nation: American Sheet Music, 1870–1885.
URL: http://memory.loc.gov/ammem/smhtml/smhome.html

Search using the keywords jubilee singers *or by the individual song title.*

Sheet Music—Spirituals:

"Deep River." Arranged by H. T. Burleigh. 1917. *Historic American Sheet Music, 1850–1920.*
URL: http://scriptorium.lib.duke.edu/sheetmusic/n/n06/n0694/

"Go down, Moses; Let my people go! Negro spirituals." Arranged by H. T. Burleigh. 1917.
Historic American Sheet Music, 1850–1920.
URL: http://scriptorium.lib.duke.edu/sheetmusic/n/n07/n0708/

"The Gospel Train." Arr. By D. C. A. 1881. *Music for the Nation: American Sheet Music, 1870–1885.*
  URL: http://memory.loc.gov/ammem/smhtml/smhome.html

  Search by song title.

"I'm Going to Sing All the Way." 1880. *Music for the Nation: American Sheet Music, 1870–1885.*
  URL: http://memory.loc.gov/ammem/smhtml/smhome.html

  Search by song title.

"Oh, Rise and Shine." Arranged by J. R. Murray. 1881. *Music for the Nation: American Sheet Music, 1870–1885.*
  URL: http://memory.loc.gov/ammem/smhtml/smhome.html

  Search by song title.

"Swing Low, Sweet Chariot, Negro Spirituals." Arranged by H. T. Burleigh. 1917. *Historic American Sheet Music, 1850–1920.*
  URL: http://scriptorium.lib.duke.edu/sheetmusic/n/n06/n0697/

"Swing Low, Sweet Chariot." Arranged by J. R. Murray. 1881. *Music for the Nation: American Sheet Music, 1870–1885.*
  URL: http://memory.loc.gov/ammem/smhtml/smhome.html

  Search by song title.

"What Kind of Shoes Are You Going to Wear?" Sung by the Jubilee Singers. 1880. *Music for the Nation: American Sheet Music, 1870–885.*
  URL: http://memory.loc.gov/ammem/smhtml/smhome.html

  Search by song title.

Sheet Music—Other Popular Songs:

"Annie Laurie. Scotch Ballad." 1850. *Historic American Sheet Music, 1850–1920.*
  URL: http://memory.loc.gov/ammem/award97/ncdhtml/hasmhome.html

  Search term: annie laurie *(match this exact phrase).*

Bishop, Henry R. "Home Sweet Home." [1870] *Historic American Sheet Music, 1850–1920.*
  URL: http://memory.loc.gov/ammem/award97/ncdhtml/hasmhome.html

  Search term: mid pleasures *(match this exact phrase).*

Audio Recordings:

Bland, James A. "Oh, Dem Golden Slippers." Linda Gill, soloist. Real Audio Version. *Music for the Nation: American Sheet Music, 1870–1885.*
  URL: http://memory.loc.gov/ammem/smhtml/audiodir.html#7901966

"Down on Me." Performer: Vera Hall. 1939. *The John and Ruby Lomax 1939 Southern States Recording Trip.*
  URL: http://memory.loc.gov/ammem/lohtml/lohome.html

  Search term: Hall, Vera *in Performer Index. Audio file.*

"Home in the Rock." Performer: Vera Hall. 1939. *The John and Ruby Lomax 1939 Southern States Recording Trip.*
  URL: http://memory.loc.gov/ammem/lohtml/lohome.html

  Search term: Hall, Vera *in Performer Index. Audio file.*

Books

Allen, William Francis, Charles Pickard Ware, and Lucy McKim Garrison. *Slave Songs of the United States.* New York: A. Simpson & Co., 1867. Electronic Edition. *Documenting the American South.* Univ. of North Carolina Chapel Hill Libraries.

URL: http://docsouth.unc.edu/church/allen/allen.html.

"© This work is the property of the University of North Carolina at Chapel Hill. It may be used freely by individuals for research, teaching and personal use as long as this statement of availability is included in the text.

The electronic edition of this book which was originally published in 1867 contains the words and music to 136 songs collected mainly from slaves on plantations on St. Helena Island of the Port Royal Islands."

Allen, William Francis, Charles Pickard Ware, and Lucy McKim Garrison, comp. *Slave Songs of the United States.* Bedford, MA: Applewood Books, [1995].
Originally published in 1867.

Cooper, Michael L. *Slave Spirituals and the Jubilee Singers.* New York: Clarion Books, 2001.
In addition to telling the story of the Fisk Jubilee Singers, Cooper provides the musical origins of spirituals in African call and response and revivals or camp meetings. Especially interesting are the firsthand accounts from slaves living on the Sea Islands south of Charleston, South Carolina, and the numerous spiritual lyrics.

Crawford, Richard. "Make a Noise! Slave Songs and Other Black Music to the 1880s." In *America's Musical Life: A History.* New York: W. W. Norton, 2001.
Crawford provides the history of the publication Slave Songs of the United States *(Allen, 1867), and an explanation of the* shout *and its origins. Differences between the oral and published versions of spirituals are noted.*

Du Bois, W. E. B. *The Souls of Black Folk.* Chapter XIV: The Sorrow Songs. 1903. *Bartleby.com; Great Books Online.*
URL: http://www.bartleby.com/114/14.html
Also available from Dover Publications.

Dunbar, Paul Laurence. "Negro Music." In *In His Own Voice: The Dramatic and Other Uncollected Works of Paul Laurence Dunbar.* Edited by Herbert Woodward Martin & Ronald Primeau. With a foreword by Henry Louis Gates, Jr. Athens, OH: Ohio Univ. Press, 2002.
Dunbar describes hearing the Dahomeyans singing African music at the World's Columbian Exposition in Chicago in 1893 and realizing the similarity with African-American music. He contends that only black people can sing the plantation songs, which reflect the conditions they have endured.

Evans, Mari. "Early Shouts and Spirituals." In *The Long Road to Freedom: An Anthology of Black Music.* N.p.: n.d.
Includes a description of the ring-shout *and musicologist Alan Lomax's explanation of the spiritual "Kneebone." The accompanying CD includes various spirituals and shouts.*

Evans, Mari. "The Underground Railroad and the War." In *The Long Road to Freedom: An Anthology of Black Music.* N.p.: n.d.
Describes the use of spirituals as a means of sending messages on the Underground Railroad. The accompanying CD includes the spirituals "Steal Away to Jesus" and "Many Thousan' Gone."

Higginson, Thomas Wentworth. "Colonel of the First Black Regiment." In *The Magnificent Activist: The Writings of Thomas Wentworth Higginson (1823–1911).* Edited by Howard N. Meyer. [New York]: Da Capo Press, 2000.
Meyer includes six of Higginson's writings on the men of his regiment and the spirituals.

Higginson, Thomas Wentworth. *The Complete Civil War Journal and Selected Letters.* Edited by Christopher Looby. Chicago: The Univ. of Chicago Press, 2000.
Higginson's diaries and letters provide a fascinating account of life in a Civil War camp, with special attention to the music of the African-American troops.

Lloyd, Ruth, and Norman, arr. *The American Heritage Songbook.* New York: American Heritage Pub. Co., 1969.
A comprehensive collection of American songs from colonial America through the nineteenth century. The history of each song is given.

Medearis, Angela Shelf, and Michael R. "The African Connection." In *Music*. New York: Twenty-First Century Books, 1997.
Medearis explores the African roots of African-American music, the use of spirituals in the Underground Railroad, and the role of the Fisk Jubilee Singers in popularizing the spirituals.

Oliver, Paul. "Spiritual. Black." In Vol. 18 of *The New Grove Dictionary of Music and Musicians*. Edited by Stanley Sadie. London: Macmillan Publishers; New York: Grove's Dictionaries of Music, 1995.
Oliver's detailed article is divided into four sections: Early collections, African and European sources, Texts, and After 1870.

Southall, Geneva H. "Jubilee Singers, (Fisk)." In Vol. 2 of *The New Grove Dictionary of American Music*. Edited by H. Wiley Hitchcock and Stanley Sadie. London: Macmillan Press; New York: Grove's Dictionaries of Music, 1986.
A brief history of the Fisk Jubilee Singers.

Southern, Eileen. "Dissemination of the Spirituals." In *The Music of Black Americans: A History*. 3rd ed. New York: W. W. Norton, 1997.
Southern relates the story of the Fisk Jubilee Singers.

"Spirituals and Other Freedom Songs." In *From My People: 400 Years of African American Folklore*. Edited by Daryl Cumber Dance. New York: W. W. Norton, 2002.
Includes the lyrics and sources of many of the spirituals.

Ward, Andrew. *Dark Midnight When I Rise: The Story of the Jubilee Singers Who Introduced the World to the Music of Black America*. New York: Farrar, Straus, & Giroux, 2000.
In his exhaustive history of the Fisk Jubilee Singers, Ward describes the group from its members' beginnings as slaves or freedmen through their first tour in 1871 to the last tour in 1903. In his retelling of the history of Fisk University and its students, Ward also provides a history of the Reconstruction period. There are extensive notes and sources and sixteen pages of photographs. The endpapers contain the music of four spirituals, "Steal Away to Jesus," "The Gospel Train," "Getting Ready to Die," and "Go Down Moses."

Work, John W. "The Spiritual." In *American Negro Songs: 230 Folk Songs and Spirituals, Religious and Secular*. Mineola, NY: Dover Publications, 1998.
This is a republication of the 1940 edition. Work, a composer, educator and ethnomusicologist, was educated at Fisk University and taught there in the music department. His thesis for his master's degree in music at Columbia was American Negro Songs and Spirituals. *Work describes the singing of the Fisk Jubilee Singers and the musical elements in the spirituals collected in the book.*

CDs

"Many Thousan' Gone." Arranged and Adapted by Howard A. Roberts and Ralph Hunter. Recorded fall 1961. On compact disc 2 of *The Long Road to Freedom*. Belafonte Enterprises; Buddha Records, 2001. 74465 997562

"Steal Away to Jesus." Attributed to Nat Turner. Directed, Arranged and Conducted by Leonard de Paul. Recorded fall 1961. On compact disc 2 of *The Long Road to Freedom*. Belafonte Enterprises; Buddha Records, 2001.

BLUES

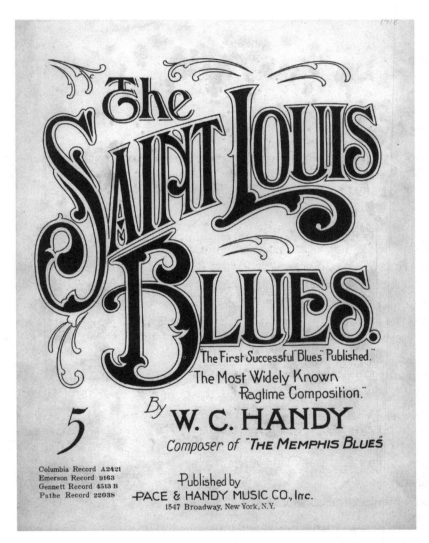

The "St. Louis Blues"/W. C. Handy. 1918. *African-American Sheet Music, 1850–1920 (from Brown University)* http://lcweb2.loc.gov/ammem/ award97/ rpbhtml/aasmhome.html

Chapter 6
W. C. Handy, 1873–1958

Composer, Musician, Cornetist

1912	1914	1924	1925
Handy publishes "The Memphis Blues"	Handy publishes "St. Louis Blues"	First performance of Gershwin's *Rhapsody in Blue*	Louis Armstrong records "St. Louis Blues" with Bessie Smith

William Christopher Handy is called the "Father of the Blues." He composed and published two of the most famous blues pieces, "St. Louis Blues" and "Memphis Blues." Handy was not the first to write and publish blues songs, but in basing his pieces on melodies and structures he heard in the Mississippi Delta from roustabouts and itinerant musicians, he was instrumental in bringing this oral tradition to a wider audience. Because Handy began his career as a minstrel performer in the late twentieth century, his life story also provides information on that aspect of music history.

In addition to composing blues music, Handy started the Pace & Handy Music Company in 1913 with Harry H. Pace. Pace eventually left the company and started the first black-owned record company, Black Swan. Handy formed a new company, Handy Brothers Music Company, and continued to publish his and others' compositions.

OBJECTIVES

Students will identify the elements of blues music.

Students will relate the history of blues music to the history of American popular music.

Students will compare copyright issues of Handy's time with those of today.

INTRODUCING THE MUSICIAN

Picture Book

Myers, Walter Dean. *Blues Journey.* Illustrated by Christopher Myers. New York: Holiday House, 2003.
In this picture book the father–son team present illustrated blues lyrics that express the plight of

African-Americans both in specific historical episodes and present-day situations. The book begins with an explanation of the history of the blues form. Also included are a glossary of terms and a timeline of the progression of blues music from 1865 to the 1960s.

Poetry

Introduce the blues pattern with Langston Hughes's poem "Po' Boy Blues."

> Hughes, Langston. "Po' Boy Blues." *Academy of American Poets: Poetry Exhibits.*
> URL: http://www.poets.org/poems/poems.cfm?prmID=1472

Compare it with Hughes's "The Weary Blues" from the same site. http://www.poets.org/poems/poems.cfm?prmID=1476

Quotations

- Author Ralph Ellison on the blues:
  . . . an impulse to keep the painful details and episodes of a brutal experience alive in one's aching consciousness, to finger its jagged grain, and to transcend it, not by the consolation of philosophy but by squeezing from it a near-tragic, near-comic lyricism. (Crawford, 2001, 557; Ellison, 1964. Shadow and Act*)*

- Trumpet player and educator Wynton Marsalis on blues:
  Blues is like the folk themes and little nuggets and kernels that are developed through the art of jazz into jazz music. You have to have that blues. Blues is like the roux in a gumbo. Now you might have a soup, and it might be killin', but if you don't have that roux, you cannot have no gumbo. People ask me if jazz always has the blues in it. I say, if it sounds good it does. (Ward, 2000, 117)

- Writer Eileen Southern on the blues:
  Generally, but not always, the blues reflects the personal response of its inventor to a specific occurrence or situation. (Southern, 1997, 333)

- Author Gary Giddins on Handy's blues:
  Yet it was Handy who organized the elements of the blues with compositional ambition, joining diverse refrains and focusing primary attention on melody. . . Not unlike Irving Berlin and his "Alexander's Ragtime Band," Handy was able to crystallize the musical moment-Fitzgerald refers to his "Beale Street Blues" as an emblematic tune in The Great Gatsby. *(Giddins, 1998, 29)*

- Author David A. Jasen on Handy's blues:
  So the blues turns out to be what Handy always said it was: it was patterned on black song, of Southern origin, a personal expression rooted in folk music but adaptable to theatrical performance, not necessarily melancholy, and not constricted to a twelve-bar pattern. (Jasen, 1998, 226)

- W. C. Handy on the blues:
  The melody of Mr. Crump *was mine throughout. On the other hand, the twelve-bar, three-line form of the first and last strains, with its three-chord basic harmonic structure (tonic, subdominant, dominant seventh) was that already used by Negro roustabouts, honky-tonk piano players, wanderers and others of their underprivileged but undaunted class from Missouri to the Gulf, and had become a common medium through which any such individual might express his personal feelings in a sort of musical soliloquy. (Handy, 1969, 99)*

- Author Will Friedwald on Handy's legacy:

  He did not actually write the melodies of his famous songs, he tells us; he cobbled them together from snatches of old Negro folk themes and blues that he'd heard here and there. As a black man, he had far greater access to the Negro subculture than any white man could have had, yet as he came from the middle class, he also had access to the publishing and profit machinery of Tin Pan Alley, which, to be sure, was true of very few Negroes at that time. (Friedwald, 2002, 40–41)

Connections to Other Musicians in This Book

- **Louis Armstrong** recorded "St. Louis Blues" with Bessie Smith. (Jasen, 1998, 246)

- Handy included excerpts from **Gershwin's** *Rhapsody in Blue* and Concerto in F in *A Treasury of the Blues*.

Periods in American History

1890s, Early Twentieth Century, World War I, Great Depression, World War II

Musical Highlights of Handy's Life: Teachers, Colleagues, Events

1873	Born in Florence, Alabama
1896	Joined the Mahara's Minstrels band as cornetist
1900	Bandmaster at the Agricultural and Mechanical College near Huntsville, Alabama
1903	Accepted a position as bandleader of the black Knights of Pythias in Clarksdale, Mississippi
1907	Took second job as bandleader with the black Knights of Pythias in Memphis, Tennessee
1909	Wrote campaign song, "Mr. Crump," for Memphis mayoral candidate Edward Hull Crump
1912	Self-published "Mr. Crump" as "The Memphis Blues" Handy scammed out of copyright
1913	Formed The Pace & Handy Music Company and published Handy's "The Jogo Blues"
1914	Vernon and Irene Castle used "The Memphis Blues" for dancing the fox trot Handy published "The St. Louis Blues" Published "The Yellow Dog Rag"
1915	Published "Joe Turner Blues"
1917	Published "Beale Street Blues"
1918	Pace & Handy opened in New York City
1920	Harry Pace left Pace & Handy; Handy joined with brother Charles to form Handy Brothers Music Company
1921	Pace formed The Pace Phonograph Company with the Black Swan label
1922	Wrote "John Henry Blues," which used folk melody
1923	Recorded on Okeh label with Handy's Orchestra
1925	Bessie Smith recorded "St. Louis Blues" with Louis Armstrong on trumpet

1926   Published *Blues: An Anthology*; included "Golden Brown Blues" with lyrics by Langston Hughes

1938   Handy Brothers published *W. C. Handy's Collection of Negro Spirituals*

1940   Handy got back the copyright to "Memphis Blues"

1941   Handy and ghostwriter Arna Bontemps wrote Handy's autobiography, *Father of the Blues*

1949   Reissued *Blues: An Anthology* as *A Treasury of the Blues*

1954   Louis Armstrong recorded *Satch Plays W. C. Handy*

1958   Died in New York

HANDY STUDENT PAGES

Inquiries

- What were the antecedents of the blues?

- What musical elements are included in blues songs?

- What is the difference between a blues song and a spiritual?

- Are blues lyrics all about despair? What emotions are included in a blues song?

- What performance techniques were used in the blues?

- How did Handy notate the unusual singing of the itinerant blues singers?

- What did the Pace & Handy Publishing Company publish?

- What arrangements were made between publishers and composers in order to get a song published?

- How were songs copyrighted during Handy's time, and who held the copyright?

- How did composers and publishers promote their songs?

- What is the story behind the "Joe Turner Blues"?

- What was the purpose of the "break" in blues songs? How did this influence jazz?

Products

- Compare the musical elements of ragtime, blues, and jazz for similarities and differences. Provide examples of these elements.

- Compare the experiences with copyright of W. C. Handy with those of Stephen Foster.

- Produce a chart that outlines the 12-bar blues structure. Provide musical examples.

- Write an explanation of how Handy, in a time of racial discrimination, was able to become a successful composer and publisher.

- In a timeline trace the history of the blues from the itinerant singers of the early twentieth century to the performers of the late twentieth century.

- Examine the lyrics of a number of blues songs and, using the pattern, write a blues song. Put the words to a melody from a Handy song and perform it.

RESEARCH RESOURCES

Web Sites
Biographical:

Gussow, Adam. " 'Make My Getaway': The Blues Lives of Black Minstrels in W. C. Handy's Father of the Blues." 2001. *African American Review.* Spring. *FindArticles.com.*
URL: http://www.findarticles.com/cf_0/m2838/1_35/74410611/p1/article.jhtml?term=gussow

In this extensive essay, Gussow contends that despite the fact that Handy's autobiography Father of the Blues *was sent to American troops in World War II, it contained material that was critical of the treatment of African-Americans in the United States.*

Morgan, Thomas L. "W. C. Handy." *BluesNet.*
URL: http://www.bluesnet.hub.org/readings/wc.handy.html

A biographical sketch of Handy's life and music from the author's book.

Oliver, Phillip. *W. C. Handy: "Father of the Blues".*
URL: http://www2.una.edu/library/handy/index.html

Includes a biography, photographs, list of works, digitized sheet music covers, and links.

"William Christopher Handy, 1873–1958." *W. C. Handy Music Festival.*
URL: http://www.wchandyfest.com/history/handybio.htm

In addition to a brief biography, the site includes a list and description of his works, and RealAudio files.

Historical:

Herman, Hawkeye. "History of the Blues." *The Blues Foundation.*
URL: http://www.blues.org/history/essays/hawkeye2.html

Beginning with a brief discussion of the blues form, Herman describes the proponents of Country Blues, Classic Blues, and Electric Blues.

Luster, Michael. "At Play in the Delta." *River of Song: Southern Fusion.*
URL: http://www.pbs.org/riverofsong/music/e3-play.html

Luster includes a history of the Delta blues from its beginnings to the artists of the late twentieth century.

Reublin, Richard A., and Robert L. Maine. "The Blues." *Parlor Songs: Popular Sheet Music from the 1800s to the 1920s.*
URL: http://www.parlorsongs.com/insearch/blues/blues.asp

A brief history of the origins of the blues, along with information on W. C. Handy.

Musical:

"American Memory Collections: All Collections." *American Memory: Historical Collections for the National Digital Library.*
URL: http://memory.loc.gov/ammem/mdbquery.html

Search for Handy's songs with the keywords handy w. c. *(match this exact phrase).*

Howze, Margaret. "St. Louis Blues." *The NPR 100.*
URL: http://www.npr.org/ramfiles/top100/20000627.top100.01.rmm

With commentary by W. C. Handy's great granddaughter, Edwina Handy DeCosta, and musicologist, Elliott Hurwit, Howze provides the history of Handy's song *"St. Louis Blues." The audio file ends with the entire 1925 recording of "St. Louis Blues" with Bessie Smith and Louis Armstrong. This ram file is available on* The NPR 100 *web site: http://www.npr.org/programs/specials/vote/100list.html*

"Learning the Blues." *Edsitement Lesson Plans.*
URL: http://edsitement.neh.gov/view_lesson_plan.asp?ID=267

This extensive lesson plan introduces students to the blues with links to articles and music.

The Lester S. Levy Collection of Sheet Music.
    URL: http://levysheetmusic.mse.jhu.edu/
Sheet music covers and music for five of Handy's songs, including "The Memphis Blues."

"Now What a Time": Blues, Gospel, and the Fort Valley Music Festivals, 1938–1943.
    URL: http://memory.loc.gov/ammem/ftvhtml/ftvhome.html

"The Fort Valley State College Folk Festival collection from the American Folklife Center consists of 104 surviving sound recordings and related written documents . . . created by John Wesley Work III, Willis Laurence James, and Lewis Jones on three recording trips to document the folk festival held at Fort Valley State College (now Fort Valley State University), Fort Valley, Georgia, in 1941 and 1943."

"The Peachite Vol. II, No. 2, Folk Festival Number, March 1944—WILLIAM C. HANDY says:"
"Now What a Time": Blues, Gospel, and the Fort Valley Music Festivals, 1938–1943.
    URL: http://memory.loc.gov/ammem/ftvhtml/ftvhome.html

Handy served as a judge for the festival. Search Full Text using the keywords william c handy *for his description of the value of the festival.*

Reublin, Richard A., and Robert L. Maine. "September 1999 Edition: The Blues." *Parlor Songs: Popular Sheet Music from the 1800s to the 1920s.*
    URL: http://www.parlorsongs.com/issues/1999-9/sep99feature.asp

Sheet music and audio files for seven blues pieces, including "Memphis Blues," "Beale Street Blues," *and* "St. Louis Blues."

Books

"Blues." In *From My People: 400 Years of African American Folklore.* Edited by Daryl Cumber Dance. New York: W. W. Norton, 2002.
In addition to the lyrics to many blues songs, this section includes the lyrics to five of Handy's songs.

Crawford, Richard. "The Jazz Age Dawns: Blues, Jazz, and a Rhapsody." In *America's Musical Life: A History.* New York: W. W. Norton, 2001.
Crawford describes the origins of the blues and examines the musical structure of "St. Louis Blues."

Evans, David. "The Birth of the Blues." In *American Roots Music.* Edited by Robert Santelli, Holly George-Warren, and Jim Brown. New York: Harry N. Abrams, 2001.
Evans provides a history of the folk-blues singers from the South and the impact of their recordings, in addition to information on W. C. Handy.

Friedwald, Will. "The St. Louis Blues (1914) words and music by W. C. Handy." In *Stardust Melodies: A Biography of Twelve of America's Most Popular Songs.* New York: Pantheon Books, 2002.
In this song biography Friedwald describes the history of its composition, a musical analysis of its form, and a chronology of all of its significant performances.

Giddins, Gary. "W. C. Handy (Birth of the Blues)" In *Visions of Jazz: The First Century.* New York: Oxford Univ. Press, 1998.
In this brief chapter Giddins explains the role Handy played in popularizing the blues.

Handy, W. C. *Blues: An Anthology. Complete Words and Music of 53 Great Songs.* Edited by W. C. Handy. With an Historical and Critical Text by Abbe Niles. With Pictures by Miguel Covarrubias. Revised by Jerry Silverman. New York: Macmillan, 1972.
Most of the songs and piano pieces in this anthology are either written by Handy or published by him. Some of them originally appeared in Blues: An Anthology, *published in 1926, and in the 1949 edition published under the new title,* A Treasury of the Blues. *The first section includes African-American folk songs that Handy heard and wrote down. Niles's introduction, "The Story of the Blues," explains the oral origins of the blues, and the musical structure of these early blues and Handy's published ones.*

Silverman has added guitar chord symbols. "Notes to the Collection" at the end of the book provide brief annotations for the songs.

Handy, W. C. *Father of the Blues: An Autobiography.* Edited by Arna Bontemps. With a Foreword by Abbe Niles. New York: Da Capo Paperback, 1991.
Handy describes his life and the development of the blues through personal stories. He vividly describes his life as a member of a minstrel show and his ups and downs in business as a publisher of sheet music.

Handy, W. C. *A Treasury of the Blues: Complete Words and Music of 67 Great Songs from Memphis Blues to the Present Day.* Edited by W. C. Handy. With an Historical and Critical Text by Abbe Niles. With Pictures by Miguel Covarrubias. New York: Charles Boni, 1949.
Most of the songs and piano pieces in this anthology are either written by Handy or published by him. Some of them originally appeared in Blues: An Anthology *published in 1926. The first section includes African-American folk songs that Handy heard and wrote down. Niles's introduction, "The Story of the Blues," explains the oral origins of the blues, and the musical structure of these early blues and Handy's published ones. "Notes to the Collection" at the end of the book provide brief annotations for the songs.*

Jasen, David A., and Gene Jones. "W. C. Handy." In *Spreadin' Rhythm Around: Black Popular Songwriters, 1880–1930.* New York: Schirmer Books, 1998.
This section on Handy not only outlines the high points of his career, but also analyzes the music for its unique elements and discusses the various performances and recordings of Handy's compositions.

Southern, Eileen. "Precursors of Jazz." In *The Music of Black Americans: A History.* 3rd ed. New York: W. W. Norton, 1997.
Southern lists the characteristics of the blues and provides a brief biography of W. C. Handy.

Work, John W. "The Blues." In *American Negro Songs: 230 Folk Songs and Spirituals, Religious and Secular.* Mineola, NY: Dover Publications, 1998.
This is a republication of the 1940 edition. Work, a composer, educator and ethnomusicologist, was educated at Fisk University and taught there in the music department. His thesis for his master's degree in music at Columbia was American Negro Songs and Spirituals. *In this chapter he describes the musical elements of the blues, discusses W. C. Handy's contribution and an interview with "Ma" Rainey.*

Wyman, Bill, and Richard Havers. *Bill Wyman's Blues Odyssey: A Journey to Music's Heart & Soul.* New York: A DK Publishing Book, 2001.
With many photographs and reproductions of album covers and sheet music covers, Wyman and Havers tell the story of the blues from its African roots to its rock and roll successors. A list of suggested recordings is included.

CDs

Bill Wyman's Blues Odyssey. Various artists. Document Records, 2001. 2 compact discs. DOCD-32-20-1.
These historic recordings range from Mamie Smith in 1926 to B. B. King in 1951.

Handy, W. C. "Joe Turner Blues." Featured vocalist: Gloria Lynne. Piano: Herman Foster. Compact disc 4 of *The Long Road to Freedom: An Anthology of Black Music.* Belafonte Enterprises; Buddha Records, 2001. 74465 997562.

Handy, W. C. "The St. Louis Blues." Bessie Smith. Compact disc one of Say It Loud! A Celebration of Black Music in America. Rhino Entertainment, 2001. CD R2 76660/A53891

May be copied for classroom use. *American Musicians Making History* by Donna B. Levene. Portsmouth, NH: Teacher Ideas Press, ©2004.

RAGTIME

Maple Leaf Rag. Composed by Scott Joplin. Sedalia, MO: John Stark & Son, 1899. *The Lester S. Levy Collection of Sheet Music*. http://levysheetmusic.mse.jhu.edu/index.html. Permission to use the above picture kindly granted by the American Tobacco Co.

Chapter 7
Scott Joplin, ca. 1867–1917

Composer, Pianist, Teacher

1899	1904	1908	1914
Maple Leaf Rag published	Wrote *Cascades*, inspired by the St. Louis World's Fair	Published manual *School of Ragtime*	Handy published "St. Louis Blues"

Scott Joplin, named the "King of Ragtime" during his career, composed "classic" piano rags. (Southern, 1997, 320–1) Though not the first to publish ragtime pieces, Joplin refined the form and added innovative melodies and harmonies. Trained in music, he sought to elevate ragtime from its saloon beginnings. Later in life, he expanded into other classical forms by composing the opera *Treemonisha*.

The popularity of ragtime was short-lived, but its signature syncopation was adopted in the popular songs and jazz pieces that followed. Ragtime music and Joplin himself had a revival in the 1970s with the movie *The Sting*.

OBJECTIVES

Students will be able to list the elements of ragtime music.

Students will be able to explain the musical influences on ragtime music and how it affected the music that followed it.

Students will be able to describe the publishing industry during Joplin's time.

INTRODUCING THE MUSICIAN

Piano Roll

Listen to the piano roll of Joplin playing his *Maple Leaf Rag*. (Levang) Find out from the students whether they know the piece or type of music and ask for their responses to the music.

Piano Music

Examine Joplin's sheet music from any of the sources below for its musical elements and musical difficulty.

> Joplin, Scott. *Complete Piano Rags.* Edited by David A. Jasen. New York: Dover Publications, 1988.
>
> *The Lester S. Levy Collection of Sheet Music.*
> URL: http://levysheetmusic.mse.jhu.edu/index.html
>
> *University of Colorado Digital Music Collection.*
> URL: http://www-libraries.colorado.edu/mus/smp/index.html

Quotations

- February 28, 1901 article in the *St. Louis Globe-Democrat*:

  Director Alfred Ernst of the St. Louis Choral Symphony Society believes that he has discovered, in Scott Joplin of Sedalia, a negro, an extraordinary genius as a composer of ragtime music. (Berlin, 1994, 94)

- Monroe Rosenfeld, songwriter and journalist, on Joplin in *the St. Louis Globe Democrat*, June 7, 1903:

  St. Louis boasts of a composer of music who, despite the ebony hue of his features and a retired disposition, has written possibly more instrumental successes in the line of popular music than any other local composer. His name is Scott Joplin, and he is better known as "The King of Rag-Time Writers," because of the many famous works in syncopated melodies which he has written. He has, however, also penned other classes of music and various vocal numbers of note. (Berlin, 1994,120)

- Article on Joplin in the *American Musician and Art Journal*, Dec. 13, 1907:

  Ragtime of the better order still has a hold on the public. Of the higher class of ragtime Scott Joplin is an apostle and authority. Joplin doesn't like the light music of the day: he is delighted with Beethoven and Bach, and his compositions, though syncopated, smack of the higher cult. (Berlin, 1994, 72)

- Joplin on playing rags in his manual *School of Ragtime*:

  To assist amateur players in giving the "Joplin Rags" that weird and intoxicating effect intended by the composer is the object of this work... We wish to say here, that the "Joplin ragtime" is destroyed by careless or imperfect rendering, and very often good players lose the effect entirely, by playing too fast. They are harmonized with the supposition that each note will be played as it is written, as it takes this and also the proper time divisions to complete the sense intended. (Joplin, 1988, xii, xiv)

Connections to Other Musicians in This Book

- Joplin contended that **Irving Berlin's** "Alexander's Ragtime Band" used a theme from his opera *Treemonisha*. (Berlin, "Scott Joplin")

- Cakewalk picture advertising **Cook** and **Dunbar's** *Clorindy, or The Origin of the Cakewalk* was on the cover of Scott Joplin's *Maple Leaf Rag*. (See Chapter 2)

Periods in American History

Tin Pan Alley era, 1893 World's Fair, 1904 St. Louis World's Fair

Musical Highlights of Joplin's Life: Teachers, Colleagues, Events

1867	Born near Texarkana, Texas
1881 or 1882	Mother bought piano
1891	Member of the Texarkana Minstrels
1893	Chicago World's Fair
1894	Arrived in Sedalia Toured with Texas Medley Quartette
1897	*Harlem Rag* by Tom Turpin published as first instrumental ragtime piece by an African American
1898	Maple Leaf Club incorporated; Joplin one of charter members
1899	Joplin's *Original Rags* published by Carl Hoffman in Kansas City Joplin's *Maple Leaf Rag* published by John Stark, Sedalia, Missouri Finished the folk ballet, *The Ragtime Dance*
1900	Collaborated with his pupil Arthur Marshall in publishing *Swipesy Cakewalk*
1901	Copyright of *Sun Flower Slow Drag* with student Scott Hayden Moved to St. Louis, Missouri Published *Peacherine Rag* and *Easy Winners* President Theodore Roosevelt led a cakewalk at a Christmas party at the White House
1902	Published *The Strenuous Life, A Breeze from Alabama, Elite Syncopations,* and *The Entertainer*
1904	St. Louis World's Fair Wrote *The Chrysanthemum* and dedicated it to Freddie Alexander whom he married that year. She died two months later. Wrote *The Cascades*, which refers to the Cascades Gardens at the St. Louis World's Fair
1905	Moved to Chicago Alice Roosevelt, daughter of Theodore Roosevelt, requested that the Marine Band play *Maple Leaf Rag*
1906	*Heliotrope Bouquet*, written by Joplin and Louis Chauvin, published *Maple Leaf Rag* recorded by the Marine Band
1907	Moved to New York near "Black Bohemia" Copyrighted *Searchlight Rag, Gladiolus Rag,* and *Rose Leaf Rag.* Met Joseph F. Lamb and persuaded Stark to publish Lamb's rags
1908	Published his manual *School of Ragtime* Started publishing his rags with Seminary Music Wrote *Fig Leaf Rag, Sugar Lane,* and *Pine Apple Rag*
1909	Joined the Colored Vaudeville Benevolent Association
1911	Published piano–vocal score of opera *Treemonisha*
1917	Died in New York City
1970	Musicologist Joshua Rifkin recorded *Piano Rags by Scott Joplin* on the Nonesuch label

1971	New York Public Library published *The Collected Works of Scott Joplin*
1972	*Treemonisha* premiered at the Atlanta Memorial Arts Center
1973	Gunther Schuller and the New England Conservatory Ragtime Ensemble recorded *The Red Back Book*, which won a Grammy for best chamber recording
1974	Joplin's music used in film score of *The Sting*
1976	Joplin awarded a Bicentennial Pulitzer Prize

JOPLIN STUDENT PAGES

Inquiries

- What are the elements of piano ragtime music?

- What musical forms preceded ragtime music, and how were they incorporated into piano rags?

- What made Joplin's rags different from other rags published during the same time?

- What was the relationship between Joplin and his publisher Stark? How did this compare to the publishing practices of the time?

- What are the musical elements in Joplin's opera *Treemonisha*? Why was this piece significant in the history of American music?

- What is the cakewalk, and how does it relate to ragtime music?

- Why did people object to ragtime music?

- What are the musical differences between the two-step, the cakewalk, and the march?

- How has ragtime music influenced classical composers?

- What musical forms followed that were based on ragtime?

Products

- Present the sheet music covers of Joplin's piano rags in a multimedia presentation. Describe the pictures as they relate to the time period and society's attitudes and discuss the changes from the early publications to the later ones.

- In a multimedia presentation compare the sheet music covers of Joplin's "classic ragtime" and the ragtime songs of the minstrel shows.

- Using the sheet music available online, point out the musical elements of ragtime.

- Present musical examples of the march, the cakewalk, and the two-step.

- Present the six exercises from Joplin's *School of Ragtime*. Show musical examples that demonstrate the lesson.

- Assemble recordings of classical music that have been influenced by the original rags. Play the sections that include ragtime elements and describe the elements of ragtime included.

- Describe the plot of the opera *Treemonisha*. Explain what Joplin is telling the audience about African-Americans.

RESEARCH RESOURCES

Web Sites
Biographical:

Albrecht, Theodore. "Joplin, Scott." *The Handbook of Texas Online.*
    URL: http://www.tsha.utexas.edu/handbook/online/articles/view/JJ/fjo70.html

A short biography with detailed information on Joplin's Texas background and a chronology of his compositions.

Berlin, Edward A. "A Biography of Scott Joplin (c1867–1917)." *The Scott Joplin International Rag Foundation.*
    URL: http://www.scottjoplin.org/biog.htm

A biographical sketch by the author of King of Ragtime: Scott Joplin and His Era.

Berlin, Edward A. "Scott Joplin (c.1867–1917)" *Classical Net.*
    URL: http://www.classical.net/music/comp.lst/joplin.html

Berlin describes Joplin's personal life, music, and the events in the revival of his music.

Schuman, Michael. "Joplin's Ragtime Plays on in His Old St. Louis Home." *JSOnline Milwaukee Journal Sentinel.*
    URL: http://www.jsonline.com/dd/destnat/jun99/joplin13061199.asp

A description of Scott Joplin House State Historic Site in St. Louis, Missouri.

Historical:

Giddins, Gary. "Weatherbird: Bad Haircut, Good Ragtime." *The Village Voice.*
    URL: http://www.villagevoice.com/issues/0148/giddins.php

Giddins describes a release by Delmark of Brunson Campbell, the only white pupil of Scott Joplin, playing piano rags.

Schuman, Michael A. "Joplin's Ragtime Music Lives on in St. Louis." *The Salt Lake Tribune,* 1996. *Jazz by Mail.*
    URL: http://www.jazzbymail.com/rosebud/saltlake.html

This article describes the Scott Joplin House State Historic Site in St. Louis, Missouri, and provides information of Joplin's life.

"Timeline: 1890–1899." *Historic American Sheet Music: Rare Book, Manuscript, and Special Collections Library, Duke University.*
    URL: http://scriptorium.lib.duke.edu/sheetmusic/timeline-1890.html

Contains the sheet music for Joplin's Original Rags.

Musical:

Historic American Sheet Music, 1850–1920.
    URL: http://memory.loc.gov/ammem/award97/ncdhtml/hasmhome.html

Search the collection using the keywords joplin scott. *Includes sheet music for Joplin's* Searchlight Rag *and* Original Rags. *The following notice appears on the first page of* Searchlight Rag: *"Notice: Do not play this piece fast. It is never right to play 'Ragtime' fast. Composer."*

The Lester S. Levy Collection of Sheet Music.
    URL: http://levysheetmusic.mse.jhu.edu/index.html

Search using the keywords Scott Joplin. *Includes the sheet music for* Rosebud, Pine Apple Rag, Palm Leaf Rag, Maple Leaf Rag *(two editions),* Felicity Rag, The Entertainer, The Favorite, *and* Antoinette.

Levang, Rex. "100 Years of the Maple Leaf Rag.: *music.mpr.org.*
    URL: http://music.mpr.org/features/9905_ragtime/index.shtml

Background information on the genesis of The Maple Leaf Rag *and a "Ragtime Timeline."*

Reublin, Richard A. and Robert L. Maine. "Ragtime." *Parlor Songs; Popular Sheet Music from the 1800s to the 1920s.*
      URL: http://www.parlorsongs.com/insearch/ragtime/ragtime.asp

Includes a description of the elements of ragtime music and a short biography of Scott Joplin. This page links to two previous issues on ragtime music that describe various sheet music pieces. These pieces can be heard and seen using the Sibelius Scorch notation software.

Trachtman, Warren. *Ragtime Piano MIDI Files.*
      URL: http://www.trachtman.org/ragtime/

A collection of public domain MIDI files of piano rags by Scott Joplin, James Scott, and many others.

University of Colorado Digital Music Collection.
      URL: http://www.libraries.colorado.edu/mus/smp/index.html

Includes the digitized sheet music of Joplin's Search-Light Rag, Antoinette, Euphonic Sounds, Pineapple Rag, *and* Country Club, *as well as rags by James Scott, Arthur Marshall, Joseph F. Lamb, Charles Johnson, and Tom Turpin.*

Books

Berlin, Edward A. *King of Ragtime: Scott Joplin and His Era.* New York: Oxford Univ. Press, 1994.
      Through exhaustive research Berlin verifies information about Joplin's life and explains what information is suspect. He includes much information about the publishing practices of the time and analyzes many of the Joplin's compositions. Extensive notes, a bibliography, and a list of all Joplin's pieces are provided.

Blesh, Rudi and Harriet Janis. *They All Played Ragtime.* New York: Oak, 1971.
      This comprehensive history of ragtime contains complete scores and lists of the compositions with publication dates and publishers.

Crawford, Richard. "Scott Joplin and the Rise of Ragtime." In *America's Musical Life: A History.* New York: W. W. Norton, 2001.
      Crawford includes a musical analysis of Maple Leaf Rag.

Joplin, Scott. *Complete Piano Rags.* Edited by David A. Jasen. New York: Dover Publications, 1988.
      Contains all of Joplin's thirty-eight rags in facsimile with the original sheet music covers and Joplin's School of Ragtime: 6 Exercises for Piano. *Jasen's introduction provides a brief biography of Joplin's life.*

Medearis, Angela Shelf. *Treemonisha.* From the opera by Scott Joplin. Illustrated by Michael Bryant. New York: Henry Holt, 1995.
      Medearis followed the plot line of Joplin's opera Treemonisha *but adapted the story for this picture book. Her "Author's Note" explains her changes. An Afterword relates the history of the composition and its performances.*

Shipton, Alyn. "Scott Joplin: King of Ragtime." In *Jazz Makers: Vanguards of Sound.* New York: Oxford University Press, 2002.
      Shipton explain's the elements of ragtime in jazz and Joplin's role in perfecting that form. Includes a discography, further reading, and a web site.

Southern, Eileen. *The Music of Black Americans: A History.* New York: W. W. Norton, 1997.
      Southern explains the history of ragtime and its elements in her chapter, "Precursors of Jazz." In "Singers, Instrumentalists, and Composers" she describes Joplin's opera Treemonisha.

CDs

Scott Joplin's Treemonisha: Original Cast Recording. Gunther Schuller, conductor. Betty Allen, Carmen Balthrop, Raymond Bazemore, and others, singers. Polygram Records. 1992. 435709. Two compact discs.
      Cast recording of the Houston Grand Opera performance in 1975.

MUSICAL THEATER

Alexander's Ragtime Band. New York, Ted Snyder, 1911. *Historic American Sheet Music, 1850–1920 (from Duke University).* http://memory.loc.gov/ammem/award97/ncdhtml/ hasmhome.html

Chapter 8
Irving Berlin, 1888–1989

Songwriter

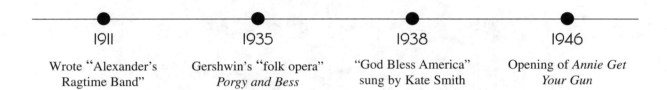

1911	1935	1938	1946
Wrote "Alexander's Ragtime Band"	Gershwin's "folk opera" *Porgy and Bess*	"God Bless America" sung by Kate Smith	Opening of *Annie Get Your Gun*

Irving Berlin, considered the greatest American songwriter by his contemporaries Jerome Kern and George Gershwin, began his career at thirteen as a "busker," or street performer. (Furia, 1998, 1) He worked his way up to singing waiter, and at age twenty-two was hired as a lyricist. His first big hit was "Alexander's Ragtime Band." Berlin, unlike most of the other popular song writers of his time, wrote both the music and the lyrics of his songs and concentrated almost exclusively on composing the popular 32-bar song. He lived to be 101 and never stopped writing songs.

His lifetime output was extraordinary in quantity, quality, and variety, despite the fact that he never learned to read or write music and could only play in one key, playing primarily on the black keys of the piano. (Furia, 1998, 34) He continued to adapt to reflect the popular culture, and many of his songs became hits. In addition to writing many popular songs for the musical *Annie Get Your Gun*, Berlin also wrote the perennial favorites "White Christmas" and "Easter Parade."

OBJECTIVES

Students will be able to describe the process of publishing songs in Tin Pan Alley.

Students will demonstrate how popular songs reflect the popular culture of the times.

Students will understand Irving Berlin's role as mirror to the changing culture of the American people.

Students will understand the life of an immigrant in the late nineteenth and early twentieth centuries.

INTRODUCING THE MUSICIAN

Song

Play the following segment on Irving Berlin's "Alexander's Ragtime Band." Discuss with students what they know about the song or the composer.

> Stamberg, Susan. "Alexander's Ragtime Band." *The NPR 100.*
>   URL: http://www.npr.org/ramfiles/atc/20000320.atc.06.rmm
>
> *Stamberg along with Berlin biographer, Laurence Bergreen, and ragtime pianist, Virginia Eskin, describe the 1911 phenomenal success of "Alexander's Ragtime Band." Recordings of Al Jolson and Bessie Smith singing the song are included.*

Song Lyrics

Provide students with lyrics from Berlin's songs in the form of poetry. Ask them to analyze the poems for their rhyme, rhythm, and story. Discuss the relationship between poems and song lyrics.

Quotations

- Berlin on popular songs:
  The mob is always right. A good song embodies the feelings of the mob and a songwriter is not much more than a mirror which reflects those feelings. (Giddins, 1998, 38)

- William G. Hyland in *Commentary*, Oct. 1990:
  Paradoxically, . . . he had no style . . . no category of popular music eluded him. He could write love songs, waltzes, ragtime, swing, jazz, or novelties. (Furia, 1998, 3)

- Tom Shone in *The New York Observer*:
  The birth of ragtime, the jazz age, the arrival of radio, the movies, the talkies, the heyday of the musical: Berlin's 101 years encompassed them all. To read The Complete Lyrics of Irving Berlin *is, at times, like reading one long epic poem, mapping the contours of the American century in metric form . . . ("Complete . . .")*

- Berlin on writing both words and music:
  I can compose them together and make them fit. I sacrifice one for the other. If I have a melody I want to use, I plug away at the lyrics until I make them fit the best part of my music and vice versa. (Furia, 1998, 37)

- Berlin in *New York Herald Tribune*, Oct. 10, 1933:
  There are some persons who need no distortion to caricature, and the same is true of much of the world's news . . . It is satire in itself and has only to be photographically reproduced to be the most gorgeous kind of irony. (Furia, 1998, 153)

- Berlin on songwriting from article in *Melody Maker*, Nov. 6, 1954:
  Three-fourths of that quality which brings success to popular songs is the phrasing. I make a study of it—ease, naturalness, every-day-ness—and it is my first consideration when I start on lyrics. "Easy to sing, easy to say, easy to remember and applicable to everyday events" is a good rule for a phrase. (Furia, 1998, 43)

- Film historian Gerald Mast on the film *Alexander's Ragtime Band*:
  Alexander's Ragtime Band *is the first film musical to realize that the history of American popular music is the history of America. Irving Berlin is a historian; to hear his songs is to read that history. . . . Over twenty-seven years, the actors don't age. Nor do the songs.*

Ageless, ever fresh and young, the songs are America—a union of past and present, dance dive and concert hall. No previous Hollywood musical demonstrated a closer bond between social history and cultural artifact. (Furia, 1998, 186)

- Composer and writer David Schiff on writing popular songs:
  Berlin brought his idiosyncratic technique to the most rigorously circumscribed musical and poetic form since the days of the troubadours or the great haiku poets. The tune-smith had to say "I love you" in just thirty-two bars, divided squarely into four eight-bar groups, and the melody had to be singable and memorable. Its range could not exceed an octave by much, and it had to have a "hook" that would set it apart from other songs (Schiff, 1996)

Connections to Other Musicians in This Book

- Berlin admired **Stephen Foster** and had his picture in his office. (Furia, 1998, 48)

- *Of Thee I Sing* with music by the **Gershwins** opened at the Berlin's Music Box Theatre.

- Berlin was a friend of both Ira and **George Gershwin**.

- **Woody Guthrie** wrote "This Land Is Your Land" in response to Berlin's "God Bless America." (See Chapter 9)

- **Bert Williams** sang Berlin's song "You Cannot Make Your Shimmy Shake on Tea" in *Ziegfeld's Follies of 1919*. (Furia, 1998, 84)

Periods in American History

The Twentieth Century: Tin Pan Alley era, World War I, Great Depression, World War II

Musical Highlights of Berlin's Life: Teachers, Colleagues, Events

1888	Born in Siberia as Israel Baline
1893	Baline family landed in New York City
1901	Became a street "busker"
1902	Became a "singing stooge" at Tony Pastor's Music Hall
1904	Got job as singing waiter at the Pelham Café and Dance Hall
1907	Wrote lyrics for first song, "Marie from Sunny Italy" Got job as singing waiter at Jimmy Kelly's restaurant
1910	Wrote lyrics for "Sadie Salome Go Home," sung by Fannie Brice in *Ziegfeld Follies* Hired as staff lyricist for Waterson & Snyder
1911	Wrote hit song "Alexander's Ragtime Band" Became partner in Waterson & Snyder
1912	After death of his first wife, Dorothy Goetz, wrote "When I Lost You"
1914	Wrote songs for Broadway musical *Watch Your Step*, starring dancers Vernon and Irene Castle; memorable song from show: the "counterpoint song," "Play a Simple Melody" Started own music publishing company, Irving Berlin, Inc. ASCAP founded

1918	Became naturalized citizen Drafted and sent to Camp Upton in Yaphank, Long Island Wrote and produced *Yip! Yip! Yaphank* with a cast of 300 soldiers; memorable song: "Oh! How I Hate to Get Up in the Morning"
1919	Wrote songs for *Ziegfeld Follies of 1919*; memorable song: "A Pretty Girl Is Like a Melody"
1920	Built and opened The Music Box Theatre
1921	Wrote the *Music Box Revue of 1921*; memorable song: "Say It with Music"
1926	Belle Baker sang "Blue Skies" as an interpolated song in Rodgers and Hart's musical *Betsy*
Late 1920s	Opened a Hollywood office
1929	Hollywood musical film *Puttin' on the Ritz*; memorable song: "Puttin' on the Ritz"
1931	*Of Thee I Sing* with music by the Gershwins opened at the Music Box Theatre
1932	Rudy Vallee sings "Say It Isn't So" on radio and it becomes hit "How Deep Is the Ocean"–verseless song Broadway hit musical *Face the Music* with Moss Hart, playwright, and George Kaufman, director; memorable song: "Let's Have Another Cup of Coffee"
1933	Revue with Moss Hart, *As Thousands Cheer*; starred Ethel Waters who sang "Harlem on My Mind," a tribute to Josephine Baker; memorable songs: "Supper Time," a song about a lynching sung by Ethel Waters; "Easter Parade"
1934	On cover of *Time* magazine
1935	Film *Top Hat*, starring Fred Astaire and Ginger Rogers; memorable songs: "Cheek to Cheek" and "Top Hat, White Tie, and Tails"
1938	Film *Alexander's Ragtime Band* "God Bless America" sung by Kate Smith on Armistice Day, Nov. 11, 1938
1942	Film *Holiday Inn*; memorable song: "White Christmas" *This Is the Army* opened on Broadway, July 4
1945	Awarded the Medal of Merit
1946	*Annie Get Your Gun* opened on Broadway; many memorable songs, including "There's No Business Like Show Business"
1948	*Easter Parade* film with Fred Astaire and Judy Garland
1950	Broadway show *Call Me Madam*, starring Ethel Merman; memorable song: "You're Just in Love"
1954	Film *White Christmas* with Bing Crosby, Danny Kaye, and Rosemary Clooney; memorable songs: "Count Your Blessings Instead of Sheep" and "Sisters"
1966	Revival of *Annie Get Your Gun*
1988	Tribute at Carnegie Hall
1989	Died in New York City

BERLIN STUDENT PAGES

Inquiries

- What was vaudeville and where does it fit in the performance continuum with minstrel shows and musical theater?

- What was Tin Pan Alley and what was its role in the music publishing business?

- How were popular songs promoted? Where was the sheet music sold?

- What is ASCAP and why was it formed?

- What case concerning ASCAP came before the Supreme Court?

- What is BMI and how did it affect ASCAP?

- Why did "hillbilly" songs start to become popular in the 1930s? How did this affect Tin Pan Alley?

- How were songs used during World War I and II? How were the songs different for each war?

- What were the *Ziegfeld Follies*? How did they differ from Broadway musicals?

- Who belonged to the Round Table at the Algonquin Hotel? How did they influence the culture of the 1920s?

- What was T. S. Eliot's poem "The Waste Land" about? How did it relate to song lyrics of the same time?

- What effect did the advent of films have on Tin Pan Alley?

- How did the advent of radio affect Tin Pan Alley?

- How did popular songs reflect and influence politics?

- When did Broadway musicals become integrated and why?

- What was the interaction between new songs and new dances of the period?

- Why and how did the song "White Christmas" become so popular?

- How was the song "White Christmas" used during World War II and the Viet Nam War?

- Why was Berlin's World War II musical *This Is the Army* a significant event in the history of America's race relations?

Products

- Compile a dictionary of Tin Pan Alley terms, such as *singing stooge, interpolated song, song plugger, sob songs,* and *busker.*

- Compile a chart of twentieth-century America by decade using Berlin's songs to explain the major events or the cultural climate of each decade.

- Trace the events surrounding the writing and performance of Berlin's "God Bless America" and the history of the song through the present day.

- Write a paper on the various techniques used by Berlin in his lyrics, using examples from the songs.

- Describe how Berlin's show *Yip! Yip! Yaphank* from World War I differed from his World War II show *This Is the Army*.

- Using Berlin's early years working in the Bowery and Chinatown as a basis, describe the economic and political atmosphere in New York City in the early twentieth century.

- Portray the "melting pot" of New York City's immigrant population with the sheet music of Berlin and other Tin Pan Alley composers.

- Investigate the copyright issues during the early twentieth century and write a paper explaining the role of ASCAP and the changes needed as radio and films became prevalent.

- Choose a political or social topic during the twentieth century and find Berlin songs that address it.

- Using lyrics from Berlin's songs, describe events or topics in the administrations of the presidents during Berlin's lifetime.

- Compare the lyrics of Berlin's song about lynching, "Supper Time," with "Strange Fruit" sung by Billie Holiday.

- Using Schiff's description of the components of a popular song (see quotation above), find examples of Berlin's music that fit the description.

RESEARCH RESOURCES

Web Sites
Biographical:

"Berlin, Irving." *The Rodgers & Hammerstein Organization.*
URL: http://www3.rnh.com/bios/Show_bio.asp?Bio_Name1=Berlin,+Irving

This biography page contains links to quotes about Berlin, a listing of his shows on Broadway, and a listing of his films.

Schiff, David. "For Everyman, by Everyman." March 1996. *The Atlantic Online.*
URL: http://www.theatlantic.com/issues/96mar/everyman/everyman.htm

In reviewing Charles Hamm's Irving Berlin: Early Songs, *composer and teacher David Schiff writes his own analysis of Berlin's music, providing examples of lyrics and citing the influence of his immigrant experiences with language.*

Weatherby, W. J. "Irving Berlin: Full Score and One Key." September 25, 1989. *Guardian Unlimited: Obituary.*

URL: http://www.guardiancentury.co.uk/1980-1989/Story/0,6051,110503,00.html

Weatherby writes an obituary that covers Berlin's "rags to riches" life story.

Historical:

Barrett, Mary Ellen. "Opening Night: July 4, 1942 *This Is the Army.* Broadway Theatre, New York."
Happy Talk: News of the Rodgers & Hammerstein Organization, Autumn, '99.
URL: http://www.rnh.com/news/fall99/rnh7.htm

Irving Berlin's daughter, Mary Ellen Barrett, recalls the opening night of This Is the Army *when she was fifteen.*

Bergreen, Laurence. "Irving Berlin, *This Is the Army.*" *Prologue*, Summer 1996. *NARA.*
URL: http://www.archives.gov/publications/prologue/summer_1996_irving_berlin_1.html

Bergreen describes the revue that Berlin wrote during World War II. "This essay is based on a talk given by Mr. Bergreen at the National Archives on July 11, 1995, on his book As Thousands Cheer: The Life of Irving Berlin *(Viking, 1990)."*

"The Complete Lyrics of Irving Berlin: 'Mapping the Contours of the American Century.' " *Happy Talk: News of the Rodgers & Hammerstein Organization*, Winter '02.
URL: http://www.rnh.com/news/winter2002/cloib.html

This description of the book The Complete Lyrics of Irving Berlin *includes quotes from reviews and a statement of the historical breadth of the lyrics' subjects.*

Musical:

"American Memory Collections: All Collections." *American Memory: Historical Collections for the National Digital Library.*
URL: http://memory.loc.gov/ammem/mdbquery.html

Search for Berlin's early songs using the search term irving berlin *(match all of these words).*

Berlin, Irving. "On Stephen Foster." *Today's Speeches, The HistoryChannel.com.*
URL: www.historychannel.com/speeches/archive/speech_18.html

This page includes a paragraph about Stephen Foster and an audio file of Berlin talking about Foster's songs.

Evans, Everett. "And God Bless Irving Berlin." *Houston Chronicle.* Dec. 8, 2001.
URL: http://www.chron.com/cs/CDA/story.hts/ae/books/reviews/1160655

This lengthy review of The Complete Song Lyrics of Irving Berlin *includes some of the song lyrics and a biographical sketch of Berlin's life and his legacy.*

"God Bless America." *American Treasures of the Library of Congress.*
URL: http://www.loc.gov/exhibits/treasures/trm019.html

This page includes a description of the writing of the song "God Bless America" and pictures of the original manuscript and the final proof. These items are in the Irving Berlin Collection at the Library of Congress.

"Irving Berlin." *Charles H. Templeton Sheet Music Collection, Mississippi State Univ. Libraries.*
URL: http://library.msstate.edu/ragtime/irvingberlin/irvingberlin.html

The collection presents twenty-four of Berlin's song in PDF format.

Lunden, Jeff. "White Christmas." *The NPR 100.*
URL: http://www.npr.org/ramfiles/atc/20001225.atc.06.rmm

Lunden, author Jody Rosen, and Berlin's daughter Linda Emmit discuss the history of "White Christmas" and the reasons for its popularity. The link to the ram file is on http://www.npr.org/programs/specials/vote/100list.html.

Stamberg, Susan. "Alexander's Ragtime Band." *The NPR 100.*
URL: http://www.npr.org/ramfiles/atc/20000320.atc.06.rmm

Stamberg along with Berlin biographer, Laurence Bergreen, and ragtime pianist, Virginia Eskin, describe the 1911 phenomenal success of "Alexander's Ragtime Band." Recordings of Al Jolson and Bessie Smith singing the song are included. The link to the ram file is on http://www.npr.org/programs/specials/vote/100list.html.

Books

Berlin, Irving. *The Complete Lyrics of Irving Berlin.* Edited by Robert Kimball and Linda Emmet. New York: Alfred A. Knopf, 2001.
Each song lyric is prefaced with the copyright date and sometimes an explanation of its history. Seventy-two photographs are included.

Furia, Philip. *Irving Berlin: A Life in Song.* With the assistance of Graham Wood. Irving Berlin Songography compiled by Ken Bloom. New York: Schirmer Books, 1998.
As Furia relates Berlin's life in music, he analyzes the lyrics and their relationship with the music to show the genius of Berlin.

Furia, Philip. "Ragged Meter Man: Irving Berlin." In *The Poets of Tin Pan Alley: A History of America's Great Lyricists.* New York: Oxford Univ. Press, 1990.
In analyzing Berlin's lyrics Furia concentrates on the "ragged" rhyming schemes.

Giddins, Gary. "Irving Berlin (Ragging the Alley)" In *Visions of Jazz: The First Century.* New York: Oxford Univ. Press, 1998.
Within the recounting of Berlin's life and numerous memorable hit songs, Giddins also explains what makes Berlin's songs so memorable.

Groce, Nancy. *New York: Songs of the City.* New York: Watson-Guptill, 1999.
Groce describes a number of Berlin's songs about New York, including "Easter Parade." She also includes articles on Tin Pan Alley and ASCAP.

Jablonski, Edward. *Irving Berlin: American Troubadour.* New York: Henry Holt, 1999.
This biography contains Berlin's personal and professional life and includes many anecdotes about Berlin and his many colleagues in music, film, and literary circles.

McFarlane, Gavin. "Performing Rights [Copyright Collecting] Societies." In Vol. 3 of *The New Grove Dictionary of American Music.* Edited by H. Wiley Hitchcock and Stanley Sadie. London: Macmillan Press; New York: Grove's Dictionaries of Music, 1986.
This article describes ASCAP (American Society of Composers, Authors and Publishers) and BMI (Broadcast Music, Inc.).

CDs

Capitol Sings Irving Berlin. Various artists. Capitol. 1992.
This collection of Irving Berlin songs contains titles pulled from the Capitol Records archives, so the singers include Judy Garland, Peggy Lee, Nat King Cole, and many others.

Irving Berlin Favorites: A Songwriters Collection. Park South Records. 2002.
Contains twenty-one Berlin songs.

Chapter 9
Rags to Riches and Patriotism in America

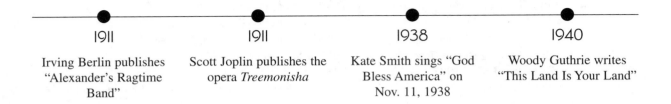

1911	1911	1938	1940
Irving Berlin publishes "Alexander's Ragtime Band"	Scott Joplin publishes the opera *Treemonisha*	Kate Smith sings "God Bless America" on Nov. 11, 1938	Woody Guthrie writes "This Land Is Your Land"

Irving Berlin (1888–1989), the longest living song writer of popular songs of the twentieth century, wrote two very successful and enduring songs that have maintained a significant role in popular culture over the years. They also have direct connections to pieces by two other musicians in this book.

"ALEXANDER'S RAGTIME BAND" BY IRVING BERLIN

Berlin added lyrics to an instrumental piece he had written, and the 1911 song "Alexander's Ragtime Band" became an enormous hit. (Berlin, 2001, 31) However, the song's title is a misnomer. The song has some raglike syncopation, but it isn't written in ragtime form. Instead of the usual 2/4 march time of ragtime piano pieces, "Alexander's Ragtime Band" is in 4/4 meter. During this time piano rags had begun to lose popularity, but the use of the term *rag* maintained its appeal among the public so that it was commonly used in popular song titles.

As described in the NPR segment below, the name "Alexander" was a mocking name for an African-American. (Stamberg) Neither the song itself nor the sheet music cover give any indication that the piece is in the minstrel format, however, its title connects it to that older tradition.

The popularity of the song gave rise to some controversy. Scott Joplin contended that Berlin based "Alexander's Ragtime Band" on a melody from his opera *Treemonisha*. Berlin's inability to read music prompted a number of accusations of plagiarism during his early career. (Berlin, 1994)

OBJECTIVES

Students will distinguish between a classic piano rag and a ragtime song.

Students will determine what ingredients were essential in a popular song of Berlin's time.

Students will define "intellectual property" and determine how and when copyright is violated.

INTRODUCING THE SONG

Stamberg, Susan. "Alexander's Ragtime Band." *The NPR 100.*
URL: http://www.npr.org/ramfiles/atc/20000320.atc.06.rmm

Stamberg along with Berlin biographer, Laurence Bergreen, and ragtime pianist, Virginia Eskin, describe the 1911 phenomenal success of "Alexander's Ragtime Band." Recordings of Al Jolson and Bessie Smith singing the song are included.

"Alexander's Ragtime Band" Student Pages

Inquiries

- What was the meaning of the title "Alexander's Ragtime Band"? Why would this title induce people to purchase the sheet music?

- Why is "Alexander's Ragtime Band" not a ragtime piece as defined by the classic rags of Scott Joplin?

- What other songs' melodies are quoted in "Alexander's Ragtime Band?"

- Why did this song become so popular?

- What is the basis for Joplin's contention that Berlin stole his theme?

- How was music copyrighted during this period? What legal recourse did composers have in protecting their works?

- How do Berlin's lyrics draw the audience into the song?

Products

- Compare the musical elements of "Alexander's Ragtime Band" with those of Joplin's "A Real Slow Drag" from the opera *Treemonisha*.

- Find other sheet music from the time of "Alexander's Ragtime Band" with the word "rag" in the title and compare them for similarities and differences.

- Compare the lives of Joplin and Berlin during this time period; examine their ages and the extent of their success in the music publishing field.

- Describe the process of copyrighting a song.

RESEARCH RESOURCES

Web Sites

"American Memory Collection: All Collections." *American Memory: Historical Collections for the National Digital Library*.
URL: http://memory.loc.gov/ammem/mdbquery.html

Search for Berlin's sheet music, including "Alexander's Ragtime Band," by using the keywords irving berlin *(match all of these words)*.

Berlin, Edward A. "Scott Joplin (ca. 1867–1917)." *Classical Net*.
URL: http://www.classical.net/music/comp.1st/joplin.html

In this biographical article Edward A. Berlin describes the reasons that Joplin claimed Irving Berlin "stole" his melody.

Reublin, Richard A., and Robert L. Maine. "Music by the Great Irving Berlin." *Parlor Songs: In Search of American Popular Songs 1800s–1920s*. November, 1998 edition.

URL: http://www.parlorsongs.com/issues/1998-11/nov98feature.asp

Sheet music covers and MIDI files of a number of Berlin's songs.

Stamberg, Susan. "Alexander's Ragtime Band." *The NPR 100.*
URL: http://www.npr.org/ramfiles/atc/20000320.atc.06.rmm

Stamberg along with Berlin biographer, Laurence Bergreen, and ragtime pianist, Virginia Eskin, describe the 1911 phenomenal success of "Alexander's Ragtime Band." Recordings of Al Jolson and Bessie Smith singing the song are included. The ram file is available on the NPR 100 *site: http://www.npr.org/programs/specials/vote/100list.html.*

University of Colorado Digital Sheet Music Collection.
URL: http://www-libraries.colorado.edu/mus/smp/index.html

Search the ragtime collection for copies of "Alexander's Ragtime Band" and other rag music.

Books

Berlin, Edward A. *King of Ragtime: Scott Joplin and His Era.* New York: Oxford Univ. Press, 1994.
Locate "Alexander's Ragtime Band" in the index for pages that relate the story of Joplin's relationship to the song.

Berlin, Irving. "Alexander's Ragtime Band." In *The Complete Lyrics of Irving Berlin.* Edited by Robert Kimball and Linda Emmet. New York: Alfred A. Knopf, 2001.
The introduction to the song lyrics provides a portion of the article "The Boy Who Revived Ragtime" by Bernard Wolf who recounted the story Berlin told him about the composing of the song. Also included are two statements by Berlin explaining the history of the song.

Giddins, Gary. "Irving Berlin (Ragging the Alley)" In *Vision of Jazz: The First Century.* New York: Oxford Univ. Press, 1998.
Giddins relates the controversy surrounding "Alexander's Ragtime Band."

CDs

Scott Joplin's Treemonisha: Original Cast Recording. Gunther Schuller, conductor. Betty Allen, Carmen Balthrop, Raymond Bazemore, and others, singers. Polygram Records. 1992. 435709. Two compact discs.
Cast recording of the Houston Grand Opera performance in 1975.

"GOD BLESS AMERICA" BY IRVING BERLIN

Irving Berlin wrote his first version of "God Bless America" during World War I for his musical revue *Yip! Yip! Yaphank*. However, he decided not to use it, and the piece was set aside. During the warlike climate of the 1930s Berlin revised the song to express his love of America, and Kate Smith introduced it on Armistice Day, Nov. 11, 1938. (Berlin, 2001, 321–22) Subsequently it was recorded by both Smith and Bing Crosby. The song has remained popular through the years and has often been suggested as an alternative to the current national anthem. In the aftermath of the events of September 11, 2001, it experienced a resurgence of popularity and playing time in the media.

Patriotism is a common theme in songs. However, the love of country is expressed in many different ways. Though Woody Guthrie's song "This Land Is Your Land" has also been nominated as a possible national anthem, its form of patriotism includes criticism of America. In this song Guthrie acted on the folk tradition of "borrowing" tunes or words by using the melody from a song sung by the Carter family, "When the World's on Fire," and adapting Berlin's "God Bless America" lyrics. Guthrie wrote the words as a response to Berlin's "God Bless America"; some say it was a "Marxist response." He felt that Berlin's song ignored the plight of the American people he represented, specifically those who were homeless because of the Dust Bowl. He originally titled his song "God Blessed America." (Spitzer)

OBJECTIVES

Students will identify the elements of a patriotic song.

Students will compare various patriotic songs to determine different points of view about patriotism.

Students will describe the impact of patriotic songs on citizens.

INTRODUCING THE SONG

"From the Mountains to the Prairies, America Rediscovers Its '#1 anthem'." *Happy Talk: News of the Rodgers & Hammerstein Organization*, Winter '02.
URL: http://www.rnh.com/news/winter2002/GBA.html

In the aftermath of September 11, 2001, Irving Berlin's song "God Bless America" became the most popular patriotic song. This article relates the instances in which the song was sung and a history of its beginnings.

Spitzer, Nick. "This Land is Your Land." *The NPR 100*.
URL: http://www.npr.org/ramfiles/atc/20000703.atc.05.rmm

In this segment on Guthrie's "This Land Is Your Land" Spitzer discusses how it is related to Berlin's "God Bless America." The ram file is available on The NPR 100 *web site: http://www.npr.org/programs/specials/vote/100list.html.*

"God Bless America" Student Pages

Inquiries

- What is the history of the writing of Berlin's song "God Bless America"?

- How was the song viewed at the time of its writing and in later times?

- Why did Guthrie use Berlin's song as a basis for "This Land Is Your Land"?

- Why is Guthrie's song called a "Marxist response to 'God Bless America' "?

- Why did Guthrie's song get published without some of the lyrics?

- What is a patriotic song? What elements make it a patriotic song?

- Why did "God Bless America" become more popular after 9/11 than other patriotic songs?

Products

- Compare the lyrics of Berlin's "God Bless America" with those of Woody Guthrie's "This Land Is Your Land," showing the similarities and the differences.

- Examine the illustrations of the picture books by Jakobsen and Munsinger (see **Books**) and demonstrate the use of illustration to reflect patriotism. Describe the similarities and differences in the illustrations.

- Investigate the performance history and use of each song, especially how they have been used in the twenty-first century.

- Discuss what elements need to be in a patriotic song, giving examples from songs.

- Discuss Berlin's statement: "A patriotic song is an emotion, and you must not embarrass an audience with it, or they'll hate your guts. It has to be right, and the time for it has to be right." ("From the Mountains to the Prairies...") How does this statement apply to "God Bless America" and "This Land Is Your Land?"

- Both "God Bless America" and "This Land Is Your Land" have been suggested as alternative national anthems for the United States. Present an argument for the adoption of one of these songs as a national anthem.

RESEARCH RESOURCES

Web Sites

"From the Mountains to the Prairies, America Rediscovers Its '#1 anthem'." *Happy Talk: News of the Rodgers & Hammerstein Organization,* Winter '02.
URL: http://www.rnh.com/news/winter2002/GBA.html

In the aftermath of September 11, 2001, Irving Berlin's song "God Bless America" became the most popular patriotic song. This article relates the instances in which the song was sung and a history of its beginnings.

"God Bless America." *American Treasures of the Library of Congress.*
   URL: http://www.loc.gov/exhibits/treasures/trm019.html

A brief history of the song and a description of Berlin's writing and revising process.

Spitzer, Nick. "This Land is Your Land." *The NPR 100.*
   URL: http://www.npr.org/ramfiles/atc/20000703.atc.05.rmm

In this segment on Guthrie's "This Land Is Your Land" Spitzer discusses how it is related to Berlin's "God Bless America." The ram file is available on The NPR 100 *web site: http://www.npr.org/-programs/specials/vote/100list.html.*

Woody Guthrie Foundation and Archives.
   URL: http://www.woodyguthrie.org/images/OrigThisLand.jpg

Copy of handwritten words to "This Land Is Your Land" including the original line, "God blessed America for me."

Books

Berlin, Irving. "God Bless America." In *The Complete Lyrics of Irving Berlin.* Edited by Robert Kimball and Linda Emmet. New York: Alfred A. Knopf, 2001.
This introduction to the lyrics describes when Berlin initially wrote the song, and the revisions he made for the 1938 rendition by Kate Smith.

Berlin, Irving. *God Bless America.* Illustrations by Lynn Munsinger. New York: HarperCollins, 2002.
Through the illustrations to Berlin's song lyrics, Munsinger portrays a bear family responding to their love of the United States in the aftermath of September 11, 2001. A note at the end of the book tells of Berlin's establishment of the God Bless America Fund that donates proceeds from the song to the Girl Scouts and Boy Scouts. The note also mentions that the trustees of the fund plan to contribute to the children of New York City who were affected by the tragedy.

Furia, Philip. "God Bless America." In *Irving Berlin: A Life in Song.* With the Assistance of Graham Wood. *Irving Berlin Songography* compiled by Ken Bloom. New York: Schirmer Books, 1998.
Furia relates the history of the song and the controversy in 1938 over attempts to make it the national anthem.

Guthrie, Woody. *This Land Is Your Land.* With a Tribute by Pete Seeger. Paintings by Kathy Jakobsen. Boston: Little, Brown, 1998.
Accompanying the verses to the song are Jakobsen's illustrations of natural landmarks in the U.S. and of significant places in Guthrie's life.

Klein, Joe. *Woody Guthrie: A Life.* New York: Delta, 1999.
Klein describes the reason that Guthrie wrote "This Land Is Your Land" and includes the lyrics to the song. The index lists a number of pages under "God Bless America," "God Blessed America," and "This Land Is Your Land."

CDs

"God Bless America: For the Benefit of the Twin Towers Fund." Various artists. New York: Columbia Records/Sony Entertainment, 2001. CK 86300.
Includes "God Bless America" sung by Celine Dion and "This Land Is Your Land" sung by Pete Seeger.

Chapter 10
George Gershwin, 1898–1937
Composer, Pianist

1919	1924	1925	1935
Jolson performs Gershwin's "Swanee"	*Rhapsody in Blue* performed by Whiteman's orchestra	Performance of *Concerto in F*	First performance of *Porgy and Bess*

George Gershwin began his musical training by working in Tin Pan Alley as a piano player for the music publisher Remick. However, he understood the importance of learning music theory and classical forms, so he studied under a number of piano and composition teachers, including Henry Cowell. As his songs became popular in Broadway shows, he started to compose pieces in longer forms. His *Rhapsody in Blue* and *American in Paris* are standard works in symphony orchestras' repertoires, demonstrating Gershwin's appeal to both popular music and classical music patrons. The culmination of his blending of popular and classical styles is his "folk opera" *Porgy and Bess.*

OBJECTIVES

Students will determine the role that popular music played in the lives of Americans in the early twentieth century.

Students will understand the role that George Gershwin played in the development of American music.

Students will identify the musical styles and forms of Gershwin's music.

Students will understand the role of Tin Pan Alley in the dissemination of sheet music and its reflection of the popular social views.

INTRODUCING THE MUSICIAN

Audio

Listen to discussions of two of Gershwin's pieces on *The NPR 100* web site: http://www.npr.org/programs/specials/vote/100list.html.

Hilgart, Art. "I Got Rhythm." *The NPR 100.*
    URL: http://www.npr.org/ramfiles/top100/20000726.top100.01.rmm
Lunden, Jeff. "Rhapsody in Blue." *The NPR 100.*
    URL: http://www.npr.org/ramfiles/top100/20000627.top100.02.rmm

Quotations

- Gershwin on music:

  True music must repeat the thoughts and aspirations of the people and the time. My people are American. My time is today. ("George Gershwin," Smithsonian*)*

- Gershwin on composing *Rhapsody in Blue*:

  It was on the train, with its steely rhythms . . . I frequently hear music in the very heart of noise. And there I suddenly heard—and even saw on paper—the complete construction of the rhapsody from beginning to end. I heard it as a sort of musical kaleidoscope of America—of our vast melting pot, of our incomparable national pep, of our blues, our metropolitan madness. (Greenberg, 1998, 65)

- Author Richard Crawford on the impact of *Rhapsody in Blue*:

  Bringing together three separate strands of musical development—the rise of blues as a popular song form, the spread of jazz as an instrumental music, and the push for artistic modernism in the classical sphere—the Rhapsody in Blue *has since come to be reckoned both an American classic, and a piece emblematic of its time. (Crawford, 2001, 574)*

- Bernstein on *Rhapsody in Blue* in a 1955 article in *Atlantic Monthly*:

  The Rhapsody *is not a composition at all. It's a string of separate paragraphs stuck together, the themes are terrific—inspired, God-given. I don't think there has been such an inspired melodist on this earth since Tchaikovsky. But if you want to speak of a composer, that's another matter. Your* Rhapsody in Blue *is not a real composition in the sense that whatever happens in it must seem inevitable. You can cut parts of it without affecting the whole. (Greenberg, 1998, 74)*

- Gershwin on melody and harmony in a 1924 interview:

  I think of melody as a line, a single thread—as the body of the music, and the harmony as the clothes you put on it. I can take a melody and harmonize it a thousand different ways. (Greenberg, 1998, 93)

- Author Rodney Greenberg on Gershwin songs:

  Gershwin's mature songs are peerless as a basis for improvisation by jazz soloists. This is because of the richness of their melodic scheme, and the sheer number of chord changes he is capable of achieving in thirty-two bars. (Greenberg, 1998, 94)

- Author Will Friedwald on "I Got Rhythm":

  When one considers the musical makeup of 'I Got Rhythm,' the song seems predestined to become a jazz classic; Gershwin, an improviser himself, almost seems to have designed it as a template for improvisation and variation. (Friedwald, 2002, 186)

- Critic A. Walter Kramer on *Porgy and Bess*:

  Mr. Gershwin has written a score of amazing fluency, in an idiom readily recognizable as his own, filled with melodic, harmonic, and rhythmic interest, rising at times to strong emotional climaxes and quite free, at all points, from dullness. Call it "folk opera," if you will. I find it a natural development of the music this composer has written for years for his musical comedies, in which he has more than once attained to passages of distinction. (Kramer, 1998, 114)

Connections to Other Musicians in This Book

- Gershwin's song "I Got Rhythm" has been sung and played by various musicians, including **Duke Ellington** and **Dizzy Gillespie**. (Hilgart)

- Gershwin's song "Summertime" was performed by **Charlie Parker, Dizzy Gillespie, Duke Ellington,** and **Louis Armstrong** with Ella Fitzgerald. (Friedwald, 2002)

- **Ellington** criticized Gershwin's *Porgy and Bess*. (Lunden, "Porgy and Bess," 2002)

- **Benny Goodman** played in the jazz bands for *Strike Up the Band* and *Girl Crazy*. (See Chapter 13)

- **Bernstein** often conducted and performed *Rhapsody in Blue* and *An American in Paris*. (See Chapter 20)

- In the process of researching for the writing of *Porgy and Bess,* Gershwin listened to Gullah Negroes on James Island off the coast of Charleston, South Carolina, perform a **spiritual** "shout." (Greenberg, 1998, 178)

- Gershwin's song "Swanee" took its title from **Foster's** "Old Folks at Home." (Crawford, 2001, 573)

Periods in American History
Tin Pan Alley era, World War I, Great Depression

Musical Highlights of Gershwin's Life: Teachers, Colleagues, Events

1898	Born in New York City
1914	Quit high school and began job as song plugger, playing sheet music for the publisher Remick in Tin Pan Alley
1918	Employed by publisher Max Dreyfus to compose songs
1919	Composed the score for the musical comedy *La, La, Lucille* Singer Al Jolson put Gershwin's song "Swanee" into his new show
1924	Gershwin's piano and orchestra piece, *Rhapsody in Blue*, is performed by Paul Whiteman's band with Gershwin as the pianist in "An Experiment in Modern Music" concert
1924	Performance of Broadway show *Lady, Be Good!*
1925	Performance of piano concerto, Concerto in F, with the New York Symphony Orchestra
1925	On cover of July *Time* magazine–first American-born musician to appear there
1930	Performance of Broadway show *Girl Crazy*, with Ethel Merman singing "I Got Rhythm"
1932	All-Gershwin concert at Lewisohn Stadium in New York City
1934	Premiere of Gershwin's *Variations on "I Got Rhythm"*
1935	First performance of *Porgy and Bess*
1937	Died in Hollywood, California

GERSHWIN STUDENT PAGES

Inquiries

- Using Gershwin's life as an example, what was the process in which Tin Pan Alley publishers promoted new sheet music?

- Why is Gershwin's music considered a turning point in American music?

- Why is *Rhapsody in Blue* considered an important piece in the history of American music?

- How does the popular music of a time period reflect the events and thinking of the time?

- Why was *Porgy and Bess* considered such a revolutionary opera? What were the reactions of the African-American community?

- Which elements of African-American music did Gershwin incorporate in *Porgy and Bess*?

- How did Gershwin's Jewish background affect his music?

- What makes Gershwin different from other Tin Pan Alley composers?

- Why did Gershwin change from composing popular songs to longer classical forms?

Products

- Leonard Bernstein and George Gershwin are similar in their backgrounds and musical development. Compare the two musicians using excerpts from their works as examples.

- Using Gershwin as an example, describe in a flowchart or timeline the process of publishing a song in Tin Pan Alley.

- Describe the musical elements that Gershwin used in his music. Provide musical examples using audio clips.

- Compile the reactions to Gershwin' opera *Porgy and Bess* by critics both at the time of its production and later productions. Write a critical analysis of the opera describing both the music and libretto.

- Produce a multimedia presentation on *Rhapsody in Blue* that includes musical excerpts, a history of its performances, and opinions on its musical aspects by musicians and critics.

- Using Bernstein's scripts (*The Leonard Bernstein Collection, ca. 1920–1989.* http://memory.loc.gov/ammem/lbhtml/lbhome.html) present an analysis of *An American in Paris*, including musical examples.

RESEARCH RESOURCES

Web Sites
Biographical:

"George Gershwin." *American Masters.*
URL: http://www.pbs.org/wnet/americanmasters/database/gershwin_g.html.

A concise biography that lists Gershwin's important compositions and their significance in American musical history.

Jolley, J. Clark. "George Gershwin." *GershwinFan.com.*
URL: http://www.gershwinfan.com/biogeorge.html

A brief biography that describes Gershwin's life in periods.

Parisi, Brandi. "Who Could Ask for Anything More? A Century of George Gershwin." *Music.mpr.org.*
URL: http://music.mpr.org/features/9809_gershwin/index.shtml.

A lengthy biography with a link to a Gershwin discography and audio ram links to Rhapsody in Blue, *"Embraceable You," and* Concerto in F: Allegro Agitato.

Historical:

"George Gershwin." *Smithsonian National Portrait Gallery.*
URL: http://www.npg.si.edu/exh/brush/gersh.htm

Portrait of Gershwin by Arthur Kaufmann.

Gutman, Peter. "George Gershwin and the Rhapsody in Blue." *Classical Notes.*
URL: http://www.classicalnotes.net/features/gershwin.html

A description of the original performance of Rhapsody in Blue *by Gershwin and Paul Whiteman's orchestra.*

Standifer, James. "The Complicated Life of Porgy and Bess." *Humanities: The Magazine of the National Endowment for the Humanities,* November/December 1997.
URL: http://www.neh.gov/news/humanities/1997-11/porgy.html

Standifer provides a history of the writing of Porgy and Bess *and a history of its performances and the reactions of critics and audiences.*

White, Raymond A. "The Gershwin Legacy: Library Celebrates Contributions of George and Ira." *LC Information Bulletin, September 1998.*
URL: http://www.loc.gov/loc/lcib/9809/gershwin.html

This article describes and quotes from the George and Ira Gershwin Collection in the Library of Congress.

Musical:

"American Memory Collections: All Collections." *American Memory: Historical Collections for the National Digital Library.*
URL: http://memory.loc.goc/ammem/mdbquery.html

Search using keywords gershwin george *(match all of these words).*

Bernstein, Leonard. "Thursday Evening Previews Scripts: [Untitled] [typescript with emendations in pencil], December 11, 1958." *The Leonard Bernstein Collection, ca. 1920–1989.*
URL: http://memory.loc.gov/ammem/lbhtml/lbhome.html

Search with keyword gershwin. *Bernstein compares the jazz elements in Gershwin's* An American in Paris *with Milhaud's* Creation of the World.

Bernstein, Leonard. "Young People's Concerts Scripts: The Road to Paris [typescript with emendations in pencil], January 18, 1962." *The Leonard Bernstein Collection, ca. 1920–1989.*
URL: http://memory.loc.gov/ammem/lbhtml/lbhome.html

Search with keyword gershwin. *Bernstein analyzes* An American in Paris.

Copland, Aaron. "American Music since 1930 [unpublished writings.]" *The Aaron Copland Collection, ca. 1900–1990.*
URL: http://memory.loc.gov/ammem/achtml/achome.html

Search with keyword gershwin. *On image 5 Copland mentions Gershwin's "folk-opera"* Porgy and Bess.

"George Gershwin." *DownBeat.com.*
URL: http://www.downbeat.com/artists/artist_main.asp?sect=bio&aid=222&aname=George+Gershwin

Includes links to recordings and videos. Many of the tracks of the recordings are accessible through audio files.

"George Gershwin." *The Music Beat.*
URL: http://musicbeat.searchbeat.com/classical/george-gershwin.htm

Lists recommended recordings of Gershwin's music.

Gershwin, George. "Swanee." *African-American Sheet Music, 1850–1920 (from Brown University).*
URL: http://memory.loc.gov/ammem/award97/rpbhtml/aasmhome.html

Search with keyword gershwin. *1919 voice and piano edition of "Swanee" with picture of Al Jolson on cover.*

Hilgart, Art. "I Got Rhythm." *The NPR 100.*
URL: http://www.npr.org/ramfiles/top100/20000726.top100.01.rmm

Hilgart traces the many variations of Gershwin's "I Got Rhythm" from its first appearance in 1930 in Girl Crazy *to Stephen Sondheim's version sung by Madonna in the 1990 movie* Dick Tracy. *On* The NPR 100 *web site: http://www.npr.org/programs/specials/vote/100list.html.*

Lunden, Jeff. "Porgy and Bess." *The NPR 100.*
URL: http://www.npr.org/ramfiles/wesun/20001008.wesun.16.rmm

Using interviews with historians and reviews from the premier of Porgy and Bess *in 1935, Lunden explores the reception of Gershwin's opera, which opened on Broadway as musical theater. Duke Ellington and other African-Americans criticized the work. Some music historians present the influence of Jewish music on Gershwin's opera. On* The NPR 100 *web site: http://www.npr.org/programs/specials/vote/100list.html.*

Lunden, Jeff. "Rhapsody in Blue." *The NPR 100.*
URL: http://www.npr.org/ramfiles/top100/20000627.top100.02.rmm

Lunden describes Gershwin's 1924 piece Rhapsody in Blue *as a "fusion of musical elements: classical, Tin Pan Alley, and jazz." Written in about three weeks for a performance with Paul Whiteman's orchestra in Aeolian Hall in New York City, this piece introduced the classical world to Gershwin's music. On* The NPR 100 *web site: http://www.npr.org/programs/specials/vote/100list.html.*

"Porgy and Bess." *American Treasures of the Library of Congress: Imagination.*
URL: http://lcweb.loc.gov/exhibits/treasures/tri008.html

A brief description of the history of Porgy and Bess *and two digital images of two of the original manuscript pages of the music.*

Books

Atkinson, Brooks, and Olin Downes. " 'Porgy and Bess,' Native Opera, Opens at the Alvin." *New York Times*, October 11, 1935. In *Gershwin in His Time: A Biographical Scrapbook, 1919–1937.* Edited, with an Introduction, by Gregory R. Suriano. Foreword by Marvin Hamlisch. New York: Gramercy Books, 1998.
Reviews of Porgy and Bess *by the theater and music critics of the* New York Times.

Crawford, Richard. "Gershwin and the *Rhapsody in Blue.*" In *America's Musical Life: A History.* New York: W. W. Norton, 2001.

Crawford describes the historic concert "Experiments in Modern Music" in which Gershwin first performed Rhapsody in Blue. *He also analyzes the music.*

Crawford, Richard. "Gershwin, George." In Vol. 2 of *The New Grove Dictionary of American Music.* Edited by H. Wiley Hitchcock and Stanley Sadie. London: Macmillan Press; New York: Grove's Dictionary of Music, 1986.
Crawford covers Gershwin's life, popular songs, and concert works.

Davenport, Marcia, and Ruth Woodbury Sedgwick. "Rhapsody in Black." *Stage,* November 1935. In *Gershwin in His Time: A Biographical Scrapbook, 1919–1937.* Edited, with an Introduction, by Gregory R. Suriano. Foreword by Marvin Hamlisch. New York: Gramercy Books, 1998.
Davenport reviews Porgy and Bess *as an opera, and Sedgwick reviews it as a play.*

Friedwald, Will. "I Got Rhythm (1930) music by George Gershwin, words by Ira Gershwin." In *Stardust Melodies: The Biography of Twelve of America's Most Popular Songs.* New York: Pantheon Books, 2002.
Friedwald describes the response of the audience to Ethel Merman's performance of "I Got Rhythm" in the musical Girl Crazy. *He then recounts the numerous jazz permutations on the song, in particular, those by Armstrong, Ellington, Fitzgerald, Gillespie, Parker, and Monk.*

Friedwald, Will. "Summertime (1935) music by George Gershwin, words by DuBose Heyward." In *Stardust Melodies: The Biography of Twelve of America's Most Popular Songs.* New York: Pantheon Books, 2002.
Friedwald describes the writing of Gershwin's "lullaby," "Summertime," in which contrary to his collaborations with his lyricist brother Ira, Gershwin wrote the music to DuBose Heyward's lyrics. This method emphasized the operatic tradition of writing the music to the libretto. Friedland also enumerates the many various recordings of the song by operatic, pop, and jazz singers and jazz instrumentalists.

Gershwin in His Time: A Biographical Scrapbook, 1919–1937. Edited, with an Introduction, by Gregory R. Suriano. Foreword by Marvin Hamlisch. New York: Gramercy Books, 1998.
Suriano has collected writings by and about Gershwin from 1919–1937. The introduction includes information on Gershwin's life and his music. The reviews cover many of Gershwin's pieces, including Rhapsody in Blue, An American in Paris, Of Thee I Sing, *and* Porgy and Bess.

Greenberg, Rodney. *George Gershwin.* London: Phaidon Press, 1998.
Greenberg not only describes Gershwin's personal and musical life, but also includes analysis of his compositions, including Rhapsody in Blue *and* Porgy and Bess.

Heyward, DuBose. "Porgy and Bess Return on Wings of Song." *Stage,* October 1935. In *Gershwin in His Time: A Biographical Scrapbook, 1919–1937.* Edited, with an Introduction, by Gregory R. Suriano. Foreword by Marvin Hamlisch. New York: Gramercy Books, 1998.
In this article Heyward, the author of Porgy, *describes the genesis of the opera* Porgy and Bess *and his collaboration with Gershwin.*

Kramer, A. Walter. "Gershwin's 'Porgy and Bess' Hailed in New York." *Musical America,* October 25, 1935. In *Gershwin in His Time: A Biographical Scrapbook, 1919–1937.* Edited, with an Introduction, by Gregory R. Suriano. Foreword by Marvin Hamlisch. New York: Gramercy Books, 1998.
Kramer's review examines the performers, the music, and the libretto.

Reef, Catherine. *George Gershwin: American Composer.* Greensboro, NC: Morgan Reynolds, 2000.
In this brief biography intended for students, Reef describes Gershwin's personal life and the high points of his career.

Vernon, Roland. *Introducing Gershwin.* Parsippany, NJ: Silver Burdett Press, 1996.
This brief introduction to Gershwin includes many photographs of the period and sidebars explaining the historical events in American history during Gershwin's life.

CDs

Feinstein, Michael. *Michael & George: Feinstein Sings Gershwin.* Ball Entertainment/Terwilliker; Concord Records, 1998. CCD-4849-2.
> *Includes liner notes by Feinstein describing each song. Feinstein sings above the original piano roll of "Swanee" played by Gershwin.*

Gershwin, George. *Gershwin Plays Gershwin: The Piano Rolls.* Realized by Artis Wodehouse. Elektra Entertainment, 1993. 79287-2.

For more listings of CDs look at the above web sites for *Downbeat.com* and *The Music Beat.*

JAZZ

Jazzin' the cotton town blues; Novelty song. 1917. New York, New York, M. Witmark & Sons, 1917. *Historic American Sheet Music, 1850–1920 (from Duke University).* http://memory.loc.gov/ammem/award97/ncdhtml/hasmhome.html

Chapter II
Louis Armstrong, 1901–1971
Horn Player, Scat Singer, Music Ambassador

1926	1928	1935	1956
Recorded "Heebie Jeebies"—scat singing	Recorded "West End Blues"	First performance of Gershwin's *Porgy and Bess*	Armstrong and his All Stars perform with N. Y. Philharmonic

Louis Armstrong is probably the best-known jazz performer in the history of jazz. He revolutionized jazz by initiating the improvised jazz solo. His virtuosic trumpet playing has been the model for subsequent jazz trumpet players. He also added scat singing to the repertoire of jazz. Armstrong was criticized at times for his antics on stage, especially by the younger jazz musicians who were sensitive to anything that reminded them of the minstrel days. (Ward, 2002, 353) Armstrong, however, was popular both in the United States and abroad, acting as a musical ambassador to many parts of the world.

OBJECTIVES

Students will define the musical elements of jazz, especially the jazz of New Orleans in the early part of the twentieth century.

Students will determine why Louis Armstrong is considered one of the most influential jazz musicians in the history of jazz.

Students will understand the role of the black jazz musician in jazz's history and the history of the United States.

INTRODUCING THE MUSICIAN

There are many accounts of Armstrong's early life and the musical influences in New Orleans. Include these two picture books with Armstrong's own reminiscences and the biographical information in books and on the Internet to evoke the early days of jazz in New Orleans.

Picture Books

Schroeder, Alan. *Satchmo's Blues*. Illustrated by Floyd Cooper. New York: A Doubleday Book for Young Readers, 1996.

In this fictional recreation of the childhood of Louis Armstrong, Schroeder and Cooper capture the sights and sounds of Armstrong's neighborhood, "back o' town" in New Orleans. As young Armstrong works to earn money to buy a horn in a pawn shop, he hears the cornetist Bunk Johnson and other jazz players.

Orgill, Roxane. *If I Only Had a Horn: Young Louis Armstrong*. Illustrated by Leonard Jenkins. Boston: Houghton Mifflin, 1997.

This fictional account of Armstrong's childhood includes many true facts about his life, including singing for money in a quartet of boys, hearing Joe Oliver on the cornet, and learning to play the cornet in the Colored Waifs' Home for Boys.

Audio Clip

Burnett, John. "West End Blues." *The NPR 100*.
URL: http://www.npr.org/ramfiles/watc/20000806.watc.08.rmm

With audio clips and interviews Burnett presents the case that Armstrong's recording of "West End Blues" was a turning point in the development of jazz.

Quotations

- Author Ralph Ellison comparing Armstrong's music to T. S. Eliot's poetry:
  Consider that at least as early as T. S. Eliot's creation of a new aesthetic for poetry through the artful juxtapositioning of earlier styles, Louis Armstrong, way down the river in New Orleans, was working out a similar technique for jazz. (Ellison, 2001, 69)

- Ralph Ellison in 1976 interview with Robert G. O'Meally when asked about identifying with Africa:
  My strength comes from Louis Armstrong and Jimmy Rushing, Hot Lips Page and people on that level, Duke Ellington, Mrs. Breaux, Mark Twain—all kinds of American figures who have been influenced by and contributed to that complex interaction of background and cultures which is specifically American. *(Ellison, 2001, 286)*

- Jazz critic and author Gray Giddins on Armstrong's vocabulary:
  Louis is believed to have coined or popularized in his early years . . . chops, jive, scat, gutbucket, mellow and solid and Pops, Face, and Daddy. (Giddins, 1998, Satchmo, *74)*

- Giddins on Armstrong's achievements:
  Danny Barker, the New Orleans-born guitarist . . . has suggested that Armstrong's greatest achievement was to jettison the jaunty second-line two-beat rhythm of New Orleans in favor of the evenly distributed four-four beat that is the basis of swing. Indeed, the swing era has been characterized as orchestrated Armstrong. (Giddins, 1998, Satchmo, *81)*

- Trumpeter Max Kaminsky on Armstrong's playing:
  No one knew what swing was till Louis came along. It's more than just the beat, it's conceiving the phrases in the very feeling of the beat, molding and building them so that they're an integral, indivisible part of the tempo. (Ward, 2000, 115)

- Trumpet player and composer Wynton Marsalis on Armstrong's influence on jazz:
  When you talk about Louis Armstrong, well, you're talking about the deepest human feeling, and the highest level of musical sophistication in the same man . . . Louis

Armstrong invented a new style of playing. He created the coherent solo, fused the sound of the blues with the American popular song, extended the range of the trumpet. Louis Armstrong created the melodic and rhythmic vocabulary that all the big bands wrote music out of... Duke Ellington once said he wanted Louis Armstrong on every instrument. (Ward, 2000, 118)

Connections to Other Musicians in This Book

- Armstrong recorded **Gershwin's** *Porgy and Bess* with Ella Fitzgerald in 1956. (Giddens, 1998, 226)

- Armstrong and his All Stars performed with **Leonard Bernstein** and the New York Philharmonic in 1956. (See Chapter 20)

- Armstrong recorded **W. C. Handy's** song "St. Louis Blues" with Bessie Smith. (See Chapter 6)

- Armstrong recorded the **minstrel** song "Carry Me Back to Old Virginny." (Giddens, 1998)

- Armstrong and **Woody Guthrie** were both musicians that loved language and playing with words.

Periods in American History
Jazz Age (1920s), World War I, Great Depression, World War II, Civil Rights era

Musical Highlights of Armstrong's Life: Teachers, Colleagues, Events

1901	Born in New Orleans, Louisiana
Circa 1907	Sang in quartet on street corners
1912	Put in Colored Waifs' Home for Boys
1913–1914	Received musical instruction from band director at Waifs' Home
1914–1917	Joe Oliver, leading trumpet play in New Orleans, taught Armstrong
1918	Oliver moved to Chicago; Armstrong took his place as cornet player in Kid Ory's band
1919	Hired by Fate Marable to perform on riverboats traveling the Mississippi River
1922	Played second cornet in King Oliver's Creole Jazz Band in Chicago
1924	Joined Fletcher Henderson Orchestra at the Roseland Ballroom in New York City
1925	Made first recording with his own group, Louis Armstrong and His Hot Five, on the Okeh label
1925	Played in the orchestra pit at the Vendome Theater, Chicago in the late 1920s; Joined a band led by Carroll Dickerson that included the pianist, Earl "Fatha" Hines
1926	Recorded "Heebie Jeebies" (scat singing)
1928	Recorded "West End Blues"
1929	Played and sang "Ain't Misbehavin'" at African-American show called *Hot Chocolates* that played at Broadway's Hudson Theater

1931	First recorded "When It's Sleepytime Down South," which became Armstrong's theme song
1944	Recorded with Billie Holiday. First Esquire All American Jazz Concert at the Metropolitan Opera House
1946	Recorded "Swing That Music"
1947	Started small group, the All Stars, that included Jack Teagarden
1956	Edward R. Murrow made the documentary *Satchmo the Great.* Recorded with Ella Fitzgerald for Verve Records
1957	Spoke out against racial injustice after the refusal of Little Rock, Arkansas, to integrate its schools
1964	*Hello Dolly* became hit
1967	Recorded "What a Wonderful World" for ABC Records
1971	Recorded the poem "The Night Before Christmas"
1971	Died in Corona, (Queens) New York

ARMSTRONG STUDENT PAGES

Inquiries

- What is jazz? What are its musical elements?

- Why is New Orleans considered the birthplace of jazz? What musical forms were present there? How did political and social events determine the course of the development of jazz?

- Investigate the phrase "blowin' the changes." What does it mean, and what does it tell us about jazz music?

- What is scat singing?

- Which jazz players in New Orleans influenced Armstrong and how?

- How did Armstrong change jazz?

- What does the term "head arrangement" mean? Why did this technique change as the bands got larger?

- Why did some people describe Armstrong as an "Uncle Tom?" What are the arguments against this opinion?

- How were Armstrong and his band received in other countries?

- What did Armstrong do to combat racial injustice?

- What are "race records" and what was their role in the recording industry?

Products

- Demonstrate the elements of jazz using Armstrong's recordings and audio files from the Internet.

- Create a product that shows the various musical forms that contributed to jazz.

- Write an essay, poem, or fictional piece that captures the flavor of Armstrong's New Orleans in the early 1900s.

- Construct a chronology of Armstrong's life based on the bands he played with or "fronted."

- Compare Armstrong the "artist" with Armstrong the "entertainer." Give examples that demonstrate Armstrong's ability at each.

- Explain the term "Uncle Tom" and discuss why some people used the term to describe Armstrong.

- Analyze the lyrics of "(What Did I Do To Be So) Black and Blue" and using the song and facts about Armstrong's life, describe Armstrong's efforts to change people's attitudes about African-Americans.

- Read Giddins's articles on the recording by Armstrong and the Mills Brothers and give an oral presentation of the event and its significance. (Giddins, *Visions*, 1998, 23–31)

- Write an essay describing the "race record" labels, such as Okeh. Describe their catalogs and their audience. Include Armstrong recordings as examples.

RESEARCH RESOURCES

Web Sites
Biographical:

"Armstrong Biography: Who is Louis Armstrong?" *Satchmo.net.*
URL: http://satchmo.net/bio/

A short biography of Armstrong with links to a Timeline, Discography, and Bibliography. Satchmo.net *also has a video tour of Armstrong's house in Corona, New York.*

Crouch, Stanley. "Louis Armstrong; the Jazz Musician." *Time 100.*
URL: http://www.time.com/time/time100/artists/profile/armstrong.html

This tribute to Armstrong emphasizes his New Orleans background and influences.

Jazz at Lincoln Center. "Louis Armstrong." *Jazz: A Film by Ken Burns: Biographies: Life and Times of the Great Ones.*
URL: http://www.pbs.org/jazz/biography/artist_id_armstrong_louis.htm

Brief biographical information with audio clips of Armstrong's music, NPR segments, and Wynton Marsalis.

"Louis Armstrong; A Cultural Legacy." *Smithsonian National Portrait Gallery.*
URL: http://www.npg.si.edu/exh/armstrong/index.htm

A brief biographical sketch with photographs.

"Louis Armstrong: Biography." *Louis Armstrong: Celebrate Satchmo's Centennial with Columbia/Legacy.*
URL: http://louis-armstrong.net/bio.html

This biography concentrates on Armstrong's recording history, beginning with the recordings for Okeh.

"Louis the First." *Time Magazine*, February 21, 1949. *Time 100.*
URL: http://www.time.com/time/time100/artists/profile/satchmo_related.html

This reprinted Time *article from 1949 begins with Armstrong's participation as King of the Zulus Parade in New Orleans and continues with a biographical sketch that includes his views on bebop, which was current at the time.*

Historical:

"A Brief History of New Orleans Jazz." *New Orleans Jazz National Historic Park.*
URL: http://www.nps.gov/neor/jazz_origins_study.html

An extensive account of the early history of New Orleans as it related to the development of jazz. It includes quotations from jazz pioneers, including Louis Armstrong.

Fleming, Thomas C. "Black Musicians and Early Radio." *The Red Hot Jazz Archive.*
URL: http://www.redhotjazz.com/smithartice.html

Fleming, a writer for the Sun-Reporter, *San Francisco's African-American weekly, recalls the jazz of the 1920s in Chico, California and his experiences buying recordings and listening to jazz on the radio.*

Hentoff, Nat. "Louis: Black and Blue and Triumphant." *Jazz Times.*
URL: http://www.jazztimes.com/finalchorus_louisarmstrong.cfm

Hentoff describes Armstrong's reactions to instances of racism.

"Jazz Origins in New Orleans, 1895–1927." *New Orleans Jazz National Historic Park.*
URL: http://www.nps.gov/neor/jazz_photo_ess_origins.html

An essay complete with photographs outlining the musicians and bands that were important in New Orleans jazz history.

Kelly, Judith, Patricia Bradford, and Consentine Morgan. "Black and Blue: Jazz in Ralph Ellison's Invisible Man." *Jazz: A Film by Ken Burns: Classroom.*
URL: http://www.pbs.org/jazz/classroom/blackandblue.htm

This lesson plan written to coordinate with the videos from Jazz: A Film by Ken Burns *uses Armstrong's performance of "Black and Blue" and Ralph Ellison's novel* Invisible Man. *There is a link to the lyrics of "Black and Blue."*

Prosperity and Thrift: The Coolidge Era and the Consumer Economy, 1921–1929.
URL: *http://memory.loc.gov/ammem/coolhtml/coolhome.html*

Search with keywords race records *in Search Full Text for information on the Okeh and Victor recording labels.*

Ross, Sam. "The Savoy Ballroom." June 14, 1939. *American Life Histories: Manuscripts from the Federal Writers' Project, 1936–940.*
URL: http://memory.loc.gov/ammem/wpaintro/wpahome.html

Ross describes an evening at the Savoy Ballroom in Chicago in which Louis Armstrong "took up a trumpet solo, rising clear and solid above the ensemble." Search the keywords louis armstrong *(match all of these words).*

Sundgaard, Arnold. "Jazz, Hot and Cold." *The Atlantic Monthly.* July 1955. *The Atlantic Monthly Online.*
URL: http://www.theatlantic.com/unbound/jazz/sundgaar.htm

Sundgaard defines jazz and supplies a chronology of its history up until the 1950s.

Musical:

"Andy Razaf: The Life & Lyrics of the Prince of Madagascar." *Riverwalk: Live from the Landing.*
URL: http://www.riverwalk.org/proglist/showpromo/razaf.htm

This show was broadcast on January 25, 2001 on Texas Public Radio's Riverwalk: Live from the Landing. *It describes the lyrics of Andy Razaf, who wrote "Black and Blue," "Honeysuckle Rose," and "Ain't Misbehavin'." A link to the complete lyrics of "Black and Blue" is included. (http://www.perfessorbill.com/lyrics/lyblckbl.htm)*

"Armstrong Biography: Discography." *Satchmo.net.*
URL: http://satchmo.net/bio/disc.shtml

A listing with descriptions of some of Armstrong's most notable recordings.

Levin, Michael. "Louis Is Superb in Carnegie Hall Concert." *Down Beat Magazine,* Feb. 26, 1947. *William P. Gottlieb: Photographs from the Golden Age of Jazz.*
URL: http://memory.loc.gov/ammem/wghtml/wghome.html

Click on Down Beat *Magazine Articles (1946–47) and find the above title for a review of Armstrong's Carnegie Hall Concert. The article lists members of Armstrong's band and the pieces they played.*

"Louis Armstrong: The Trumpeter." *Jazz Profiles from NPR.*
URL: http://www.npr.org/programs/jazzprofiles/archive/armstrong_trumpeter.html

This online version of the radio show on Armstrong is interspersed with audio tracks of people discussing Armstrong's trumpet playing.

"Louis 'Satchmo' Armstrong (1900–1971)" *The Red Hot Jazz Archive.*
URL: http://www.redhotjazz.com/louie.html

In addition to a brief biography of Armstrong, this site contains audio files from six of Armstrong's bands.

Waller, Fats. "(What Did I Do To Be So) Black and Blue?" *The Red Hot Jazz Archive.*
    URL: http://www.redhotjazz.com/lao.html.
The audio file of the July 22, 1929 Decca recording of Waller's song by The Louis Armstrong Orchestra is on this page.

Weinstock, Len. "The Origins of Jazz." *The Red Hot Jazz Archive.*
    URL: http://www.redhotjazz.com/originsarticle.html
A thoughtful explanation for the social and musical reasons that jazz originated in New Orleans. Weinstock also lists specific musical elements.

Books

Crawford, Richard. "Morton, Armstrong, and Chicago." In *America's Musical Life: A History.* New York: W. W. Norton, 2001.
Crawford analyzes some of Armstrong's recordings to point out his innovations. The role of white and black jazz bands in the Chicago area is also discussed.

Ellison, Ralph. *Living with Music: Ralph Ellison's Jazz Writings.* Edited by Robert G. O'Meally. New York: Modern Library, 2001.
O'Meally includes selections from Ellison's nonfiction and fiction writings, letters, and interviews that relate to music.

Giddins, Gary. "Louis Armstrong/Mills Brothers (Signifying)" In *Visions of Jazz: The First Century.* New York: Oxford Univ. Press, 1998.
Giddins described recordings by Armstrong and the Mills Brothers of "Carry Me Back to Old Virginny" and "Darling Nellie Gray," the former a minstrel song and the latter an abolitionist song.

Giddins, Gary. *Satchmo: The Genius of Louis Armstrong.* New York: Da Capo Press, 2001.
Giddins explores Louis Armstrong's life and his music in two sections: "The Entertainer as Artist" and "The Artist as Entertainer." The book includes many photographs, a discography, and a bibliography.

Gourse, Leslie. *Blowing on the Changes: The Art of the Jazz Horn Players.* New York: Franklin Watts, 1997.
In addition to providing biographical and musical information on the great jazz horn players, Gourse explains Armstrong's influence on jazz in the chapters "Louis 'Pops' Armstrong Blows on the Changes" and "Louis Armstrong Thrills and Influences His Whole Generation."

Haskins, James. *One Nation under a Groove: Rap Music and Its Roots.* New York: Jump at the Sun Hyperion Books, 2000.
Haskins traces rap's roots, from the call and response of African music through blues and jazz.

Shipton, Alyn. "Louis Armstrong: Ambassador Satch." In *Jazz Makers: Vanguards of Sound.* New York: Oxford Univ. Press, 2002.
Shipton relates Armstrong's musical career and his significance in jazz's history. Includes a discography, further reading, and web sites.

Ward, Geoffrey C. *Jazz: A History of America's Music.* New York: Alfred A. Knopf, 2000.
Use the index to find all the sections on Armstrong.

CDs

Armstrong, Louis. *Louis Armstrong: The Definitive. Ken Burns Jazz.* Columbia/Legacy, 2000. CK 61440.
"Heebie Jeebies," "Black and Blue," "St. Louis Blues," and "When It's Sleepy Time Down South" are included among the twenty-five tracks.

Handy, W. C. "St. Louis Blues." Bessie Smith (and Louis Armstrong). Compact disc one of *Say It Loud! A Celebration of Black Music in America.* Rhino Entertainment Company, 2001. R2 76660/A53891.

"Heebie Jeebies." Louis Armstrong & His Hot Five. Compact disc one of *Say It Loud! A Celebration of Black Music in America.* Rhino Entertainment Company, 2001. R2 76660/A53891.

Chapter 12
Duke Ellington, 1899–1974
Composer, Bandleader, Arranger, Pianist

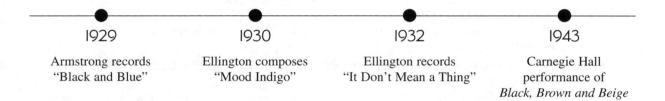

1929	1930	1932	1943
Armstrong records "Black and Blue"	Ellington composes "Mood Indigo"	Ellington records "It Don't Mean a Thing"	Carnegie Hall performance of *Black, Brown and Beige*

Edward Kennedy Ellington got his nickname "Duke" in his teens because of his "polite manners, fashionable clothes, and aristocratic bearing." (Hasse, 1993, 38) Throughout his career as a composer and bandleader, he lived up to this name, working steadily, despite racial discrimination, to use his music to portray the life of his people. Some of his compositions, such as *Black, Brown and Beige*, *My People*, and *Jump for Joy*, were programmatic and related the history of African-Americans in the United States. Ellington used his orchestra as his instrument and with this instrument changed the structure of jazz music and American music.

OBJECTIVES

Students will describe the type of jazz composed and performed in the "swing era."

Students will explain Duke Ellington's role and significance in the history of jazz.

Students will describe the makeup of a jazz orchestra and the patterns of the musical arrangements.

INTRODUCING THE MUSICIAN

Picture Book

Pinkney, Andrea Davis. *Duke Ellington: The Piano Prince and His Orchestra*. Illustrated by Brian Pinkney. New York: Hyperion Books for Children, 1998.
This picture book biography calls out to be read. The text describes the instrumentalists and their music in poetic terms. The phrases "butterscotch tones" and "silver notes" are reflected in the illustrations. Because the book also provides a lot of information on Ellington's life and his music, it is a good

introduction to a study of jazz or Ellington and his place in music. With music spilling out of instruments in colorful, swirling illustrations and words that mirror jazz's breezy style, the Pinkneys have captured Duke Ellington's sophisticated, elegant music.

Video

Duke Ellington. Scholastic. Produced for Weston Woods by Top Dog Media, Inc., adapted and directed by Ray Messecar. Westport, CT: Weston Woods, c2000. VHS.
   Based on the book, Duke Ellington: The Piano Prince and His Orchestra.

Audio Clip

Santacroce, Lou. "Mood Indigo." *The NPR 100.*
   URL: http://www.npr.org/ramfiles/atc/20001106.atc.11.rmm
   Lou Santacroce, in a segment for The NPR 100 *(http://www.npr.org/programs/specials/vote/ 100list.html#M) describes the writing of "Mood Indigo" and its musical significance.*

Quotations

- Billy Strayhorn on "the Ellington effect" in the Nov. 4, 1952 issue of *Down Beat*:
  Each member of his band is to him a distinctive tone color and set of emotions, which he mixes with others equally distinctive to produce a third thing, which I like to call the Ellington effect. Sometimes this mixing happens on paper and frequently right on the bandstand. I have often seen him exchange parts in the middle of a piece because the man and the part weren't the same character. (Hasse, 1993, 309)

- Photographer and writer, Gordon Parks, on Ellington:
  Ellington had always been my hero. Unlike . . . black Hollywood stereotypes he never grinned, he smiled; he never shuffled, he strode . . . At his performances we young blacks sat high in our seats, wanting the whites to see us; to know that this handsome, elegant, sharply dressed man playing that beautiful, sophisticated music, was one of us. (Hasse, 1993, 217)

- Ellington on his music in the article "Duke Says Swing Is Stagnant" from *Down Beat Magazine*, Feb. 1939:
  . . . our aim has always been the development of an authentic Negro music, of which swing is only one element. We are not interested primarily in the playing of jazz or swing music, but in producing musically a genuine contribution from our race. (Duke, 1993, 135)

- Ralph Ellison on hearing Ellington's orchestra as a teenager:
  And then Ellington and the great orchestra came to town; came with their uniforms, their sophistication, their skills, their golden horns, their flights of controlled and disciplined fantasy . . . They were news from the great wide world, an example and a goal; and I wish that all those who write so knowledgeably of Negro boys having no masculine figure with whom to identify would consider the long national and international career of Ellington and his band, the thousands of one night stands played in the black communities of this nation." (Ellison, 2001, 81)

- Trumpet player Wynton Marsalis on Ellington:
  You don't get the same type of spiritual high-mindedness in his sound that you have in Louis Armstrong's. Duke Ellington, he's more of a late-night person. He's the person who understands the sensuous. That's in his music and it's in his sound. When he hits one or two notes on the piano, you know he's going to take you into a late-night room where something of interest is about to take place. (Ward, 2000, 118)

Connections to Other Musicians in This Book

- At Carnegie Hall debut given plaque signed by composers, including **Aaron Copland**. (Hasse, 1993, 266)

- Ellington's "Cotton Tail," written in 1940, is built on a series of variations on the chord progressions of **Gershwin's** "I Got Rhythm." (Hasse, 1993, 266)

- Wrote composition "Portrait of Louis Armstrong." (Hasse, 1993, 390)

- Composer **Will Marion Cook** was a mentor to Ellington. (Hasse, 1993, 78)

- Recorded with **Dizzy Gillespie.** (Ward, 2001, 413)

Periods in American History

World War I, Jazz Age (1920s), Great Depression, World War II, Civil Rights era

Musical Highlights of Ellington's Life: Teachers, Colleagues, Events

1899	Born in Washington, D.C.
1918	Formed first band, Duke's Serenaders
1923	Moved to New York City and formed band, the Washingtonians
1927–32	Performed at the Cotton Club
1927	Recorded "Black and Tan Fantasy" and "Creole Love Song"
1929	Ellington and band performed in Ziegfeld's *Show Girl*; music was by George Gershwin
1930	Composed *Mood Indigo*
1932	Recorded "It Don't Mean a Thing If It Ain't Got That Swing" Played for composer Percy Grainger's music appreciation class at New York University
1933	First tour of Europe
1935	Appeared in film *Symphony in Black*
1937	Recorded "Diminuendo and Crescendo in Blue"
1938	Wrote "Battle of Swing"
1939	Ellington began his collaboration with Billy Strayhorn
1941	Premiere of Ellington's all-black musical *Jump for Joy*
1943	Premier at Carnegie Hall of *Black, Brown and Beige: A Tone Parallel to the History of the Negro in America*
1956	Newport Jazz Festival appearance
1959	Composed score for film, *Anatomy of a Murder*, which won the Academy Award Awarded Spingarn Medal by the NAACP for "the highest or noblest achievement by an American Negro during the preceding year or years" (Hasse, 1993, 338)
1960	Composed *Suite Thursday* as a tribute to John Steinbeck's novel *Sweet Thursday*
1963	Performed his *My People* at the Century of Negro Progress Exposition in Chicago

1969	Given Presidential Medal of Freedom
1970	Recorded *The New Orleans Suite*, which includes "Portrait of Louis Armstrong"
1974	Died in New York City
1999	Posthumously awarded the Pulitzer Prize

ELLINGTON STUDENT PAGES

Inquiries
- What is "swing" music?

- What is the history of the "rent parties" in Harlem? How did they affect the music of the city?

- How did segregation affect the black jazz bands? How did Duke Ellington respond to the inequalities?

- How did Ellington manage to remain successful through the decades?

- What was the unique sound of The Washingtonians?

- How did Ellington's arrangements transform the jazz bands?

- What pieces were written during Ellington's tenure at the Cotton Club? How did these reflect the racial atmosphere during that time?

- What did Ellington say about the inspiration for his music?

- What is the significance of the title of Ellington's piece *Black, Brown and Beige*?

- What was the social significance of Ellington's *Jump for Joy*

- How did Ellington's music differ from the "classic jazz" of New Orleans?

- How did Ellington respond to the rise of bebop and demise of the swing band?

- What role did radio play in the success of Ellington's band?

- What role did swing play in the dance crazes of the 30s and 40s?

Products
- Reproduce the atmosphere of the Cotton Club in Harlem in a visual and aural presentation.

- Compile a list of Ellington's pieces that relate to color and describe their genesis and influence.

- Read *Duke Ellington: The Piano Prince and His Orchestra* with accompanying sound tracks of the music that is mentioned. Produce a visual presentation that matches the colors mentioned in the book.

- Compare the pieces written during the different periods of Ellington's life and discuss their relationship to the times.

- Describe Ellington's role in swing, listing the similarities between the bands, and Ellington's distinguishing features. Elaborate on Ellington's quote, "Jazz is music; swing is business." (Hass, 1993, 203)

- Investigate the titles of Ellington's music and use them to explain Ellington's views on the role of African-Americans during that time period.

- Investigate the pieces Ellington wrote that deal with African-American history, such as *Black, Brown and Beige, Jump for Joy*, and *My People*. Use the music as a basis for an oral presentation on that history and as examples of music as a vehicle for social protest.

- Describe the pieces played during Ellington's annual concerts at Carnegie Hall. Compare them to his earlier pieces in terms of form and content.

- Trace the history of jazz from New Orleans to Chicago to New York City by describing the bands and the clubs in which they performed.

- Using the photographs in the American Memory collections and recordings compile a multimedia presentation of Duke Ellington and his orchestra during the 30s and 40s.

RESEARCH RESOURCES

Web Sites
Biographical:

"Duke Ellington; A Celebration." *Duke Ellington: Celebrating 100 Years of the Man and his Music.*
URL: http://www.dellington.org/scrapbk/scrap00.html

Designed as a scrapbook with pictures and text on facing pages, this web site presents Ellington's life, his music, and his accomplishments.

"Edward 'Duke' Ellington (1899–1974)." *The Red Hot Jazz Archive: A History of Jazz before 1930.*
URL: http://www.redhotjazz.com/duke.html

In addition to a brief biography, audio files are included for recordings of many of Ellington's orchestras.

Jazz at Lincoln Center. "Duke Ellington: Composer, Bandleader, Pianist." *Jazz: A Film by Ken Burns: Biographies, Life and Times of the Great Ones.*
URL: http://www.pbs.org/jazz/biography/artist_id_ellington_duke.htm

A short review of Ellington's music with links to web sites, including NPR's Jazz Profiles: Duke Ellington, The NPR 100: "Mood Indigo," *and audio samples of some of his pieces.*

Levi, Robert, and Molly Murphy. "Duke Ellington: the Bandleader, Part 1." *Jazz Profiles from NPR.*
URL: http://www.npr.org/programs/jazzprofiles/archive/ellington_d1.html

Interspersed in this profile of Ellington are audio files of former band members and musicians describing Ellington's rehearsal and compositional techniques.

"One Hundred Years; A Duke Ellington Timeline." *Duke Ellington: Celebrating 100 Years of the Man and his Music.*
URL: http://www.dellington.org/timeline.html

Yearly events in Ellington's life are adjacent to events in American history.

Historical:

America from the Great Depression to World War II: Black-and-White Photographs from the FSA-OWI 1935–1945.
URL: http://memory.loc.gov/ammem/fsahtml/fahome.html

Search duke ellington *for photographs of Ellington and his orchestra during the 30s and 40s.*

"Jazz in Time, History in the Key of Jazz: The Great Depression." *Jazz: A Film by Ken Burns.*
  URL: http://www.pbs.org/jazz/time/time_depression.htm

  "Primarily excerpted from Jazz: A History of America's Music," *this web site based on the Ken Burns film,* Jazz, *provides background on jazz's role during the Great Depression and the influence of swing. It also recounts the enthusiastic reception for Ellington's band as they toured Europe in 1939.*

"Spaces, Places, and Changing Faces: Cotton Club." *Jazz: A Film by Ken Burns.*
  URL: http://www.pbs.org/jazz/places/spaces_cotton_club.htm

  This site provides a brief history of New York City's Cotton Club. Especially interesting is the audio file that contains interviews with some of the dancers that performed at the Club.

"Visualizing Jazz Scenes of the Harlem Renaissance." *Jazz: A Film by Ken Burns: Classroom.*
  URL: http://www.pbs.org/jazz/classroom/visualize.htm

  Based on a few episodes of the PBS series, Jazz: A Film by Ken Burns, *this lesson's objectives are for the student to compare the literature and jazz of the Harlem Renaissance period, specifically describing the impact of jazz on the literature. The lesson feature Ellington's music and the poems of Langston Hughes.*

William P. Gottlieb: Photographs from the Golden Age of Jazz.
  URL: http://memory.loc.gov/ammem/wghtml/wghome.html

  Search duke ellington *for photographs of Ellington and has orchestra taken by Gottlieb from 1938–1948.*

Musical:

"Duke Ellington and his Orchestra." *The Red Hot Jazz Archive: A History of Jazz before 1930.*
  URL: http://www.redhotjazz.com/dukeo.html

  Includes a discography, a list of band members, a filmography, and audio links to "It Don't Mean a Thing," "Sophisticated Lady," *and others.*

Gottlieb, William P. "Duke & Group on the Cover." *Down Beat,* Nov. 4, 1946. *Down Beat Magazine Articles Written and Illustrated by William P. Gottlieb, 1946–47.*
  URL: http://memory.loc.gov/ammem/wghtml/wgdbeat.html

  The November 4, 1946 Down Beat *cover and article announces the concert at the Civic Opera in Chicago by Ellington and his band.*

MENC: The National Association for Music Education. "Ellington, Music and Color." *Duke Ellington Centennial Celebration.*
  URL: http://www.dellington.org/lessons/lesson00.html

  Five lessons with audio clips and multiple choice questions.

Santacroce, Lou. "Mood Indigo." The NPR 100.
  URL: http://www.npr.org/ramfiles/atc/20001106.atc.11.rmm

  Lou Santacroce, in a segment for The NPR 100 (http://www.npr.org/programs/specials/vote/100list.html#M) describes the writing of "Mood Indigo" *and its musical significance.*

Books

The Duke Ellington Reader. Edited by Mark Tucker. New York: Oxford Univ. Press, 1993.
  Arranged chronologically, this anthology includes magazine and newspaper articles by Ellington, music critics, and jazz historians. An interesting item is the program, including program notes, for the Carnegie Hall concert on January 23, 1943. Irving Kolodin describes the sections of Black, Brown and Beige.

Ellington, Duke. "We, Too, Sing 'America.' " In *I Hear a Symphony: African Americans Celebrate Love.* Edited by Paula L. Woods and Felix H. Liddell. New York: Doubleday, 1994.
  In this speech by Ellington on February 9, 1941 at the Annual Lincoln Day Services at Scott Methodist Church, in Los Angeles, Ellington reiterates Langston Hughes's assertion of the contributions of African-Americans to America.

Ellison, Ralph. "Homage to Duke Ellington on His Birthday." *Sunday Star*, April 27, 1969. In Ellison, Ralph. *Living with Music: Ralph Ellison's Jazz Writings.* New York: Modern Library, 2001.
Ellison recounts Ellington's influence on American life and recalls hearing Ellington's band as a teenager.

Hasse, John Edward. *Beyond Category: the Life and Genius of Duke Ellington.* New York: Simon & Schuster, 1993.
Hasse concentrates on Ellington's musical career and compositional technique. The chronological chapters are determined by the significance of that period in Ellington's life. At the end of each chapter Hasse includes explanations of some of the music from that period and recommendations of recordings.

Lawrence, A. H. *Duke Ellington and His Word: A Biography.* New York: Routledge, 2001.
Lawrence, who was a jazz trombonist in the 40s, interviewed jazz musicians who played with Ellington as he researched this biography. Of particular note are the sections at the end of the book, which include a list Ellington's various bands and their members, a chronological list of his compositions, and brief biographies of musicians who played in Ellington's bands.

Shipton, Alyn. "Duke Ellington: Music Is My Mistress." In *Jazz Makers: Vanguards of Sound.* New York: Oxford Univ. Press, 2002.
Shipton discusses Ellington's career as a bandleader, especially at a Harlem's Cotton Club. Includes a discography, further reading, and web sites.

Ward, Geoffrey C. "Jungle Music." In *Jazz: A History of America's Music.* New York: Alfred A. Knopf, 2000.
This section describes the décor, clientele, and floor show at the Cotton Club while Ellington and his orchestra were in residence. It includes Ellington's reactions to performing for a whites-only audience and how the club was advertised to tourists.

CDs

Ellington, Duke. *Duke Ellington: The Definitive. Ken Burns Jazz.* Columbia/Legacy, 2000. CK 61444.
Contains many of Ellington's popular pieces, such as "Mood Indigo", "It Don't Mean a Thing (If It Ain't Got That Swing)," and "Sophisticated Lady."

Ellington, Duke. "It Don't Mean a Thing (If It Ain't Got That Swing)." Duke Ellington & His Famous Orchestra. In *Say It Loud! A Celebration of Black Music in America.* Rhino Entertainment Company, 2001. R2 76660/A53891.

Chapter 13
Benny Goodman, 1909–1986

Clarinetist, Bandleader

1932	**1935**	**1936**	**1947**
Ellington records "It Don't Mean a Thing"	Palomar Ballroom appearance — birth of swing	Integrated jazz trio at jazz concert at Congress Hotel	Commissioned Copland's *Concerto for Clarinet*

Benny Goodman was known as the "King of Swing." Although he wasn't the first to perform swing music, his radio shows attracted a large, mostly young audience whose enthusiasm became evident at a concert at the Palomar Ballroom in California on August 21, 1935, the "night the swing era was born." (Firestone, 1993, 149) Goodman was the first white band leader to integrate his band by hiring both African-American musicians and arrangers. He began with hiring Teddy Wilson, pianist, for the Goodman Trio and later, Lionel Hampton, vibraphonist, for the Goodman Quartet. His use of small combos in his concerts was also a first. Because of his discipline in practicing, he became a virtuoso clarinet player and was able to perform and commission classical pieces, as well as produce amazing jazz solos.

OBJECTIVES

Students will recognize the elements of swing music.

Students will describe how swing music related to the political and social ideas of the time in America.

Students will identify the disparities between black and white jazz bands and musicians and determine Benny Goodman's role in promoting change.

INTRODUCING THE MUSICIAN

Picture Book

Winter, Jonah. *Once Upon a Time in Chicago: The Story of Benny Goodman*. Pictures by Jeanette Winter. New York: Hyperion Books for Children, 2000.

With illustrations that capture Chicago in the early twentieth century this picture book describes Goodman's childhood and his beginnings in music. It is an excellent introduction to the childhood of a son of immigrants in the early twentieth century. Use it as a springboard to speculate on the availability to immigrants of educational opportunities from religious groups and charity organizations. How did a childhood with these influences affect Goodman's role as an orchestra leader?

Quotations

- Louis Armstrong on jazz after ragtime:
  Later on in the years it was called jazz music, hot music, gutbucket, and now they've poured a little gravy over it and called it swing music. (Firestone, 1993, 157)

- Jazz musician Lionel Hampton on Goodman's hiring black musicians:
  As far as I'm concerned, what he did in those days—and they were hard days in 1937—made it possible for Negroes to have the chance in baseball and other fields. He was a real pioneer, and he didn't grandstand about it. He used to tell me, 'If a guy's got it, let him give it, I'm selling music, not prejudice.' (Firestone, 1993, 183–184)

- Goodman on practicing:
  Some of the guys I played with . . . didn't go around learning more about their instruments from an intellectual point of view. All they wanted was to play hot jazz, and the instrument was just a means . . . But I've always wanted to know what made music. How you do it and why it sounds good. (Ward, 2000, 135)

- Author James Lincoln Collier on Goodman's playing:
  . . . and it is these things—the varied way of dividing the beat, the terse fragments interrupted by long, soaring notes, the quick twist at the end of notes, that contributed to the enormous swing which was always present in his work. (Collier, 1989, 72)

- Author Gary Giddins on Goodman's playing:
  Goodman was a hot player whose adroit blues choruses distinguished him almost from the start during his days in Chicago. His command of every register enabled him to contrive a style of high drama and earthy swing . . . Goodman's rhythmic gait was unmistakable; his best solos combined cool legato, a fierce doubling up of notes, and the canny use of propulsive riffs. (Giddins, 1998, 161)

Connections to Other Musicians in This Book

- Performed in jazz bands for **Gershwin's** *Strike Up the Band* and *Girl Crazy*. (Firestone, 1993, 63)

- Goodman's quartet played **Gershwin's** "I Got Rhythm" on its Carnegie Hall concert in 1938. (Firestone, 1993, 213)

- **Gershwin** wrote King of Swing in honor of Goodman.

- Goodman commissioned **Copland's** *Concerto for Clarinet*. (Firestone, 1993, 250)

- Benny Goodman and His Orchestra played an arrangement of **Irving Berlin's** "Blue Skies."

- Goodman recorded **Bernstein's** *Prelude, Fugue and Riffs*. (Firestone, 1993, 421)

Periods in American History
Jazz Age (1920s), Great Depression, World War II

Musical Highlights of Goodman's Life: Teachers, Colleagues, Events

1909	Born in Chicago, Illinois
1919	Joined Kehelah Jacob Synagogue band
1920	Joined boys' band at Hull House Took private lessons from Franz Schoepp, clarinet teacher at Chicago Musical College
1922	Met Austin High Gang, which included Jimmy and Dick McPartland, Bud Freeman, Frank Teschemacher, and Jim Lanigan Heard black band of Lil Hardin, piano, Baby Dodds, drum, and Johnny Dodds, clarinet
1923	Played with Bix Beiderbecke on excursion boat Spent nights listening to bands at the Entertainer's Café (Jimmie Noone, Bessie Smith) and Lincoln Gardens (King Oliver's Creole Jazz Band with Lil Hardin, Dodds brothers, and Louis Armstrong)
1925	Went to California to join Ben Pollack's band
1927	Published *One Hundred Jazz Breaks by Benny Goodman*
1928	Pollack band went to New York and opened at the Little Club
1929	Goodman left Pollack's band Stock market crash
1930	Performed in bands for Gershwin's *Strike Up the Band* and *Girl Crazy*
1929–1933	Freelanced on radio shows, and movie sound tracks
1933	Met John Hammond and recorded jazz sides for English Columbia
1934	Put together orchestra and opened at the Billy Rose Music Hall One of three orchestras for "Let's Dance" radio show Hired Fletcher Henderson as arranger
1935	Recorded as Benny Goodman Trio with Teddy Wilson, piano, and Gene Krupa, drums Appeared at the Palomar Ballroom in California, "the night the Swing Era was born" (Firestone, 1993, 149)
1936	Jazz concert at Congress Hotel in Chicago included integrated jazz trio with Goodman, Teddy Wilson, piano, and Gene Krupa, drums Lionel Hampton on vibraphone added to form Goodman Quartet
1937	"Music Battle of the Century" with Chick Webb's orchestra at the Savoy Ballroom
1938	Carnegie Hall appearance Goodman played with the Budapest String Quartet in a Mozart quintet at Town Hall

1939	Goodman played *Rhapsody for Clarinet and Violin* by Bela Bartok in Carnegie Hall recital
	Published autobiography *Kingdom of Swing*
1940	Goodman, Szigeti (violin), and Bartok (piano), recorded *Contrasts* (formerly *Rhapsody for Clarinet and Violin*)
1947	Goodman commissioned Hindemith's *Concerto for Clarinet and Orchestra* and Copland's *Concerto for Clarinet*
1963	Recorded Bernstein's *Prelude, Fugue and Riffs*
	Goodman Quartet recorded *Together Again!*
1986	Died in New York City

GOODMAN STUDENT PAGES

Inquiries

- What is "swing" music?

- What were the reactions to swing?

- Why was Benny Goodman referred to as the "King of Swing?"

- What was Hull House, and what was its purpose?

- How was Goodman's attitude toward jazz different from the Austin High Gang?

- What was unique about Goodman as a performer, and how did this influence his success?

- Which black bands and musicians influenced Goodman in his Chicago days?

- How did the Depression affect musicians, especially Goodman?

- What American historical events helped bring jazz bands back?

- How was Goodman involved in the integration of jazz bands?

- What was the role of John Hammond in Goodman's career?

- What made the Café Society different from other cabarets in New York City?

- How were Goodman's orchestras different from other jazz orchestras?

- What part did radio play in the history of jazz, and particularly swing?

Products

- Compare Goodman's childhood and musical beginnings with that of Louis Armstrong.

- Investigate the jazz life in Chicago at the time of Goodman's start in jazz. List the clubs and the bands and explain the interactions between the white and black bands.

- Describe the role that radio played in the 1930s in the development of jazz and particularly in Goodman's career.

- Find quotes from the time period that reflect the reactions to swing. Include reactions from other countries. Explain the reasons for the various reactions.

- On a timeline plot events in Goodman's life that demonstrate his role in integrating his bands to include African-American musicians.

- Present arguments on both sides on the issue of integrating the jazz bands.

- Investigate the role of John Hammond in Goodman's career and the careers of other jazz musicians. Discuss the role of left-wing politics in the jazz world, including the role of the Café Society cabaret.

RESEARCH RESOURCES

Web Sites
Biographical:

"Benny Goodman." *Big Band and Jazz Hall of Fame.*
　　URL: http://www.jazzhall.org/jazz.cgi?@GOODMANBENNY

This biography includes quotes from other musicians and pictures of a couple of Goodman's album covers.

"Benny Goodman." *Downbeat.com Biography.*
　　URL: http://www.downbeat.com/artists/artist_main.asp?sect=bio&aid=46&aname=Benny+
　　Goodman

A brief synopsis of Goodman's career.

"Benny Goodman." *Kennedy Center Honors.*
　　URL: http://www.kennedy-center.org/programs/specialevents/honors/history/honoree/goodman.
　　html

A brief biography that relates the story of the enthusiastic reception Goodman's band received at Hollywood's Palomar ballroom during their 1935 tour.

Cooke, Mervyn. "Populist and Classicist: Benny Goodman." In *The Chronicle of Jazz. Abbeville Press.*
　　URL: http://www.abbeville.com/jazz/084.asp

In this section from the book The Chronicle of Jazz *Cooke describes Goodman's rise to his position as "King of Swing." There is a link to a section on his 1938 Carnegie Hall appearance.*

"Jazz Interviews: Benny Goodman on Jazz Legends." *BBC Radio3.* Aug. 18, 2002.
　　URL: http://www.bbc.co.uk/radio3/jazz/jazzlegends/goodmanint.shtml

Benny Goodman's story is told on eight tracks of audio files and includes interviews with Goodman, Teddy Wilson, and Lionel Hampton. The segments include the Palomar concert and the Carnegie Hall Concert. Includes a link to a profile of Goodman's life.

Wang, Richard. "Goodman, Benny [Benjamin David]." In Vol. 2 of *The New Grove Dictionary of Jazz.* 2nd ed. Edited by Barry Kernfeld. London: Macmillan Publishers; New York: Grove's Dictionaries, 2002. "Benny Goodman." *Jazz: A Film by Ken Burns: Biographies, Life and Times of the Great Ones.*
　　URL: http://www.pbs.org/jazz/biography/artist_id_goodman_benny.htm

This article, excerpted from The New Grove Dictionary of Jazz, *is interspersed with audio files of Goodman's music, including* The NPR 100 *segment on "Sing, Sing, Sing."*

Wilson, John S. "Benny Goodman, King of Swing, Is Dead." *The New York Times on the Web; On This Day, June 14, 1986.*
　　URL: http://www.nytimes.com/learning/general/onthisday/bday/0530.html

The extensive obituary on Benny Goodman that appeared in the New York Times *on June 14, 1986.*

Yanow, Scott. "Benny Goodman." *JazzSteps.com.*
　　URL: http://www.jazzsteps.com

Search under Artists for Benny Goodman. Site includes a biography and reviews of recordings.

Historical:

"Carnegie Hall Gets First Taste of Swing." *Downbeat.com: Archives: Stories: Benny Goodman.*
　　URL: http://www.downbeat.com/artists/artist_main.asp?sect=archives&aid=46&aname=Benny+
　　Goodman

This article describes the historic jazz concert at Carnegie Hall in 1938.

Dana, Robert W. "Goodman Turns Back the Clock." *Craig's Big Bands and Big Names.com.*
　　URL: http://www.bigbandsandbignames.com/BennyGoodmanReview.html

A February 17, 1956 review of an appearance by Goodman's orchestra in the Empire Room of the Waldorf-Astoria in New York City.

" 'Musical Ability Has Damn Little to Do with It': *Downbeat* Dodges the Racial Issue." *Center for History and New Media: Between the Wars.*
   URL: http://chnm.gmu.edu/courses/hist409/downbeat.html

For the course, History 409, Michael O'Malley includes the two articles from the October 15, 1939 issue of Down Beat that address the question of one article's title, "Should Negro Musicians Play in White Bands?"

"Predicted Race Riot Fades as Dallas Applauds Quartet!" *Downbeat.com: Archives: Stories: Benny Goodman.*
   URL: http://www.downbeat.com/artists/artist_main.asp?sect=archives&aid=46&aname=Benny+Goodman

An article describing the controversy of booking Goodman's integrated band for the Dallas Exposition in 1937.

Musical:

"The Most Legendary Concert in Jazz History." *Legacy Recordings.*
   URL: http://www.legacyrecordings.com/BennyGoodman/index.html

Includes a press release describing the 1938 Carnegie Hall jazz concert, and a listing of tracks, some with ram and wav audio files.

"Sing, Sing, Sing." *The NPR 100.*
   URL: http://www.npr.org/ramfiles/atc/20000131.atc.05.

A description of the Carnegie Hall concert on January 16, 1938 by biographer Russ Firestone, with clips from an audience member and Goodman. The performance of "Sing, Sing, Sing" is discussed and the segment includes the performance of the song. The RAM file is available on The NPR 100 *web site: http://www.npr.org/programs/specials/vote/100list.html*

Spelman, A. B., and Murray Horwitz. *"Benny Goodman: Ken Burns Jazz." The NPR Basic Jazz Record Library.*
   URL: http://www.nprjazz.org/links/bjrl.bgoodman.html

The transcript of this NPR segment is a review of the Goodman CD: Ken Burns Jazz: Benny Goodman *on Columbia/Legacy.*

Books

Collier, James Lincoln. *Benny Goodman and the Swing Era.* New York: Oxford Univ. Press, 1989.
   This detailed biography explores all aspects of Goodman's career and its significance. Collier, a jazz musician, also analyzes the pieces on the various recordings by Goodman.

Erenberg, Lewis A. *Swingin' the Dream: Big Band Jazz and the Rebirth of American Culture.* Chicago: University of Chicago Press, 1998.
   Erenberg, a professor of history, describes the role swing played in defining the American popular culture of the 30s and 40s. In addition he portrays the relationship between politics, in particular the Popular Front, and jazz.

Firestone, Ross. *Swing, Swing, Swing: The Life & Times of Benny Goodman.* New York: W. W. Norton, 1993.
   Firestone provides a chronological account of Goodman's professional career with details about Goodman's various bands, tours, and recording sessions.

Giddins, Gary. "Benny Goodman (The Mirror of Swing)" In *Visions of Jazz: The First Century.* New York: Oxford Univ. Press, 1998.
   Giddins describes Goodman's legacy and the reasons for his popularity.

Shipton, Alyn. "Benny Goodman: King of Swing." In *Jazz Makers: Vanguards of Sound*. New York: Oxford Univ. Press, 2002.
Shipton describes Goodman's rise from childhood poverty in Chicago to the "King of Swing." Includes a discography, further reading, and a web site.

Ward, Geoffrey C. *Jazz: A History of America's Music*. New York: Alfred A. Knopf, 2000.
Use the index to find all sections on Goodman.

CDs

Goodman, Benny. *Benny Goodman: Ken Burns Jazz*. Columbia/Legacy, 2000.
Nineteen tracks including "King Porter Stomp," "Body and Soul," and "Sing, Sing, Sing."

Goodman, Benny. *Live at Carnegie Hall: 1938 Complete*. Sony, 1999. B00002MZ2L.
This reissue of the historic Goodman concert at Carnegie Hall includes commentary by Goodman.

Sensational Swing. Benny Goodman, Tommy Dorsey, Glenn Miller, and others. ASV. 2 compact discs. AJS 239.
The pieces on the CDs were first recorded in 1932– 46. Includes the following tracks by Benny Goodman's Orchestra: "Don't Be That Way," "King Porter Stomp," "Roll 'em," "Sing Sing Sing," "Stompin' at the Savoy," and "Why Don't You Do It Right?"

Chapter 14

Jazz As Social Protest

John Hammond and the Café Society

1936	1938	1938 and 1939	1939	1941
Goodman's integrated jazz trio performs	Café Society opens	Hammond produces *From Spirituals to Swing*	Billie Holiday performs "Strange Fruit"	Ellington composes *Jump for Joy*

John Hammond was a jazz critic and impresario who influenced the world of jazz in the 1930s and 40s. He was a wealthy man who used his money to promote jazz and help musicians, especially African-Americans. Hammond was also instrumental in integrating the jazz orchestras, beginning with Benny Goodman's. He frequented the Harlem nightclubs and discovered a number of musicians, including Billie Holiday, and later Bob Dylan, Aretha Franklin, and Bruce Springsteen.

In 1938 Hammond produced *From Spirituals to Swing*, a ground-breaking concert at New York's Carnegie Hall that presented African-American music performed by African-Americans. The concert was sponsored by *New Masses,* a Communist Party journal. (Erenberg, 1998, 120) Hammond also produced a second concert of the same name in 1939. The integrated Benny Goodman Sextet performed in the 1939 concert.

Hammond's interest in social justice prompted him to help finance and book the talent for the controversial Café Society, a nightclub in Greenwich Village that was the first integrated nightclub in New York both in its entertainers and audience. Owned and operated by members of the Popular Front of the Communist Party, Café Society attracted people with a social conscience. Barney Josephson, the owner, promoted it as "the wrong place for the Right people." (Margolick, 2000, 40)

One of the first performers booked was Billie Holiday. Holiday was a jazz singer discovered by John Hammond. She recorded with Benny Goodman and had performed at the Apollo Theater in Harlem. She toured for a while with Artie Shaw's orchestra. At the time this was controversial because white bands did not hire black singers. When the Café Society opened in December 1938, Hammond convinced Josephson to hire Holiday. Her famous song "Strange Fruit" had its debut in 1939 at the Café Society. Abel Meeropol, a Jewish leftist English teacher at the Bronx's DeWitt Clinton High School, wrote the song under the pen name "Lewis Allan" and asked Holiday to perform it. (Margolick, 2000, 33, 42) It became Holiday's signature song.

OBJECTIVE

Students will understand the use of music in social protest.

JAZZ AS SOCIAL PROTEST STUDENT PAGES

Inquiries

- How did John Hammond influence the jazz bands and recordings during the 30s and 40s?

- What was the significance of the Café Society? How did it reflect the politics of the time?

- Why was the Communist Party a popular political alternative during the 1930s?

- Why did the Popular Front promote jazz?

- What was the impact of the song "Strange Fruit?" What was its significance in the history of civil rights?

- What is "agitprop"? Why does "Strange Fruit" fit into this category?

- Why was the concert *From Spirituals to Swing* a milestone in American music history?

Products

- Trace John Hammond's achievements in integrating jazz bands, listing the musicians, bands, and recordings.

- Investigate the role of the Communist Party as it related to jazz and specifically swing. Produce a chart that lists the various events sponsored by the Popular Front and the musicians that participated.

- Produce a multimedia presentation that portrays the Café Society's entertainment, slogans, and décor.

- Analyze the lyrics of "Strange Fruit" for its message and literary devices.

- Using Margolick's book, trace the history of the performances of "Strange Fruit" and relate the reactions of performers and audience members.

RESEARCH RESOURCES

Web Sites

"John Hammond." *American Masters.*
> URL: http://www.pbs.org/wnet/americanmasters/database/hammond_j.html

A brief biography that describes Hammond's role in promoting jazz artists, integrating jazz orchestras, and funding the Café Society.

Margolick, David. "Civil Rights, Civil Wrongs." *Guardian Unlimited.* February 16, 2001.
> URL: http://www.guardian.co.uk/friday_review/story/0,3605,438304,00.html

This article for the online Guardian Unlimited *contains a portion of Margolick's book* Strange Fruit.

Margolick, David. "Strange Fruit." *The Unofficial Billie Holiday Website.*
    URL: http://www.ladyday.net/stuf/vfsept98.html

The article from the September 1998 issue of Vanity Fair *that was the basis for Margolick's book on "Strange Fruit."*

Schermer, Vic. "Author David Margolick on his New Book: Strange Fruit." *All about jazz.*
    URL: http://www.allaboutjazz.com/IVIEWS/dmargolick.htm

In this interview Margolick answers questions about his book about the Billie Holiday song "Strange Fruit."

Yannow, Scott "John Hammond, Sr." *Bob Dylan Biography.*
    URL: http://bobdylanbiography.8k.com/John_Hammond/john_hammond_biography.htm

A brief biography that relates Hammond's influence on the jazz world.

Books

Erenberg, Lewis A. "Swing Left: The Politics of Race and Culture in the Swing Era." In *Swingin' the Dream: Big Band Jazz and the Rebirth of American Culture.* Chicago: Univ. of Chicago Press, 1998.

This chapter points out the influence of John Hammond and leftist groups in attacking segregation by promoting black musicians and the integration of the jazz clubs and bands. It discusses Benny Goodman's role and Duke Ellington's 1941 musical comedy, Jump for Joy, *which challenged the prevalent, stereotypical views of African-Americans.*

Firestone, Ross. *Swing, Swing, Swing: The Life & Times of Benny Goodman.* New York: W. W. Norton, 1993.

Use the index to find information on John Hammond.

Margolick, David. *Strange Fruit: Billie Holiday, Café Society, and an Early Cry for Civil Rights.* Philadelphia: Running Press, 2000.

Basing his story on interviews and reminiscences, Margolick, a contributing editor for Vanity Fair, *presents the history of the writing and performances of the controversial song "Strange Fruit." Includes a discography.*

Ward, Geoffrey C., and Ken Burns. *Jazz: A History of America's Music.* New York: Alfred A. Knopf, 2000: 269–70.

A description of the opening of the Café Society and Holiday's first performance of "Strange Fruit."

Wyman, Bill, and Richard Havers. "From Spirituals to Swing: An Evening of American Negro Music." In *Bill Wyman's Blues Odyssey: A Journey to Music's Heart & Soul.* 1st American ed. London: DK Publishing Book, 2001.

Wyman relates the background of this milestone concert in the history of American music.

CDs

From Spirituals to Swing: The Legendary 1938 & 1939 Carnegie Hall Concerts Produced by John Hammond. Vanguard Records. 1999. B00000JT6C.

A three-CD boxed set of the concerts. It includes a forty-five-page booklet and a facsimile of the Dec. 23, 1938 program.

Holiday, Billie. *Billie Holiday: The Definitive. Ken Burns Jazz.* Verve Music Group. 2000. 314 549 081-2.

Includes Holiday singing "Strange Fruit." "Recorded April 20, 1939."

Chapter 15

Bebop

Dizzy Gillespie, 1917–1993: Trumpeter, Composer, Arranger
Thelonious Monk, 1917–1982: Pianist, Composer, Arranger
Charlie Parker, 1920–1955: Alto Saxophonist, Composer, Arranger

1940s	1942	1945	1948
Beginnings of bebop at Minton's	Gillespie wrote "A Night in Tunisia"	Recording of "Ko Ko" by Parker and Gillespie	Monk recorded "Misterioso"

As swing became connected with commercial music, jazz musicians began experimenting with a new sound. Minton's Playhouse in New York was a meeting place, and in jam sessions after hours, young jazz musicians tried out the sounds that became bebop. Thelonious Monk was the house pianist at Minton's and is credited with originating the harmonies of bebop. Bebop, characterized by fast melodic runs and unusual harmonies, became the new "pure" jazz. Audiences didn't dance to bebop; they listened and appreciated the difficult improvisations.

The origin of the word *bebop* is still debated. "The new jazz was popularly known as 'bebop,' a term of dubious origin often cited as the onomatopoeic equivalent of the two-note phrases (frequently the interval of a flatted fifth) that capped many of the melodic figures improvised by the modernists." (Giddins, 1998, 261–262)

OBJECTIVES

Students will define the bebop style of jazz and compare it to the earlier forms of jazz.

Students will describe the connection between bebop music and the social atmosphere of the time period.

INTRODUCING THE MUSICIANS

Picture Books and Cassettes

Before playing the cassette to either book, ask students to speculate what Raschka's book is saying about bebop. Do the rhythms of the words or the illustrations provide clues to the music of bebop?

Raschka, Chris. *Charlie Parker Played Be Bop*. New York: Orchard Books, 1997; Pine Plains, NY: Live Oak Media, 2000. Cassette.

> *The text of* Charlie Parker Played Be Bop *mimics the rhythms of the bebop jazz style. Raschka's accompanying cassette features a jazz vocalist reading the book to the accompanying music of Dizzy Gillespie's "A Night in Tunisia". On the cassette Raschka explains that he wrote the book while listening to the music, and the rhythm of the text matches the bebop rhythm of the music.*

Raschka, Chris. *Mysterious Thelonious*. New York: Orchard Books, 1997; Pine Plains, NY: Live Oak Media, 2000. Cassette.

> *Raschka explains the colorful illustrations and high and low word placement in his book as a visual representation of Thelonious Monk's piece "Misterioso". He assigned a different color to each note in the scale. These colors line the edge of the paper, and the words added to the piece are placed on the color line that matches the tone. Jazz vocalist Richard Allen sings Raschka's words to "Misterioso" first as a solo and then above a live recording of the Thelonious Monk Quartet.*

Quotations

- Author and musician John Edward Hasse on bebop:

  > *Employing angular melodies, asymmetric phrases, heightened rhythmic complexity, a faster melodic rhythm, sometimes dizzying tempos, and extended harmonies, they [Gillespie, Parker, Monk, and Clarke] introduced a music that was intended far less for dancing than for listening in small clubs. In contrast to much of Ellington's music, in many cases the new style was "pure" or abstract music with no overt programmatic references. (Hasse, John Edward.* Beyond Category: The Life and Genius of Duke Ellington. *New York: Simon & Schuster, 1993: 290)*

- Thelonious Monk on bebop in *Down Beat* article, September 24, 1947:

  > *If my own work had more importance than any other's, it's because the piano is the key instrument in music. I think all styles are built around piano developments. The piano lays the chord foundation and the rhythm foundation, too. (Gottlieb, "Thelonious...")*

- Author Ralph Ellison comparing Charlie "Bird" Parker to a mockingbird:

  > *Peterson [author of* Field Guide to the Birds*] informs us that its song consists of "long successions of notes and phrases of great variety, with each phrase repeated a half-dozen times before going on to the next," that mockingbirds are "excellent mimics" who "adeptly imitate a score or more species found in the neighborhood," ... his [Parker's] playing was characterized by velocity, by long-continued succession of notes and phrases, by swoops, bleats, echoes, rapidly repeated bebops—I mean rebopped bebops—by mocking mimicry of other jazzmen's styles, and by interpolations of motifs from extraneous melodies, all of which added up to a dazzling display of wit, satire, burlesques and pathos. (Ellison, 2001, 67–68)*

- Author Ralph Ellison on reasons for bebop music:

  > *It was a time of big bands, and the greatest prestige and economic returns were falling outside the Negro community—often to leaders whose popularity grew from the compositions and arrangements of Negroes ... the inside-dopesters will tell you that the "changes" or chord progressions and melodic inversions worked out by the creators of bop sprang partially from their desire to create a jazz which could not be so easily imitated and exploited by white musicians to whom the market was more open simply because of their whiteness. (Ellison, 2001, 63–64)*

- Dizzy Gillespie on music after World War II:

  > *Your music reflects the times in which you live. My music emerged from the war years ... and it reflected those times ... Fast and furious, with the chord changes going*

this way and that way, it might've looked and sounded like bedlam, but it really wasn't. (Ward, 2000, 334)

Connections to Other Musicians in this Book

- Parker based his piece "Anthropology" on **Gershwin's** "I Got Rhythm." (Shipton, 2002, 139)

- Gillespie played in **Ellington's** orchestra for a while. (Owens, 2002, 36)

Period of American History
World War II and after

Musical Highlights of Lives of Gillespie, Monk, and Parker: Teachers, Colleagues, Events

1917	Gillespie born in Cheraw, South Carolina Monk born in Rocky Mount, North Carolina
1920	Parker born in Kansas City, Kansas
1939	Gillespie joined Cab Calloway Orchestra
1940	Dizzy Gillespie heard Charlie Parker play in Kansas City Gillespie, Parker, and Monk started playing in after-hour jam sessions at Minton's Playhouse and Monroe's Uptown House in Harlem Monk was house pianist at Minton's
1942	Bandleader Earl "Fatha" Hines hired Gillespie and Parker Monk toured with Gillespie in Lucky Millinder's band, accompanying the Ink Spots
1944	Monk's "Round Midnight" recorded Monk played and recorded with Coleman Hawkins Quartet
1945	Gillespie and Parker performed at the Three Deuces as part of a quintet Parker and Gillespie made bebop recordings, including "Ko Ko" Gillespie recorded his *Salt Peanuts*
1946	Gillespie formed his own band
1947	Monk recorded for Blue Note
1948	Monk recorded "Misterioso"
1950	Monk and Parker recorded together
1953	Gillespie and Parker recorded concert in Toronto
1955	Parker died in New York City, New York
1971–72	Gillespie toured with Giants of Jazz, which included Monk
1982	Monk died
1993	Gillespie died

BEBOP STUDENT PAGES

Inquiries
- What are the musical elements in bebop music?
- How did bebop differ from the jazz preceding it?
- How does the musical style of bebop reflect the time period?
- What kinds of music were other jazz artists such as Armstrong, Ellington, and Goodman performing during the bebop era?
- How did the style and fashion connected to bebop reflect the music?
- How and where was bebop developed?
- Why was bebop created at that time in the history of jazz?

Products
- Using the photographs in Gottlieb's collection, produce a multimedia presentation depicting the bebop artists. Include important events and recordings.
- Using Raschka's book *Mysterious Thelonious* as a model, make a book that illustrates a bebop piece.
- Using the *NPR Jazz: The Basic Jazz Record Library*, produce an oral presentation of significant bebop recordings and explain their significance.
- Describe the club Minton's Playhouse, listing the performers and its after-hours' role for black jazz musicians.
- Write an essay explaining the musical elements of bebop and the reasons for its development during the 1940s.

RESEARCH RESOURCES

Web Sites
Biographical:

Blake, Ron. "Monk, Thelonious (Sphere)." In Vol. 2 of *The New Grove Dictionary of Jazz.* 2nd ed. Edited by Barry Kernfeld. London: Macmillan Publishers; New York: Grove's Dictionaries, 2002. "Thelonious Monk." *Jazz: A Film by Ken Burns: Biographies: The Life and Times of the Great Ones.* URL: http://www.pbs.org/jazz/biography/artist_id_monk_thelonious.htm

> *This article, excerpted from* The New Grove Dictionary of Jazz, *includes links to audio files from* The NPR 100 *and* NPR's Basic Jazz Record Library.

"Dizzy Gillespie." *Jazzradio.org: The Official Home of Jazz From Lincoln Center.* URL: http://www.jazzradio.org/dgillespie.htm

> *A short biography of Gillespie describing his career.*

Owens, Thomas. "Gillespie, Dizzy." In Vol. 2 of *The New Grove Dictionary of Jazz.* 2nd ed. Edited by Barry Kernfeld. London: Macmillan Publishers; New York: Grove's Dictionaries, 2002. "Dizzy Gillespie." *Jazz: A Film by Ken Burns: Biographies: The Life and Times of the Great Ones.*
URL: http://www.pbs.org/jazz/biography/artist_id_gillespie_dizzy.htm

This article, excerpted from The New Grove Dictionary of Jazz, *includes links to audio files from* The NPR 100, NPR Jazz Feature *and a segment by Stanley Crouch from* Jazz: A Film *by Ken Burns.*

Patrick, James. "Parker, Charlie." In Vol. 3 of *The New Grove Dictionary of Jazz.* 2nd ed. Edited by Barry Kernfeld. London: Macmillan Publishers; New York: Grove's Dictionaries, 2002. "Charlie Parker." *Jazz: A Film by Ken Burns: Biographies: The Life and Times of the Great Ones.*
URL: http://www.pbs.org/jazz/biogr.aphy/artist_id_parker_charlie.htm

This article, excerpted from The New Grove Dictionary of Jazz, *includes links to audio files from* The NPR 100, NPR's Jazz Profiles, *and* NPR's Basic Jazz Record Library.

Yanow, Scott. "Charlie Parker." *Jazzsteps.com.*
URL: http://www.jazzsteps.com

Search for charlie parker *as Artist. Yanow's biography recounts Parker's career and recordings.*

Yanow, Scott. "Dizzy Gillespie." *Jazzsteps.com.*
URL: http://www.jazzsteps.com/

Search for dizzy gillespie *as Artist. Yanow's biography recounts Gillespie's career and recordings.*

Yanow, Scott. "Thelonious Monk." *Jazzsteps.com.*
URL: http://www.jazzsteps.com/

Search for thelonious monk *as Artist. Yanow's biography recounts Monk's career and recordings.*

Historical:

Gottlieb, Bill. "Thelonious Monk—Genius of Bop." *Downbeat,* September 24, 1947. *William P. Gottlieb: Photographs from the Golden Age of Jazz.*
URL: http://memory.loc.gov/music/gottlieb/wgpubs/1151r.jpg

Gottlieb describes interviewing Monk at Minton's Playhouse in which Monk describes bebop's beginnings in 1941. Teddy Hill, former bandleader and manager of Minton's, gives credit to Monk for starting bebop.

Gottlieb, William. "Charlie Parker and Tommy Potter." *In His Own Words: Photographs and Commentary by William Gottlieb. William P. Gottlieb, Photographs from the Golden Age of Jazz.*
URL: http://memory.loc.gov/ammem/wghtml/wgpres14.html

In an audio file Gottlieb describes the setting for a photo he took of Parker and Potter.

Gottlieb, William. "Ella Fitzgerald and Dizzy Gillespie." *In His Own Words: Photographs and Commentary by William Gottlieb. William P. Gottlieb, Photographs from the Golden Age of Jazz.*
URL: http://memory.loc.gov/ammem/wghtml/wgpres02.html

In an audio file Gottlieb describes the setting for a photo he took of Fitzgerald and Gillespie.

William P. Gottlieb—Photographs from the Golden Age of Jazz.
URL: http://memory.loc.gov/ammem/wghtml/wghome.html

Gottlieb as writer/photographer for both the Washington Post *and* Down Beat *took many photographs of jazz artists. For photographs of Gillespie, Monk, and Parker browse the Name Index.*

Musical:

"Bird's Legacy." *Jazz from Lincoln Center.*
URL: http://www.jazzradio.org/b_legacy.htm

This page includes the script for Bird's Legacy, *written by Joseph Hooper, and an audio file of the complete program.*

"Charlie Parker." *NPR Jazz Feature.*
    URL: http://www.nprjazz.org/programs/bird.feature.html

A collection of web sites of various NPR programs and ram files on Charlie Parker. Included are an excerpt from the NPR Jazz Profile *and "Ko Ko" from* The NPR 100.

Enright, Ed. "Bebop Emergence." *Downbeat's Jazz 101.*
    URL: http://www.downbeat.com/default.asp?sect=education&subsect=jazz_09

Enright provides a brief introduction to bebop.

Horwitz, Murray, and A. B. Spellman. "Charlie Parker." *NPR Jazz: The Basic Jazz Record Library.*
    URL: http://www.nprjazz.org/links/index.html#P

Links to ram files and text of the programs featuring two jazz recordings by Parker.

Horwitz, Murray, and A. B. Spellman. "Dizzy Gillespie." *NPR Jazz: The Basic Jazz Record Library.*
    URL: http://www.nprjazz.org/links/index.html#G

Links to ram files and text of the programs featuring three jazz recordings by Gillespie.

Horwitz, Murray, and A. B. Spellman. "Thelonious Monk." *NPR Jazz: The Basic Jazz Record Library.*
    URL: http://www.nprjazz.org/links/index.html#M

Links to ram files and text of the programs featuring three jazz recordings by Monk.

"Jazz from Lincoln Center: Bird's Legacy." *NPR Jazz Main Feature.*
    URL: http://www.nprjazz.org/feature/jflc010810.html

Includes links to various NPR web sites on Parker, including Morning Edition *and* Fresh Air.

Stage, Margot. "A Night in Tunisia." *The NPR 100.*
    URL: http://www.npr.org/ramfiles/watc/20000903.watc.07.rmm

This segment includes an interview with Gillespie in which he relates the story of writing "A Night in Tunisia" and recordings of various versions of "A Night in Tunisia". Stage compares the earlier version, "Interlude", with the later bebop version.

Vitale, Tom. "Koko [sic]." *The NPR 100.*
    URL: http://www.npr.org/ramfiles/wesun/20000827.wesun.14.rmm

This audio segment analyzes the musical structure of Charlie Parker's "Ko Ko", which is based on the harmonic structure of Ray Noble's "Cherokee". It also describes the unusual events that took place during the taping of the recording of "Ko Ko". The segment also includes excerpts from an interview with Parker. The ram file is available on The NPR 100 *web site: http://www.npr.org/programs/specials/vote/100list.html.*

Books

Blake, Ran. "Monk, Thelonious (Sphere)." In Vol. 2 of *The New Grove Dictionary of Jazz*, 2nd edition. Edited by Barry Kernfeld. London: Macmillan Publishers; New York: Grove's Dictionaries, 2002.
This article includes sections on Monk's life, compositions, and piano style.

Crawford, Richard. "Jazz, Broadway, and Musical Permanence." In *American's Musical Life: A History.* New York: W. W. Norton, 2001.
Crawford writes about origins of bebop and particularly about Gillespie and Parker.

Ellison, Ralph. "The Golden Age, Time Past." In *Living with Music: Ralph Ellison's Jazz Writings.* Edited by Robert G. O'Meally. New York: Modern Library, 2001.
As part of a three-part September 28, 1958 Esquire *issue on "The Golden Age of Jazz," Ellison explains what was real during that time in comparison to what is remembered.*

Ellison, Ralph. "On Bird, Bird-Watching, and Jazz." In *Living with Music: Ralph Ellison's Jazz Writings.* Edited by Robert G. O'Meally. New York: Modern Library, 2001.
Ellison compares Charlie Parker, known as "Bird," to a mockingbird and discusses his role as an entertainer.

Giddins, Gary. "Charlie Parker (Flying Home)." In *Visions of Jazz: The First Century*. New York: Oxford Univ. Press, 1998.
After a brief introduction to bebop, Giddins describes the highlights of Parker's performances. He illustrates his points with musical examples, including a lengthy section from "Ko Ko."

Gottlieb, William P. "Bop!... And All That Modern Jazz." In *The Golden Age of Jazz*. San Francisco: Pomegranate Artbooks, 1995.
As jazz critic and photographer from 1938 to 1948 for the Washington Post *and* Down Beat, *Gottlieb provides first-hand accounts and photos on jazz musicians.*

Gourse, Leslie. "Dizzy Gillespie, Charlie 'Bird' Parker, and the Bebop Revolution." In *Blowing on the Changes: The Art of the Jazz Horn Players*. New York: Franklin Watts, 1997.
Gourse describes the childhood and musical influences of both Gillespie and Parker and their careers separately and together.

Gourse, Leslie. "Thelonious Monk." In *Striders to Beboppers and Beyond: The Art of Jazz Piano*. New York: Franklin Watts, 1997.
Gourse describes Monk's career and his interactions with beboppers.

Owens, Thomas. "Bop." In Vol. 1 of *The New Grove Dictionary of Jazz*, 2nd edition. Edited by Barry Kernfeld. London: Macmillan Publishers; New York: Grove's Dictionaries, 2002.
Owens describes the origins of bop and its musical elements. He also enumerates the types of jazz that followed it.

Owens, Thomas. "Gillespie, Dizzy." In Vol. 2 of *The New Grove Dictionary of Jazz*, 2nd edition. Edited by Barry Kernfeld. London: Macmillan Publishers; New York: Grove's Dictionaries, 2002.
The article includes a section on Gillespie's life and musical style.

Patrick, James. "Parker, Charlie." In Vol. 3 of *The New Grove Dictionary of Jazz*, 2nd edition. Edited by Barry Kernfeld. London: Macmillan Publishers; New York: Grove's Dictionaries, 2002.
This articles covers Parker's life, style, and influence. It includes musical examples.

Shipton, Alyn. "Charlie Parker: Bird Lives." In *Jazz Makers: Vanguards of Sound*. New York: Oxford Univ. Press, 2002.
Shipton explains Parker's uniqueness as a jazz soloist and the highlights of his career. Includes a discography, further reading, and a web site.

Shipton, Alyn. "Dizzy Gillespie: Groovin' High." In *Jazz Makers: Vanguards of Sound*. New York: Oxford Univ. Press, 2002.
Shipton provides a detailed account of Gillespie's career and his role in promoting bebop. Includes a discography, further reading, and a web site.

Shipton, Alyn. "Thelonious Monk: Blue Sphere." In *Jazz Makers: Vanguards of Sound*. New York: Oxford Univ. Press, 2002.
Shipton concentrates on Monk's compositions and his role as a pianist in working out the harmonies and rhythms of bebop. Includes a discography, further reading, and web site.

CDs

Gillespie, Dizzy. *Dizzy Gillespie: The Definitive. Ken Burns Jazz*. Verve, 2000.
Includes "Salt Peanuts" and "A Night in Tunisia".

Monk, Thelonious. *Thelonious Monk: The Definitive. Ken Burns Jazz*. Columbia/Legacy, 2000.
Includes "Misterioso", "Rhythm-a-Ning", and "Round Midnight".

Parker, Charlie. *Charlie Parker: The Definitive. Ken Burns Jazz*. The Verve Music Group, 2000. 314 549 084-2.
Includes "Salt Peanuts", "Ko-Ko", "Ornithology", and others.

COUNTRY MUSIC

"The Little Old Cabin in the Lane." Words and Music by Will S. Hayes. Boston: Oliver Ditson, 1871. *Historic American Sheet Music, 1850–1920 (from Duke University)* URL: http://memory.loc.gov/ammem/award97/ncdhtml/hasmhome. html

Chapter 16

The Carter Family: A. P., Sara, and Maybelle

1927	1935	1937	1950
Recorded for Peer in Bristol, Tennessee	Released "Can the Circle Be Unbroken"	*Woody and Lefty Lou* radio show (Woody Guthrie)	Joined the Grand Ole Opry

Country music was born in the summer of 1927 when Ralph Peer, working for the Victor Talking Machine Co., recorded the Carter Family in Bristol, Tennessee. With the advent of radio, record producers like Peer had begun looking for new markets for their recordings. The Carter Family, including A. P. Carter, his wife Sara, and Sara's cousin and sister-in-law, Maybelle, had been singing informally at family gatherings and school and church functions, but the Bristol recording made them famous and started the country music industry. A. P. gathered songs for their recordings. Sara sang lead and played the autoharp. Maybelle sang and developed a unique style of playing the guitar that was copied by many aspiring bluegrass performers. (Seidman, 1997, 72)

As the Carter family grew, the original trio disbanded, and the performing group members fluctuated. Maybelle began performing with her daughters as The Carter Sisters and Mother Maybelle. In later years Sara and Maybelle reunited for performances. The Carter Family was the first group to be inducted into the Country Music Hall of Fame. (Seidman, 1997, 73)

OBJECTIVES

Students will define country music and describe its influences and its bluegrass successors.

Students will determine the role of the recording industry and radio in the popularity of various types of music.

Students will connect country music lyrics to the experiences of rural Americans.

INTRODUCING THE MUSICIAN

Music
Play the audio file of the Carter Family singing "Keep on the Sunny Side." Ask the students to identify the type of music, the singers, and the time period.

"Keep on the Sunny Side." *NPR Morning Edition with Bob Edwards.*
URL: http://www.npr.org/ramfiles/me/20020716.me.carter.keep.ram

Next, play the same song sung by The Whites on the sound track to the film *O Brother, Where Art Thou?* (See **CDs** below)

Quotations
- Country music singer Ralph Stanley on the music he heard as a child:
  About the first music that I heard when I was a child was some people like the Carter Family. That was on phonograph records. I never heard of radio until about 1936. My father sang the old ballads like "Pretty Polly" and "Man of Constant Sorrow." He didn't play any music, but he would sing 'em just a cappella. "Pretty Polly" and "Man of Constant Sorrow" are old traditional songs that go way, way back, I guess hundreds of years as far as I know. I really don't know who wrote them, but I would guess they maybe came over from England or somewhere. (American Root Music, 2001, 32)

- Author Mark Zwonitzer on the Carter family:
  The family's music sprang mainly from the narrow traditions of white southern gospel and the balladry that had floated for generations in the thin mountain air of Appalachia...A. P., Sara, and Maybelle were at their best when they were plying the sharper edges of private and personal pain. (Zwonitzer, 2002, 101)

- Authors Bufwack and Oermann on the importance of the Carter family:
  Country music's first star group is unmatched as a preserver and popularizer of folk and parlor songs. Maybelle's then-revolutionary guitar style helped transform the instrument from background rhythm to the dominant lead sound in pop culture. Her playing and Gene Autry's marketing of the instrument in Sears catalogs are perhaps the most significant factors in bringing the guitar to the forefront. In addition, Sara and Maybelle were essentially a duet with occasional bass vocals from A. P. and were thus the foundation female act of country music history. (Bufwack, 1993, 55)

Connections to Other Musicians in This Book
- **Woody Guthrie** borrowed melodies from the Carters' songs, "When the World's on Fire," "Wildwood Flower," and "John Hardy Was a Desperate Little Man." (Bufwack, 1993, 55–56)

Periods in American History
1920s, Great Depression, World War II, 50s and 60s Folk Revival

Musical Highlights of Carter Family's Lives: Teachers, Colleagues, Events

1891	A. P. Carter born in Poor Valley, Virginia
1898	Sara Dougherty born in Rich Valley, Virginia
1909	Maybelle Addington born in Midway, Virginia

1915	A. P. and Sara were married
1919	A. P. and Sara moved to Maces Springs, Virginia
1925	A. P., Sara, and Maybelle performed together at the schoolhouse in Maces Springs
1927	Recorded for Ralph Peer of Victor in Bristol, Tennessee First recording published with songs "Poor Orphan Child" and "Wandering Boy"
1928	Recording released with "The Storms Are on the Ocean" and "Single Girl, Married Girl" Recorded twelve songs for Peer in Camden, New Jersey, including "Will You Miss Me When I'm Gone" and "Wildwood Flower"
1931	Recorded with Jimmie Rodgers
1933	A. P. and Sara separated
1935	"Can the Circle Be Unbroken" released and became hit
1936	A. P. and Sara divorced Carter Family signed with Decca
1938	Carter Family went to Texas to broadcast on XERA's *Good Neighbor Get-Together* in Mexico
1939	Maybelle and daughters performed on XERA
1943	Original Carter Family disbanded The Carter Sisters and Mother Maybelle performed on WRNL in Richmond
1946	The Carter Sisters and Mother Maybelle joined WRVA in Richmond on the *Old Dominion Barn Dance*
1948	The Carter Sisters and Mother Maybelle joined *Midday Merry-Go-Round* on WNOX in Knoxville, Tennessee Chet Atkins performed with the Mother Maybelle and the Carter Sisters on the road
1949	Maybelle and daughters joined the Ozark Jubilee in Springfield, Missouri
1950	Maybelle and daughters joined The Grand Ole Opry in Nashville
1955	Joined a package tour that included Elvis Presley
1960	A. P. Carter died in Mount Vernon, Tennessee
1961	Flatt & Scruggs recorded *Songs of the Famous Carter Family* with Maybelle
1963	Maybelle toured with the New Lost City Ramblers beginning at the Ash Grove in Hollywood Maybelle performed at the Newport Folk Festival
1966	Recorded *Historic Reunion* with Sara and her son Joe
1970	Carter Family (A. P., Sara, and Maybelle) inducted into the Country Music Hall of Fame
1971	Maybelle recorded "Will the Circle Be Unbroken" with the Nitty Gritty Dirt Band
1975	Sara and Maybelle sang at the "First A. P. Carter Memorial Day Festival and Crafts Show."
1978	Maybelle Carter died
1979	Sara Carter Coy died.

CARTER FAMILY STUDENT PAGES

Inquiries

- What is country music? How does it differ from bluegrass music?

- What types of music did the Carter family perform? How did they find their songs? Which ones were written by the family members?

- Why is the Bristol recording session called the "birth of country music?"

- Why did Peer decide to record in Bristol? What types of pieces were recorded during the Bristol sessions?

- Why were recordings so popular with rural people in the 1920s?

- What role did radio play in the success of the Carter family and other country performers?

- Why did radio stations such as XERA broadcast from Mexico? What audience did they hope to address?

- What technological elements came together to help popularize country music?

- Why did the country music become popular during the Depression?

- Why did so many of the country songs from Appalachia contain *death* as a topic?

- Why were the recorded country songs so popular during the Dust Bowl era?

- What instruments were used in country music and why?

Products

- Search the American Memory Collections for the song "Wildwood Flower" (match this exact phrase) and compare the versions to the Carter family version. Using *The NPR 100* segment on "Wildwood Flower," explain the reasons for the variations.

- Research the role of radio during the 20s and 30s and its importance in the spread of country music. Include the border stations and the Los Angeles station of Aimee Semple McPherson.

- Produce a multimedia presentation on the role of women in country music, including song lists and audio files.

- Trace the use of Carter Family songs in the later folk revival. Include Woody Guthrie, Joan Baez, and The Nitty Gritty Dirt Band. Provide examples of the music.

- Investigate the instruments used in country music and their origins.

- Compare the motivation and intent of the commercial recordings of country performers done by Ralph S. Peer to the government-sponsored recordings of folk music. Include descriptions of the process and the equipment. (See Woody Guthrie and Folk Families lessons.)

- Investigate and describe the recording companies during the 20s and 30s. List the various labels and their catalogs. Include audio tracks.

RESEARCH RESOURCES

Web Sites
Biographical:

"The Carter Family." *Birthplace of Country Music Alliance.*
> URL: http://www.birthplaceofcountrymusic.org/heritage/biographies/carter_family.htm

> *This site provides personal and professional information about the original Carter singing group and a listing of their recordings.*

"Country Music's First Family: New Book Chronicles Legacy of the Influential Carter Family." *NPR Morning Edition with Bob Edwards*, July 16, 2002.
> URL: http://www.npr.org/programs/morning/features/2002/jul/carter/index.html

> *This page summarizes the* Morning Edition *program in which Bob Edwards discusses the Carter family and the book* Will You Miss Me When I'm Gone? The Carter Family and Their Legacy in American Music *by Mark Zwonitzer. The site includes a link to the ram file for the program and audio files of some Carter family songs. At the end of the article are related web site links.*

Gossett, Peter J. "Carter Family Genealogy." *Bluegrass West.*
> URL: http://www.silcom.com/~peterf/ideas/genealogy.htm

> *Includes birth and death dates for A. P. and Sara Carter, and Maybelle Addington Carter and their children.*

Place, Jeff. "John Hardy Was a Desperate Little Man, Selection 17." *Smithsonian Folkways: Anthology of American Folk Music. Edited by Harry Smith. Supplemental Notes on the Selections.*
> URL: http://www.folkways.si.edu/harry/anthnotes17.htm

> *Place provides background information on the Carter family and lists additional recordings.*

"Ralph S. Peer." *peermusic.*
> URL: http://www.peermusic.com/aboutus/rp1.cfm

> *A brief biography of Ralph S. Peer, who recorded the Carter family in Bristol*

Historical:

"The Birth of Country Music: Early American Influences." *Country Music Hall of Fame and Museum.*
> URL: http://www.halloffame.org/hist/time.essay2.html

> *This article cites the role of religious music in forming country music. It also describes the role of the guitar and the string bands.*

"Birthplace of Country Music—The Bristol Music Story." *Tennessee: Local Legacies.*
> URL: http://www.loc.gov/bicentennial/propage/TN/tn_s_frist3.html

> *This page contains an explanation of the "Bristol Session" and lists all of the musicians who have been influenced by the Carter family.*

Molinaro, John. "The Carter Family: Traditional Songs & Modernization." *This Land Is Your Land: Rural Music & the Depression.*
> URL: http://xroads.virginia.edu/~1930s/RADIO/c_w/carters.html

> *A brief description of the Carter family's musical career that includes a ram file of "Worried Man Blues"*

Molinaro, John. " 'There's a Contest Coming and a Ticket to Nashville': Hillbillies on the Radio." *This Land Is Your Land: Rural Music & the Depression*.
URL: http://xroads.virginia.edu/~1930s/RADIO/c_w/essay1.html

This article describes the impact of radio and recordings on the popularity of country music.

Winship, Dave. "In the Summer of 1927 . . ." *Birthplace of Country Music Alliance*.
URL: http://www.birthplaceofcountrymusic.org/heritage/1927_DWinship.htm

Winship recounts how the recording sessions by Ralph Peer in Bristol, Tennessee/Virginia began the careers of the Carter family and Jimmie Rodgers and began the country music industry.

Musical:

Dvorak, Mark. "Song Notes: A Companion to the Old Town School of Folk Music Songbook, Stories & Information." *Old Town School of Folk Music*.
URL: http://www.oldtownschool.org/resources/songnotes/

Dvorak provides information on the history of individual folk songs. "Wildwood Flower" and "Will the Circle Be Unbroken" are included.

"Song Texts of the Original Carter Family." *Bluegrass West*. Hosted by Peter Feldmann.
URL: http://www.silcom.com/~peterf/ideas/carter.htm

"The song texts here are intended for study and comparison to later country and bluegrass versions."

Spottswood, Dick. "Wildwood Flower." *The NPR 100*.
URL: http://www.npr.org/ramfiles/me/20001214.me.14.rmm

Spottswood relates the history of the song "Wildwood Flower" that the Carter family made popular. The words date from an 1860 poem "I'll Twain Mid the Ringlets," but since the song was passed down orally from mother to daughter in the Carter family, the song's lyrics changed over the years and are not the same as the original poem. Spottsword also points out that Maybelle Carter's guitar style was copied by many beginning guitarists. This ram file can be accessed at The NPR 100 *site: http://www.npr.org/-programs/specials/vote/100list.html*

"The Wildwood Flower." Performers: Mrs. Vester Whitworth, Zelmer Ward, guitar. *Voices from the Dust Bowl: The Charles L. Todd and Robert Sonkin Migrant Worker Collection, 1940–1941*
URL: http://memory.loc.gov/ammem/afctshtml/tshome.html

Recorded Aug. 1, 1940 at the Arvin FSA Camp. Search with keywords wildwood flower.

Books

American Musical Traditions. Vol. 3, British Isles Music. Jeff Todd Titon, Bob Carlin, editors. New York: Schirmer Reference, 2002.
This volume present various articles on the American musical traditions that began with the music of the British Isles. "Published in collaboration with The Smithsonian Folkways Archive."

Bufwack, Mary A., and Robert K. Oermann. "Hungry Disgusted Blues." In *Finding Her Voice: The Saga of Women in Country Music*. New York: Crown Publishers, 1993.
The authors describe the Mexican-border stations and their role in the 1930s. The chapter discusses the use of protest songs by Aimee Semple McPherson and Aunt Molly Jackson.

Bufwack, Mary A., and Robert K. Oermann. "Single Girl, Married Girl: The Carter Family and the Birth of Country Music Recording." In *Finding Her Voice: The Saga of Women in Country Music*. New York: Crown Publishers, 1993.
The authors describe the beginnings of the original Carter Family, A. P., Sara, and Maybelle, and their musical families. The chapter lists the Carter songs that have been sung by later country and rock performers.

Collins, Ace. "Can the Circle Be Unbroken." Written by A. P. Carter, based on a hymn by Ada Habersoln and Charles Gabriel. In *The Stories Behind Country Music's All-Time Greatest 100 Songs*. New York: Boulevard Books, 1996.

A. P. Carter rewrote the verses of the 1907 song "Can the Circle Be Unbroken." In 1968 Carl Perkins rewrote the song for Johnny Cash and called it "Daddy Sang Bass," and in 1972 the Nitty Gritty Dirt Band produced an album that brought together old and new country singers, including Maybelle Carter singing "Will the Circle Be Unbroken."

"Glossary." In Vol. 3, *American Musical Traditions: British Isles Music.* Jeff Todd Titon, Bob Carlin, editors. New York: Schirmer Reference, 2002.
Includes basic definitions of words connected with American music derived from the British Isles.

Malone, Bill C. "Grand Ole Opry." In Vol. 2 of *The New Grove Dictionary of American Music.* Edited by H. Wiley Hitchcock and Stanley Sadie. London: Macmillan Press; New York: Grove's Dictionaries of Music, 1986.
A short history of the Grand Ole Opry from its beginnings on WSM in Nashville in 1925.

Marrocco, W. Thomas, Mark Jacobs, and Paul C. Echols. "Peer-Southern." In Vol. 3 of *The New Grove Dictionary of American Music.* Edited by H. Wiley Hitchcock and Stanley Sadie. London: Macmillan Press; New York: Grove's Dictionaries of Music, 1986.
This brief article relates the history of the music publishing company founded by Ralph S. Peer. Southern's Concert Music Division published works by Charles Ives, featured in Chapter 21 of this book.

Seeger, Mike. "The Autoharp in Old-Time Southern Music." In Vol. 3, *American Musical Traditions: British Isles Music.* Jeff Todd Titon, Bob Carlin, editors. New York: Schirmer Reference, 2002.
The following essay is based on the liner notes Seeger wrote to accompany the 1962 album Mountain Music Played on the Autoharp *(Folkways 2365), which was reissued on CD in 1998 (Folkways F-02365). Seeger includes a section on Maybelle Carter's influence on autoharp playing.*

Seidman, Alice. "Carter Family, The Original." In *Country Music: The Encyclopedia.* Irwin Stambler & Grelun Landon. Contributors: Alice Seidman and Lyndon Stambler. New York: St. Martin's Press, 1997.
Seidman describes the Bristol, Tennessee recording session and highlights of the lives of A. P., Sara, and Maybelle. She also lists a number of their songs.

Stambler, Irwin, and Grelun Landon. "Carter, Mother Maybelle." In *Country Music: The Encyclopedia.* Contributors: Alice Seidman and Lyndon Stambler. New York: St. Martin's Press, 1997.
Maybelle Carter's guitar-playing style is described, as well as her influence on later guitar players.

Titon, Jeff Todd. "Bluegrass." In Vol. 3, *American Musical Traditions: British Isles Music.* Jeff Todd Titon, Bob Carlin, editors. New York: Schirmer Reference, 2002.
Titon describes the origins of bluegrass music, its musical elements, and the early performers.

Wolfe, Charles. "Early Country: Treasures Untold." In *American Roots Music.* Edited by Robert Santelli, Holly George-Warren, Jim Brown. Foreword by Bonnie Raitt. New York: Harry N. Abrams, 2001.
Wolfe describes the recording of the Carter family by Ralph Peer for Victor.

Wolfe, Charles. "The Legend That Peer Built: Reappraising the Bristol Sessions." In *The Country Reader: Twenty-Five Years of the Journal of Country Music.* Edited by Paul Kingsbury. Foreword by Chet Flippo. Nashville: The Country Music Foundation Press & Vanderbilt Univ. Press, 1996.
Wolfe describes the Bristol recording sessions, dispelling some of the legends and providing insight into the recording industry of the time.

Wyman, Bill. *Bill Wyman's Blues Odyssey.* With Richard Havers. New York: DK Publishing Book, 2001.
Use the index to find information on the Carter family and the landmark recording Anthology of American Folk Music.

Zwonitzer, Mark with Charles Hirshberg. *Will You Miss Me When I'm Gone? The Carter Family and Their Legacy in American Music.* New York: Simon & Schuster, 2002.
This biography examines the lives of the Carter family, including the original performing trio of A. P.,

Sara, and Maybelle, and also Maybelle and her daughters. Zwonitzer portrays the personal life of the family members as it relates to their music.

CDs

Carter, A. P. "Single Girl, Married Girl." On Vol. 3: Songs of *Anthology of American Folk Music.* Edited by Harry Smith. Washington, D.C.: Smithsonian Folkways Recordings, 1997.
Smith's "newspaper headline" that describes the song: "Single Girl: Dressed Fine, Goes to Store Buys, Going Where Please. Married Girl: Wears Any Kind, Rocks Cradle Crys, Baby on Knees." Smith's Anthology *also includes "John Hardy Was a Desperate Little Man," "Engine One-Forty-Three," and "Little Moses" by the Carter Family.*

"O Brother, Where Art Thou?" Music from a film by Joel Coen & Ethan Coen. Mercury Records, 2000. 088 170 069-2.
Includes "Keep on the Sunny Side" written by A. P. Carter and "In the Highways" written by Maybelle Carter.

Will the Circle be Unbroken. Nitty Gritty Dirt Band. 30th Anniversary Edition. Produced by William E. McEuen for Aspen Recording Society, Colorado. Produced for Reissue by John McEuen. Capitol Records, 2002. 2 compact discs. 0777-7-46589-2-8. LC-0249.
In addition to many other country stars, Mother Maybelle Carter is featured on "Keep on the Sunny-side," "I'm Thinking Tonight of My Blue Eyes," "Wildwood Flower," and "Will the Circle Be Unbroken."

FOLK MUSIC

Our Singing Country

A Second Volume of American Ballads and Folk Songs

COLLECTED AND COMPILED BY

JOHN A. LOMAX

Honorary Consultant and Curator of the Archive of American
Folk Song of the Library of Congress

AND

ALAN LOMAX

Assistant in Charge of the Archive of American
Folk Song of the Library of Congress

RUTH CRAWFORD SEEGER

Music Editor

New York · The Macmillan Company · 1941

Title Page of 1941 edition of *Our Singing Country: A Second Volume of American Ballads and Folk Songs*. Lomax, John A., and Alan Lomax, comp. Ruth Crawford Seeger, Music Editor. *Our Singing Country: A Second Volume of American Ballads and Folk Songs*. New York: The Macmillan Co., 1941.

Chapter 17
Folk Families: Lomax and Seeger

1927	1934	1941
Carl Sandburg publishes *American Songbag*	John and Alan Lomax publish *American Ballads and Folk Songs*	Lomaxes and Ruth Crawford Seeger publish *Our Singing Country*

Just as there are families of folk songs, there are families in folk song. The two families that contributed greatly to the preservation of folk songs and the revival of their use in popular culture are the Lomax and Seeger families. A study of these two families and their connections to each other provide a history of folk music from the early twentieth century to the present. Members of these families collected folk songs, wrote folk songs, performed folk songs, published folk songs, and continue to be involved with folk songs today.

OBJECTIVES

Students will understand the importance of preserving the folk tradition.

Students will describe the role of government in the 1930s in preserving the folk tradition.

Students will understand the political relationships between the leftist movement and the music during the 1930s.

INTRODUCING THE MUSICIANS

Quotations

- Judith Tick, the author of *Ruth Crawford Seeger: A Composer's Search for American Music* in her introduction to *Our Singing Country*:
  Instead of treating folk music as some kind of antiquarian relic, the Lomaxes touted the modernity of the material. No more quaintness, no more stereotypes of folk song as an example of primitive simplicity. Over and over, the literary commentary embedded music in lived experience . . . This approach to folk music made OSC a 'functional songbook' in

*Alan Lomax's eyes. The term is barely used now, but back then it stood for a new
approach to the field, which Alan Lomax, along with other New Deal culture advocates
like B. H. Botkin and Charles Seeger, actively promoted. They stressed the meaning of
the material to the community and its relationship to 'acculturation'— the way singers
and songs adapted to change.* (Our Singing Country, 2000, xv–xvi)

Lomax Family

Though John Lomax (1867–1948) studied English literature in college, his interest in folk
music was based on his life in Texas. Encouraged by his folklore professors at Harvard, he collected cowboy songs and published them in 1910 as the anthology *Cowboy Songs and Other
Frontier Ballads*.

Lomax persuaded the Library of Congress to provide him with an electric recording machine,
and in 1933 as honorary consultant to the Archive of American Folk Song, John and his
eighteen-year-old son Alan (1915–2002) set out for the south to record American folk songs,
specifically those of "Negroes." These songs were added to the Library of Congress collection
and in 1934 were published as *American Ballads and Folk Songs*. At the Louisiana State
Penitentiary in Angola, the Lomaxes discovered and recorded Huddie Ledbetter, later known as
Lead Belly. (Crawford, 2001, 609–10) John Lomax's second wife, Ruby Terrill Lomax, accompanied him on his later Southern states trips in the role of transcriber and writer of liner notes.
("Ruby Terrill Lomax")

In 1937 Congress began funding the Archive of American Folk Song, and Alan Lomax was
hired as a staff member and began collecting trips of his own in Kentucky, Ohio, Michigan,
Indiana, and Vermont. In a number of instances, other federal projects worked in conjunction
with the Library of Congress. For instance, Zora Neale Hurston, as a member of the Federal
Writer's Project, was on the Lomax expedition to Florida.

Alan Lomax traced the start of the folk song revival to 1933 and its impetus to the New Deal
programs of the Roosevelt administration. Lomax wrote in the anthology *Folk Song USA* (1947):

*The collector goes where book-learning is not. He lives with the underprivileged. He
brings back the proof in their songs and stories and dances that these folks are expressive
and concerned about the beautiful and the good . . . the folklorist has the duty to speak as
the advocate of the common man.* (Crawford, 2001, 610–11)

Alan Lomax promoted folk songs in a number of radio programs, "Back Where I Come
From" and a folk music series for CBS's "American School of the Air." He also participated as
a singer in the "Grapes of Wrath Evening" in New York's Forrest Theater in March 1940. The
concert was arranged to make money for the migrant farm workers. This landmark folk concert
included other now well-known artists such as Lead Belly and Burl Ives, and was the first time
Lomax heard Woody Guthrie. Shortly afterward, Lomax recorded Guthrie at the Archive of
American Folk Song. (Crawford, 2001, 611, 613, 615)

At this time Guthrie also met Pete Seeger who was working at the Archive.
The Lomax and Seeger families overlapped in 1941 with the publication of *Our Singing Country*.
Alan and John collected the songs, and Ruth Crawford Seeger, Pete Seeger's stepmother, tran-
scribed and edited the musical notation. Bess Lomax Hawes writes of the classically trained
Crawford Seeger's contribution:

*She tackled the presentation on paper of a fiddle tune like "Bonaparte's Retreat" with the
same precision, determination, and awe that she would have devoted to a brilliantly realized cadenza from a Mozart violin concerto. Ruth listened, and listened, and then listened*

some more. She used the recording for what she believed it to be—a true record of the music as played or sung. She took as her basic assumption that the music was sounding the way the player wanted it to sound—not like a failed imitation of something else. (Hawes)

After serving in World War II Lomax became Director of Folk Music at Decca Records and continued to collect folk songs, produce albums of folk music, concertize, and lecture. Lomax produced the prize-winning PBS folklore series, "American Patchwork," in 1990.

Seeger Family

Folksinger Pete Seeger came naturally to music. His mother, Constance DeClyvver Edson, was a violinist, and his father, Charles Louis Seeger (1886–1979), taught music theory, history, and composition. Both were on the faculty at New York City's Julliard Institute. Charles Seeger also taught at the New School for Social Research, a New York institution with radical political leanings. After Charles Seeger's second marriage to Ruth Crawford (1901–1953) in 1932, both became involved with the Composers' Collective of New York, an organization connected to the Communist Party that sought to provide music for the education of the workers. (Pescatello, 1992, 110)

Their connection to folk music and ultimately the Lomaxes began around 1935 when Charles took a position with the New Deal's Resettlement Administration whose charge was to use music to "encourage social integration" in the new settlements. (Pescatello, 12, 126) His next position with the Federal Music Project continued his work of collecting and publishing folk music.

Ruth Crawford Seeger was trained as a classical composer and published a number of pieces before she became Seeger's pupil. Studying in Chicago she became friends with composers Henry Cowell and Edgar Varèse and poet Carl Sandburg. Her first foray into folk music was in writing piano accompaniments to some of the songs in Sandburg's *American Songbag* (1927). (Seeger, 1992, 102)

Pete Seeger was exposed early in his life to folk music when his father was collecting folk songs. Seeger learned that there were many versions of the same song. At age seventeen, Seeger met the folk song collector, Alan Lomax; and at the age of twenty, he met folksinger and writer, Woody Guthrie. Guthrie often borrowed and changed melodies from other folk songs. Learning from Guthrie, Seeger noted:

> *One can make up a new song by changing around an old song. Who cares if it is not completely original? The aim in this world is to do a good job, not to try and prove how original one can be. (Seeger, 1993, 12)*

Seeger's friendship with Lomax and Guthrie turned into collaboration as they worked on a collection of folk songs that became *Hard Hitting Songs for Hard-Hit People*. Lomax provided access to the songs in the Archive of American Folk Song, Seeger transcribed the songs and words, and Guthrie wrote the introductions. Some of Guthrie's songs were also included. This project began in 1940, but the book was not published until the 60s. Guthrie also gave Seeger advice about earning some money. In 1940 Seeger decided to hitchhike and ride the freights across the U.S. Guthrie advised him to learn "half a dozen well-known commercial country songs, worth a quarter in any Western bar." (Seeger, 1993, 18)

In late 1940 Seeger, Lee Hayes, and Mill Lampell started singing for left-wing fundraising parties in New York City and formed the group, the Almanac Singers. By 1941 Woody Guthrie had joined them and they added "win-the-war" ballads to their repertoire. After the war Seeger and others began publishing the *People's Songs* bulletin. The song "We Will Overcome," an early version of the 60s protest song, "We Shall Overcome," was published. (Seeger, 1993, 32)

In 1949 Seeger formed the singing group the Weavers. In 1950 *Sing Out!*, a successor to *People's Songs,* printed "The Hammer Song" on the cover of its first issue. This song, written by Seeger and Hayes, was later popularized by Peter, Paul, and Mary as "If I Had a Hammer." Because of blacklisting the Weavers disbanded in 1952. Seeger earned money by recording albums for Moe Asch's Folkways label.

Connections to Other Musicians in This Book

- **Aaron Copland** was connected to both the New School for Social Research and the Composers' Collective of New York. (Pollack, 1999, 58, 278)

- **Copland** used the fiddle tune "Bonyparte" from *Our Singing Country* for the "Hoedown" movement of *Rodeo.* (See Chapter 19)

- Charles Seeger wrote articles about **Charles Ives**, whose music was promoted by their mutual friend Henry Cowell. (Pescatello, 1992, 94)

Periods in American History

World War I, Great Depression, World War II, 50s and 60s Folk Revival

Musical and Historical Connections for Further Research

Almanac Singers	Global Jukebox—multimedia database
"American Patchwork"—PBS series	Hurston, Zora Neale
American Songbag by Carl Sandburg	Lead Belly
Archive of American Folk Song	*People's Songs*
Asch, Moe	Peter, Paul, and Mary
Blacklisting	*Sing Out!*
Federal Music Project	*"We Shall Overcome"*
Folkways Records	Weavers

FOLK FAMILIES STUDENT PAGES

Inquiries

- What are the similarities and differences between the folk songs that were collected by Lomax and the ones written by Guthrie and Seeger?

- How did the role of the U.S. government impact the collection of folk songs? Compare the acquisition of folk songs to that of life histories and photographs. Was there a political role?

- Why were many of the folksingers of the 1930s connected in some way to communism or leftist politics?

- What is the mission of the Library of Congress today? Has it changed since the 1930s?

- What was Alan Lomax's role in preserving folk songs? How did it differ from earlier folk song preservation?

- Where did the Lomaxes go to collect folk songs, and why?

- How did Pete Seeger differ in his use of folk songs?

- What are Pete Seeger's views on the role of folk songs and the practice of changing them to suit topical needs?

- What roles did Ruby Terrill Lomax and Ruth Crawford Seeger play in the history of folk music? How and why did their roles differ from that of their husbands?

- How did Ruth Crawford Seeger popularize folk music? What role did folk songs play in American education? How are they used in today's music classes?

Products

- Choose songs from a folk song anthology that relate to each other and perform them, explaining the relationship.

- Construct a timeline that shows the interactions between the various members of the Lomax and Seeger families that relate to the promotion of folk music.

- Chart the various folk song preservation trips that the Lomaxes took and describe the types of songs collected and the musicians that were recorded.

- Write a biographical sketch of the life of Ruth Crawford Seeger that illustrates her contribution to both classical and American folk music.

- Choose a folk song that appears in different anthologies and trace its history and the changes in the song in various anthologies.

- Produce a chart that describes the various government agencies that supported the collection and preservation of folklore and folk music. Include the names of musicians, writers, and artists who were involved with these endeavors.

- Produce a discography of the reissues of the Lomax recordings. Include the interviews of singers such as Woody Guthrie.

RESEARCH RESOURCES

Web Sites

Biographical:

Alan Lomax

"The Alan Lomax Collection: Timeline." *Rounder.*
    URL: http://www.rounder.com/rounder/artists/lomax_alan/timeline.htm
A chronology of Alan Lomax's life until 1993.

Conan, Neal. "Alan Lomax Remembered." *Talk of the Nation, NPR.*
    URL: http://www.npr.org/ramfiles/totn/20020724.totn.02.ram
Shortly after Lomax's death on July 19, 2002, Neal Conan, guests Nick Spitzer, Pete Seeger, and Worth Long, and callers reminisced about Alan Lomax's life and life's work—folklore.

The Alan Lomax Website.
    URL: http://www.alan-lomax.com/
A timeline of Lomax's life from his birth to 1993.

John Lomax

"John Avery Lomax (1867–1948)." *Southern Mosaic: The John and Ruby Lomax 1939 Southern States Recording Trip.*
    URL: http://memory.loc.gov/ammem/lohtml/lojohnbio.html

This biography gives a brief description of Lomax's life especially as it relates to the collection of folk songs for the Archive of American Folk Songs.

Ruby Terrill Lomax

"Ruby Terrill Lomax (1886–1961)" *Southern Mosaic: The John and Ruby Lomax 1939 Southern States Recording Trip.*
    URL: http://memory.loc.gov/ammem/lohtml/lorubybio.html

This biographical sketch describes the role of Ruby Terrill Lomax, John Lomax's second wife, in the collecting and recording trips sponsored by the Archive of American Folk Song.

Pete Seeger

"Pete Seeger." *The Kennedy Center Honors.*
    URL: http://kennedy-center.org/programs/specialevents/honors/history/honoree/seeger.html
This article lists the highlights of Seeger's career.

"Pete Seeger, Performer." *The Rock and Roll Hall of Fame and Museum.*
    URL: http://rockhall.com/hof/inductee.asp?id=185
A brief biographical sketch and timeline for Seeger's 1996 induction into The Rock and Roll Hall of Fame.

Ruth Crawford Seeger

Seeger, Mike. "Thoughts of Silver Spring, 1938." *ISAM Newsletter, Fall 2001, Volume XXXI, No. 1.*
    URL: http://depthome.brooklyn.cuny.edu/isam/rcsmike.html

Mike Seeger reminisces about his childhood and the wealth of music and fascinating visitors to the Seeger home.

Tick, Judith. "Ruth Crawford Seeger: A Virtual Autobiography." *ISAM Newsletter, Fall 2001, Volume XXXI, No.1.*
> URL: http://depthome.brooklyn.cuny.edu/isam/rcstick.html

Tick intersperses her biographical material about Ruth Crawford Seeger's life with quotations from her letters.

Historical:

California Gold: Northern California Folk Music from the Thirties.
> URL: http://lcweb2.loc.gov/ammem/afccchtml/cowhome.html

Sidney Robertson Cowell began collecting folk music as an assistant to Charles Seeger in the Resettlement Administration. She collected the California music for the WPA California Folk Music Project. This site contains information on the process of collecting music in the article "The Ethnographic Experience: Sidney Robertson Cowell in Northern California." http://lcweb2.loc.gov/ammem/afccchtml/cowsonek.html. Especially interesting is Cowell's "Instructions to WPA Staff" in the "Research Material." http://lcweb2.loc.gov/ammem/afccchtml/cowfield.html

Hawes, Bess Lomax. "Reminiscing on Ruth." *ISAM Newsletter, Spring 2002.*
> URL: http://depthome.brooklyn.cuny.edu/isam/hawes1.html

Bess Lomax Hawes describes the contributions of her brother Alan Lomax and Ruth Crawford Seeger to the anthology Our Singing Country. *Ruth, with her classical background, provided the musical foundation, while Alan, with his extensive interaction with the folk musicians, represented the role of the musicians' lives in the music.*

Kennedy, Stetson. "A Florida Treasure Hunt." *Florida Folklife from the WPA Collections, 1937–1942.*
> URL: http://memory.loc.gov/ammem/flwpahtml/ffpres01.html

Kennedy relates his experiences as a "Junior Interviewer" for the Works Progress Administration recording folk songs in Florida in the 1930s for the Library of Congress. His reminiscences include working with Zora Neale Hurston. The collection includes songs collected and sung by Hurston.

Lomax, Alan. "1939 Annual Report: Excerpt from the Archive of American Folk-Song Annual Report, 1930–1940" *Southern Mosaic: The John and Ruby Lomax 1939 Southern States Recording Trip.*
> URL: http://memory.loc.gov/cgi-bin/query/r?ammem/lomax:@field(DOCID+ar0001)

Lomax's report to the Archive on the various expeditions for collecting folk songs. He mentions the trip by John and Ruby Lomax and also notes recordings supervised by Charles Seeger for the Special Skills Division of the Resettlement Division.

"Voice Clips." *The Folk Music Archives.*
> URL: http://folkmusicarchives.org/voiceclips.htm

Voice clips of Pete Seeger and others relating the story of the writing of "Where Have All the Flowers Gone" and its permutations.

Musical:

"The Alan Lomax Collection." *Rounder Records.*
> URL: http://www.rounder.com/rounder/artists/lomax_alan/

Rounder's listing of the Lomax Collection includes audio files of excerpts of the songs.

Bernstein, Leonard. "Young People's Concerts Scripts: Folk Music in the Concert Hall [typescript on blue paper with emendations in blue and black pencil, yellow fragment pasted on page 9], April 9, 1961." *The Leonard Bernstein Collection, ca. 1920–1989.*
> URL: http://memory.loc.gov/ammem/lbhtml/lbhome.html

Bernstein gives his definition of a folk song and how it is determined by the geography and speech patterns of the country of its origin. Search in the Title Index for this script.

Edwards, Bob. "America's Folk Music Anthology: 50 Years Later, Harry Smith's Music Collection Still Rings True." *NPR Morning Edition with Bob Edwards.*

URL: http://www.npr.org/programs/morning/features/2002/jul/anthology/index.html

Edwards explains the influence on folk musicians of Harry Smith's Anthology of America's Folk Music *set of recordings.*

Key, Susan. "Maverick Icons." *American Mavericks Program Notes.*
URL: http://www.americanmavericks.com/prog_notes/june_09.html

In her analysis of Ruth Crawford Seeger's andante movement from the 1931 String Quartet, Key explains why Crawford Seeger was a "straddler of two worlds" in her work in both the classical and folk traditions.

Neff, Maryl. "Folk Music: American Folk Legends." *Media Usage in the American Folk Music Community.*
URL: http://www.coe.ufl.edu/courses/EdTech/Vault/Folk/Guthrie-Seeger-Lomax.htm

As part of a summary of Neff's doctoral dissertation on the folk music community, this page provides a brief history of the contributions of Woody Guthrie, Pete Seeger, and John and Alan Lomax.

Straus, Joseph N. "Ruth Crawford Seeger's Contributions to Musical Modernism." *ISAM Newsletter, Fall 2001, Volume XXXI, No. 1.*
URL: http://depthome.brooklyn.cuny.edu/isam/rcstraus.html

Straus discusses the musical elements of Seeger's classical compositions.

Tick Judith. "[Crawford Seeger, Rissolty Rossolty]" *American Symphony Orchestra, Dialogues & Extensions.*
URL: http://www.americansymphony.org/dialogues_extensions/96_97season/4th_concert/rissolty.cfm

An analysis of Crawford Seeger's orchestral fantasia Rissolty Rossolty *for a March 12, 1997 concert by the American Symphony Orchestra.*

Tick, Judith. "Ruth Crawford Seeger's Different Tunes." *ISAM Newsletter, Spring 2001, Volume XXX, No. 2.*
URL: http://depthome.brooklyn.cuny.edu/isam/tick.html

Tick discusses the reasons for the renewed interest in Crawford Seeger's music and presents the response to her String Quartet 1931.

Books

Crawford, Richard. "All That Is Native and Fine: American Folk Song and Its Collectors." In *American's Musical Life; A History.* New York: W. W. Norton, 2001.
Beginning with Harvard's Francis James Child's The English and Scottish Popular Ballads *and covering the Lomaxes, Seegers, and Woody Guthrie, Crawford explains the history and business of folk music in America.*

Filene, Benjamin. *Romancing the Folk: Public Memory & American Roots Music.* Chapel Hill: The Univ. of North Carolina Press, 2000.
In addressing what is "roots music" and how it has been packaged and presented, Filene provides a history of folk song collection and an analysis of the performers who promoted the songs.

Jabbour, Alan. "The Flowering of the Folk Revival." In *American Roots Music.* Edited by Robert Santelli, Holly George-Warren, and Jim Brown. New York: Harry N. Abrams, 2001.
Jabbour traces the folk movement from the 1930s to the revival in the 1950s and 60s. The contributions of the Seegers and Lomaxes are included.

Pescatello, Ann M. *Charles Seeger: A Life in American Music.* Pittsburgh: Univ. of Pittsburgh Press, 1992.
This thorough biography of Seeger's life and musical theories also provides information on Ruth Crawford Seeger.

Seeger, Laura Vaccaro. *I Had a Rooster: A Traditional Folk Song.* Foreword by Pete Seeger. New York: Viking, 2001.

This picture book is the result of collaboration of many members of the Seeger family. Based on an idea of Ruth Crawford Seeger, the book is illustrated by Laura Vaccaro Seeger, the wife of Mike Seeger's son Chris. The accompanying compact disc includes songs sung by Pete Seeger and Crawford Seeger's children, Mike and Peggy.

Seeger, Pete. *Where Have All the Flowers Gone: A Singer's Stories, Songs, Seeds, Robberies.* Edited by Peter Blood. Bethlehem, PA: Sing Out Publication, 1993.
"This book tells the story of one person's attempts, over a long lifetime, to put together new songs. Sometimes changing old songs slightly, adding new words to old melodies, or new melodies to old words. Combining traditions from many lands. If you're looking for songs, skip ahead. Ignore the personal chit-chat between the songs. But if you're curious about the life of a musician in 20th century America, here goes." (First paragraph of Pete Seeger's book.)

Tick, Judith. "Washington: 1936–1953." In *Ruth Crawford Seeger: A Composer's Search for American Music.* New York: Oxford Univ. Press, 1997.
In this section of Tick's biography of Ruth Crawford Seeger, she describes Crawford Seeger's role as transcriber for Our Singing Country *and as an educator promoting folk songs to the young, culminating in her publication,* American Folk Songs for Children.

Folk Music Anthologies

Lomax, John A., and Alan Lomax. *American Ballads and Folk Songs.* With a Foreword by George Lyman Kittredge. New York: Dover Publications, 1994.
Originally published in 1934, this anthology includes a wide variety of songs collected by the Lomaxes. Many are introduced with a history of the song or the circumstances of its field recording.

Lomax, John A., and Alan Lomax, comps. *Our Singing Country: Folk Songs and Ballads.* Music Editor, Ruth Crawford Seeger. Introduction to the Dover edition by Judith Tick. Mineola, NY: Dover Publications, 2000.
This reprint of the original 1941 edition is introduced by Judith Tick, the author of Ruth Crawford Seeger: A Composer's Search for American Music.

Music Educators National Conference. *Get America Singing . . . Again!* A Project of the Music Educators National Conference. Foreword by Pete Seeger. Milwaukee: Hall Leonard, 1996.
MENC published these two songbook volumes as part of their campaign "to establish a common song repertoire." The songbooks are available in both a Singer's Edition and a Piano/Vocal/Guitar edition. Both folk songs and copyrighted songs are included.

Sandburg, Carl. *The American Songbag.* With an Introduction by Garrison Keillor. San Diego: A Harvest Book; Harcourt Brace, 1990.
Originally published in 1927, this collection of folk songs includes some arrangements by Ruth Crawford Seeger.

Seeger, Ruth Crawford. *American Folk Songs for Children in Home, School and Nursery School: A Book for Children, Parents and Teachers.* Illustrated by Barbara Cooney. Garden City, NY: Doubleday, 1948.
In the prefatory material Seeger addresses the question "Why American Folk Music for Our Children?" For some of the songs Seeger includes historical information and suggestions for using it with children.

CDs

This Land Is Your Land: Song of Freedom. Various artists. Vanguard Records, 2002. 79710–2.
Includes "If I Had a Hammer" and "Kumbaya" sung by the Weavers.

Seeger, Pete. *If I Had a Song . . . : The Songs of Pete Seeger.* Vol. 2. Various artists. Appleseed Records, 2001.

Seeger, Pete. *Where Have All the Flowers Gone: The Songs of Pete Seeger.* Vol. 1. Various artists. Appleseed Records, 1998.

Terkel, Studs. *Voices of Our Time: Five Decades of Studs Terkel Interviews.* Tape 1. The Chicago Historical Society, 1999. HBP 65178.
Terkel interviewed Pete Seeger in 1955 and Alan Lomax in 1959.

A Treasury of Library of Congress Field Recordings. Selected and Annotated by Stephen Wade. Various performers. Rounder Records Corp., 1997. 3719.
Wade selected performances recorded between 1933 and 1942 for the Library of Congress's Archive of American Folk Song. Most of the recordings were collected by the Lomaxes.

Chapter 18
Woody Guthrie, 1912–1967
Balladeer, "Poor Folkist", Troubadour, Folk Poet

1935	1940	1943	1946
Wrote "Dusty Old Dust"	Wrote "This Land Is Your Land"	Copland wrote *Fanfare for the Common Man*	Recorded his children's songs

Woody Guthrie, a self-professed "poor folkist," traveled throughout the United States in the 30s and 40s singing his songs at labor rallies, at Dust Bowl camps, and on the radio. (Hoog) Inevitably he met Alan Lomax and Pete Seeger, kindred spirits in their interest in people and their music. The three collaborated on *Hard Hitting Songs for Hard-Hit People*. (Klein, 1999, 166)

Guthrie became the voice of the people, often using existing folk tunes and adding words to fit the situation. He became the advocate and eventually the symbol of the common man. His song "This Land Is Your Land," written as a testament to the rights of the neglected people of the United States, has become a widely known American anthem.

OBJECTIVES

Students will define a folk song.

Students will understand the role of a folk song writer as both a reflector of the times and an influence on the times.

Students will understand the role songs played in workers' lives in the 1920s–1940s.

INTRODUCING THE MUSICIAN

Picture Books

Guthrie, Woody. *This Land Is Your Land.* Paintings by Kathy Jakobsen. Boston: Little, Brown, 1998.
The text of this well-known folk song is illustrated with paintings of the areas of the United States mentioned in the song. The borders of the pages include lyrics from Guthrie's songs. The book also includes a tribute by folksinger Pete Seeger, a brief biography of Guthrie, and the melody line and chords of the song.

Guthrie Songs Listed in *This Land Is Your Land*

Biggest Thing That Man has Ever Done	Over the Waves and Gone Again
Do Re Mi	Pastures of Plenty
Dust Can't Kill Me	Pretty Boy Floyd
Dust Storm Disaster	Ramblin' Round
Going Down the Road	Roll On Columbia
Grassey Grass Grass & Dance Around	Seamen Three
Hard Travelin'	So Long, It's Been Good to Know Yuh
Howdido	Talking Subway Blues
I Ain't Got No Home	This Train is Bound for Glory
Little Seed	Tom Joad
My Daddy Flies a Ship in the Sky	Union Maid
New York Town	Woody and Lefty Lou's Theme Song
Oklahoma Hills	

Christensen, Bonnie. *Woody Guthrie: Poet of the People.* New York: Alfred A. Knopf, 2001.

This picture book biography includes many of the events that shaped Guthrie's career as a folksinger of the people. The words to "This Land Is Your Land" are printed across the top of the "woodcut-like" illustrations. Some of the lyrics of his songs are woven into the text, and the complete set of verses of "This Land Is Your Land" is printed at the end of the book.

Audio

Guthrie, Woody. *Woody Guthrie; Library of Congress Recordings.* Recorded by Alan Lomax. 1988. Woody Guthrie Publications; Rounder Records. CD 1041/2/3.

Play portions of the first CD in this collection as an introduction to Guthrie.

Spitzer, Nick. "This Land is Your Land." *The NPR 100.*
URL: http://www.npr.org/ramfiles/atc/20000703.atc.05.rmm

Provides background information on Guthrie's song, "This Land Is Your Land." Includes Guthrie's definition of a folk song. This ram file can be accessed on The NPR 100 *site: http://www.npr.org/programs/ specials/vote/100list.html#T.*

Text

Bernstein, Leonard. "Young People's Concert Scripts: Folk Music in the Concert Hall [typescript on blue paper with emendations in blue and black pencil, yellow fragment pasted onpage 9], April 9, 1961." *The Leonard Bernstein Collection, ca. 1920–1989.*
URL: http://memory.loc.gov/ammem/lbhtml/lbhome.html

This script includes Bernstein's definition of folk music and its use in classical music. Use as basis for discussion of folk songs. Search by keywords folk music scripts *(match all of these words).*

Quotations

• Guthrie in 1941 letter to Alan Lomax:

A folk song ought to be pretty well satisfied just to tell the facts and let it go at that. You hadn't ought to try to be too funny because if you just tell folks the truth they'll laugh at

every other word. The best of all funny stories have got a mighty sincere backbone...
People that laugh at songs laugh because it made them think of something and they
want you to leave a good bit to their guesswork and imagination and it takes on a
friendly and warm atmosphere like you was thanking them for being good listeners and
giving them credit for being able to guess the biggest part of the meaning. (Guthrie,
Pastures of Plenty, *1990, 47–48)*

- Guthrie on folk songs:
  A folk song is whats wrong and how to fix it or it could be whose hungry and where
  their mouth is or whose out of work and where the job is or whose broke and where the
  money is or whose carrying a gun and where the peace is... (Guthrie, Pastures of Plenty,
  1990, 50)

- Guthrie after listening to a radical speech in a camp near Redding, California and
  then singing with two "Okie" girls: (Guthrie, *Bound for Glory*, 253)
  [The music] done something a lot better, something that's harder to do, something you
  need ten times more. It cleared your head up, that's what it done, caused you to fall
  back and let your draggy bones rest and your muscles go limber like a cat's.
  *(*Hard Travelin', *1999, 80)*

- Arlo Guthrie on his father's songs in an interview for *American Roots Music*:
  My dad's songs were really written to make certain people feel as though they had some
  kind of value. Because they were told from where they work and from the countries they
  had immigrated from that they did not. People were being controlled by others who had
  a lot of money... And so they stepped in—my dad, Pete Seeger, Lead Belly and the
  Lomaxes... They sang and wrote and collected the songs in the books that were songs
  for educating people; songs for organizing people; songs for indoctrinating people. They
  had to change the world because the world was crushing them. (Guthrie, Arlo)

- John Steinbeck on Guthrie:
  Working people sing of their hopes and of their troubles, but the rhythms have the beat
  of work... This work is the song and the song is the people... Woody is just Woody.
  Thousands of people do not know he has any other name. He is just a voice and a guitar.
  He sings the songs of a people and I suspect that he is, in a way, that people. Harsh
  voiced and nasal, his guitar hanging like a tire iron on a rusty rim, there is nothing
  sweet about Woody, and there is nothing sweet about the songs he sings. But there is
  something more important for those who will listen. There is the will of a people to
  endure and fight against oppression. I think we call this the American Spirit. (Hard
  Hitting Songs for Hard-Hit People, *1999, 9)*

- Alan Lomax on Guthrie:
  At first glance Woody was not an impressive figure, especially to a Texan. Slight of build,
  windburnt, Apache-eyed, thin-lipped, wiry and with a curly bush of dusty hair under his
  semi-Stetson—I'd seen hundreds of his type in Panhandle towns. He was as familiar as
  cockleburrs or the tumbleweed, built to last, to cling, to prick your conscience and be
  forgotten. Then, in conversation, his voice bit at the heart. A low, harsh voice with velvet
  at the edges, the syllables beautifully enunciated, the prose flowing with a professional
  writers' balance of sentence and with the salt of a folk wit. (Guthrie, Woody Guthrie;
  Library of Congress, *1988, CD liner notes)*

Connections to Other Musicians in This Book

- Collaborated with **Pete Seeger** and **Alan Lomax** to write *Hard Hitting Songs for Hard-Hit People*. (Klein, 1999, 166)

- Wrote "This Land Is Your Land" as a reaction to **Irving Berlin's** song "God Bless America." (See Chapter 9)

- Guthrie used the tune from the **Carter Family's** "Wildwood Flower" for his song "The Sinking of the Reuben James" (Klein, 1999, 217), and their tune "When the World's on Fire" for "This Land Is Your Land." (*Hard Travelin'*, 1999, 59)

Periods in American History

Great Depression, Great Dust Bowl (1930s), World War II, McCarthyism (1950s)

Musical Highlights of Guthrie's Life: Teachers, Colleagues, Events

1912	Born in Okemah, Oklahoma
1929	Learned to play guitar
1935	Major dust storm, wrote "Dusty Old Dust"
1937	*Woody and Lefty Lou* radio show
1940	Wrote "This Land Is Your Land"
	Met Pete Seeger at benefit concert for California farmworkers arranged by actor Will Geer
	Started working on *Hard Hitting Songs for Hard-Hit People*
	Alan Lomax recorded Guthrie for the Library of Congress (sixty-six songs and monologues)
	First commercial recording–*Dust Bowl Collection* on Victor Records
1941	Wrote songs for the Bonneville Power Administration
	Joined singing group Almanac Singers
1943	Wrote autobiography *Bound for Glory*
1944	Guthrie and Cisco Houston recorded more than 160 songs during six-week period for Moe Asch, including "This Land Is Your Land"
1946	Wrote songs about Sacco and Vanzetti
	Began writing children's songs; recorded them for Moe Asch
1952	Diagnosed with Huntington's Chorea
1961	Visited in hospital by Bob Dylan
1967	Died in Queens, New York
1988	Inducted posthumously into the Rock and Roll Hall of Fame

GUTHRIE STUDENT PAGES

Inquiries

- What is a folk song? Why were they popular during the 1930s?

- What social issue is Guthrie addressing in "This Land is Your Land"? Why is it called "a Marxist response to 'God Bless America' "? (Spitzer, "This Land…")

- What do the lyrics and pictures in the book *This Land Is Your Land* tell us about Woody Guthrie's life and philosophy?

- Why did Guthrie write the song "Tom Joad," a song that tells the story of *The Grapes of Wrath* by Steinbeck? Who is the intended audience? How do the lyrics of Guthrie's songs fit into his definition of a folk song? How does using a song to express an idea differ from using fiction?

- What historical events and ideas are reflected in Guthrie's songs?

- How and where is Guthrie's song "This Land Is Your Land" used now?

- Search the *American Life Histories: Manuscripts from the Federal Writers' Project, 1936–1940* for information about the migrant workers' life in the camps. What role did music play in their lives?

- Guthrie read and admired the poetry of Walt Whitman. How are Whitman's words and Guthrie's words similar, and how are they different?

- How did Guthrie's songs affect the labor movement?

- How and why did Guthrie's songs change during World War II?

Products

- Analyze the lyrics of some of Guthrie's songs and write an essay about his social beliefs.

- Examine Guthrie's letters in the collection *Woody Guthrie and the Archive of American Folk Song: Correspondence 1940–1950* and in the book *Pastures of Plenty* and compile a group of quotes that distill Guthrie's views.

- Write a narrative that correlates the labor movement events with the Guthrie songs about labor.

- Find photographs in *America from the Great Depression to World War II: Black-and-White Photographs from the FSA-OWI, 1935–1945* that reflect the people in Guthrie's songs. (Use the Geographic Location Index.) Produce a slide show that includes Guthrie's lyrics that relate to the photographs.

- Look at a timeline of American history from the 1920s to the 1960s. Choose folk songs from *Hard Hitting Songs for Hard-Hit People* and fit them into the timeline. For example, "Tom Joad" relates to Steinbeck's *Grapes of Wrath* and the Dust Bowl era.

- Create a map that lists the places mentioned in Guthrie's songs and the relevant lyrics from the songs.

- Produce a visual presentation using the photographs of the Dust Bowl with captions from Guthrie's lyrics.

- Produce a radio show with performances of Guthrie's songs and quotations. This can be modeled on the Lomax interview.

- Perform Guthrie's children's songs for a group of younger children. Act them out.

- Write an essay detailing the uses of the song "This Land Is Your Land" from the time it was written to the present day.

- Compare Irving Berlin's song "God Bless America" with Guthrie's "This Land Is Your Land."

- Give an oral presentation of a typical day in the life of an "Okie," including audio excerpts of their songs.

- Pete Seeger (Seeger, 1993, 142) and Mary Katherine Aldin (*Hard Travelin'*, 1999, 6) refer to Guthrie's habit of adapting older tunes for his songs. Research these examples and compare the original tunes to Guthrie's. Include the Carter Family songs.

- Compile quotations by Guthrie that illustrate his philosophy of life and the role of music.

- Investigate Guthrie's life and songs at the Smithsonian Magazine *Woody Guthrie Online Gallery* and at the *Woody Guthrie Foundation and Archives*. Trace the places he lived and correlate his life to the events depicted in his songs.

- Investigate the historical event of the sinking of the *Reuben James* and discuss the impact of Guthrie's song "Reuben James."

RESEARCH RESOURCES

Web Sites
Biographical:

"Biography." *Woody Guthrie Foundation and Archives.*
URL: http://www.woodyguthrie.org/biography.htm

Extensive biography with numerous photographs, a selected discography, bibliography, and filmography.

Guthrie, Arlo. "Oral Histories: Arlo Guthrie." *American Roots Music.*
URL: http://www.pbs.org/americanrootsmusic/pbs_arm_oralh_arloguthrie.html

In an interview with Arlo Guthrie for the PBS series American Roots Music *Guthrie answers questions about his father and Lead Belly.*

Jackson, Mark Allan. "Rambling Round: The Life and Times of Woody Guthrie." *Woody Guthrie and the Archive of American Folk Song: Correspondence, 1940–1950.*
URL: http://memory.loc.gov/ammem/wwghtml/wwgessay.html

This biography of Guthrie includes photographs from the Library of Congress American Memory Collections and the Woody Guthrie Foundation and Archives.

Lomax, Alan. "Oral Histories: Alan Lomax." *American Roots Music.*
URL: http://www.pbs.org/americanrootsmusic/pbs_arm_oralh_alanlomax.html

Lomax answers questions about Woody Guthrie and Lead Belly as part of the PBS series American Roots Music.

"Remembering Woody Guthrie: an Online Photo Gallery." *Smithsonian Magazine*, May 2000.
URL: http://www.smithsonianmag.si.edu/smithsonian/issues00/may00/highopener_may00. html

Photos of Guthrie through the years.

Rock and Roll Hall of Fame and Museum, Inductee: Woody Guthrie, 1988.
URL: http://www.rockhall.com/hof/inductee.asp?id=115

Contains brief biographical information.

Woody Guthrie and the Archive of American Folk Song; Correspondence 1940–1950.
URL: http://memory.loc.gov/ammem/wwghtml/

Mainly correspondence from the 1940s between Guthrie and the Archive of American Folk Song. The collection also contains a biographical essay, timeline, bibliography, and discography.

"Woody Guthrie: Dust Bowl Balladeer." *This Land Is Your Land: Rural Music and the Depression.*
URL: http://xroads.virginia.edu/%7E1930s/RADIO/c_w/guthrie.html

Brief biography with quotes and drawings by Guthrie.

Historical:

America from the Great Depression to World War II: Black-and-White Photographs from the FSA-OWI, 1935–1945.
URL: http://memory.loc.gov/ammem/fsahtml/fahome.html

A digitized collection of over 112,000 black-and-white photographs and 1,600 color photographs collected under the direction of Roy Emerson Stryker for the Farm Security Administration and Office of War Information during the years 1935–1942. (Keyword searches: dust storm, migrant camp, workers union).

American Life Histories: Manuscripts from the Federal Writers' Project, 1936–1940.
URL: http://memory.loc.gov/ammem/wpaintro/wpahome.html

2,900 life histories written by the staff of the Folklore Project of the Federal Writers' Project for the U.S. Works Progress Administration (WPA) from 1936-1940. (For keywords read the "Learn More About It!

U.S. History" page: *http://memory.loc.gov/ammem/ndlpedu/collections/wpa/history.html) (Keyword search:* union songs).

Fanslow, Robin A. "The Migrant Experience." *Voices from the Dust Bowl: The Charles L. Todd and Robert Sonkin Migrant Worker Collection, 1940–41.*
    URL: http://memory.loc.gov/ammem/afctshtml/tsme.html

An article that provides background information on the migrant camps visited by Charles L. Todd and Robert Sonkin.

Voices from the Dust Bowl: The Charles L. Todd and Robert Sonkin Migrant Worker Collection, 1940–41.
    URL: http://memory.loc.gov/ammem/afctshtml/tshome.html

Audio recordings, photographs, and song texts collected from the central California migrant camps by Todd and Sonkin for the Archive of American Folk Song.

Musical:

Bernstein, Leonard. "Young People's Concert Scripts: Folk Music in the Concert Hall [typescript on blue paper with emendations in blue and black pencil, yellow fragment pasted onpage 9], April 9, 1961." *The Leonard Bernstein Collection, ca. 1920–1989.*
    URL: http://memory.loc.gov/ammem/lbhtml/lbhome.html

Search folk music scripts *(images 4 and 5).*

Guthrie, Woody. "This Land Is Your Land." *Woody Guthrie Foundation and Archives.*
    URL: http://www.woodyguthrie.org/images/OrigThisLand.jpg

Copy of handwritten words to "This Land Is Your Land" including the original line, "God blessed America for me."

Hoog, Ann. "Woody Guthrie—This Land is Your Land." *Educational Cyber PlayGround.*
    URL: http://www.edu-cyberpg.com/Music/woodieguthrie.html

Explains the contents of the All Things Considered *piece that aired Monday, July 3, 2000 as part of* The NPR 100 *and includes the missing verses of "This Land is Your Land."*

Spitzer, Nick. "This Land is Your Land." *The NPR 100.*
    URL: http://www.npr.org/ramfiles/atc/20000703.atc.05.rmm

Spitzer relates the history of "This Land is Your Land" as one of the pieces chosen for National Public Radio's NPR 100, "some of the most significant works of American music in the last century." The segment includes part of Alan Lomax's 1940 interview with Guthrie. This ram file is available on The NRP 100 *web site: http://www.npr.org/programs/specials/vote/100list.html*

Woody Guthrie Foundation and Archives.
    URL: http://www.woodyguthrie.org/this_land_is_your_land.htm

Description of the information gathered by Kathy Jakobsen from the Woody Guthrie Archive for the book This Land Is Your Land.

Books

Guthrie, Woody. *Bling Blang.* Pictures by Vladimir Radunsky. Cambridge, MA: Candlewick Press, 2000.
    This is a picture book of Guthrie's children's song "Bling Blang". Sheet music on reverse side of jacket.

Guthrie, Woody. *Bound for Glory.* Illustrated with Sketches by the Author. Foreword by Pete Seeger. E. Rutherford, NJ: New American Library, 1995.
    Guthrie's autobiography of the first thirty years of his life includes his experiences as a child in Okemah, Oklahoma, and as a rider of the rails. His narrative style is similar to the style of his songs. The 1976 Dutton edition includes an introduction by Studs Terkel.

Guthrie. Woody. *Hard Hitting Songs for Hard-Hit People.* Compiled by Alan Lomax. Notes on the songs by Woody Guthrie. Music transcribed and edited and with a new afterword by Pete Seeger. Lincoln, NE: Univ. of Nebraska Press, 1999.

This compilation of songs from the Depression was begun by Alan Lomax in the late 1930s. Woody Guthrie wrote some of the songs and all the introductions to the songs, and Pete Seeger transcribed the music from 78 rpm records. John Steinbeck wrote the foreword. The book wasn't published until the 60s. This edition adds a new afterword by Pete Seeger. Most of the photographs were taken by photographers working for the Farm Security Administration in the 1930s.

Guthrie, Woody. *Howdi Do*. Pictures by Vladimir Radunsky. Cambridge, MA: Candlewick Press, 2000.
A picture book version of Guthrie's children's song "Howdi Do." Sheet music on reverse side of jacket. CD included that contains "Howdi Do," "Bling Blang," and "My Dolly."

Guthrie, Woody. *Pastures of Plenty: A Self-portrait*. Edited by Dave Marsh and Harold Leventhal. New York: HarperCollins, 1990.
A compilation of Guthrie's unpublished writings, ranging from handwritten notes on calendars to letters to newspaper and magazine articles.

Guthrie, Woody. *The Woody Guthrie Songbook*. Edited by Harold Leventhal and Marjorie Guthrie. New York: Grosset & Dunlap, 1976.
Includes sixty of Guthrie's songs, including "This Land Is Your Land," "Talking Dust Bowl," "Tom Joad," and "Do Re Mi." Actor Will Geer writes about performing with Guthrie in the California migrant camps, and Edward Robbin describes Guthrie's radio show on California station KFVD.

Klein, Joe. *Woody Guthrie: A Life*. New York: Delta Trade Paperbacks, 1999.
Paperback edition of the 1980 Alfred A. Knopf edition, with a new afterword by the author. Klein had access to Woody Guthrie's papers and the cooperation of Marjorie Guthrie and other family and friends in producing this exhaustive biography of Guthrie.

Partridge, Elizabeth. *This Land Was Made for You and Me: The Life & Songs of Woody Guthrie*. New York: Viking, 2002.
Beginning each chapter with a quote from Guthrie and including many photographs and drawings, Partridge tells the story of Guthrie's life in a personal, flowing narrative.

Santelli, Robert, and Emily Davidson, eds. *The Life and Legacy of Woody Guthrie*. Hanover, NH: Wesleyan Univ. Press, 1999.
A book of essays from the presentations at the conference, Hard Travelin': The Life and Legacy of Woody Guthrie. *The essays cover Guthrie's life, creative output, and social and political issues.*

Seeger, Pete. "This Land Is your Land." In *Where Have All the Flowers Gone: A Singer's Stories, Songs, Seeds, Robberies*. Edited by Peter Blood. Bethlehem, PA: Sing Out Corp., 1993.
In this anthology of writings and songs, Seeger often describes his experiences with Guthrie and Guthrie's songs, including "This Land Is Your Land."

CDs

Folkways: A Vision Shared: A Tribute to Woody Guthrie & Leadbelly. Various artists. Columbia, 1988. CK 44034.
Includes "Pretty Boy Floyd," "Do, Re, Mi," and "This Land Is Your Land" by Woody Guthrie, among others.

Guthrie, Woody. *Woody Guthrie; The Asch Recordings*, Vol. 1–4. Compiled by Jeff Place and Guy Logsdon. Annotated by Guy Logsdon and Jeff Place. Smithsonian Folkways Recordings, 1999. SFW CD 40112.
Moses (Moe) Asch recorded Woody Guthrie from 1944 to 1954. Place and Logsdon have transferred some of the original recordings in the Moses Asch/Folkways Records Archives.

Guthrie, Woody. *A Tribute to Woody Guthrie: Highlights from Concerts at Carnegie Hall, 1968, Hollywood Bowl, 1970*. Words and music by Woody Guthrie. Narrations by Peter Fonda, Will Geer, Robert Ryan. Warner Bros. Records, 1976. 9 26036-2.
Performances by Joan Baez, Judy Collins, Bob Dylan, Jack Elliott, Arlo Guthrie, Richie Havens, Country Joe McDonald, Odetta, Tom Paxton, Earl Robinson, and Pete Seeger. Includes a performance of "This Land Is Your Land" with narration by Will Geer.

Guthrie, Woody. *Woody Guthrie; Library of Congress Recordings.* Recorded by Alan Lomax. 1988. Woody Guthrie Publications; Rounder Records. 1041/2/3.
These recordings made by Woody Guthrie and Alan Lomax for the Library of Congress in March 1940 include twenty-nine songs interspersed with monologues by Guthrie in response to questions from Lomax. Guthrie discusses his personal life and the effects of the Dust Bowl on him and people he observed.

"This Land Is Your Land." In *This Land is Your Land: Songs of Freedom.* Various artists. Vanguard Records, 2002. 79710-2.
The song is sung by Cisco Houston.

CLASSICAL MUSIC

SIMPLE GIFTS

'Tis the gift to be sim-ple, 'tis the gift to be free, 'Tis the gift to come down where we ought to be, And when we find our-selves in the place just right, 'Twill be in the val-ley of love and de-light. When true sim-pli-ci-ty is gain'd, To bow and to bend we shan't be a-sham'd, To turn, turn will be our de-light 'Till by turn-ing, turn-ing we come round right.

"Simple Gifts." In *The Gift to be Simple: Songs, Dances and Rituals of the American Shakers.* By Edward Deming Andrews. New York: Dover Publications, 1962.

Chapter 19
Aaron Copland, 1900–1990
Composer, Conductor, Pianist

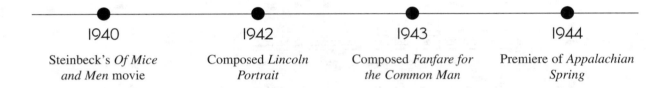

1940	1942	1943	1944
Steinbeck's *Of Mice and Men* movie	Composed *Lincoln Portrait*	Composed *Fanfare for the Common Man*	Premiere of *Appalachian Spring*

Aaron Copland is known as the "Dean of American Music." His early compositions used jazz elements in an attempt to portray an American sound. Later, he incorporated folk songs such as "Simple Gifts" into his pieces. Eventually, Copland's style and sound became synonymous with American music. Bernstein described Copland's Third Symphony as containing many of the elements of American music: "jazz rhythms, and optimism, and wide-open spaces, and simplicity, and sentimentality, and a mixture of things from all over the world." (Bernstein, *Young People's…*)

OBJECTIVES

Students will be able to identify the elements in classical music that make it "American."

Students will determine Aaron Copland's role in the history of American music.

Students will identify the role of musicians in the politics of the 1950s.

INTRODUCING THE MUSICIAN

Picture Book

"Simple Gifts," a Shaker hymn, was written around 1848. Aaron Copland used the melody in the ballet *Appalachian Spring* and in his song set, *Old American Songs, Set I*. Raschka's book *Simple Gifts* can be used as an introduction to the music of Aaron Copland on two levels. It introduces the reader to a song that was used by Copland in one of his most popular pieces. It also can be used as a way of introducing the sparseness or "simplicity" of Copland's music.

Raschka, Chris. *Simple Gifts: A Shaker Hymn*. New York: Henry Holt, 1998.
   Using oil crayon on pastel paper, Raschka patterned his illustrations for the Shaker hymn "Simple Gifts" on "Dark Voyage," a painting by Paul Klee. Raschka's "simple gifts" include a cat, a blue jay, a

squirrel, a turtle, and a rabbit. The animals "turn, turn" and the stylized flowers "bow" and "bend." An explanation of the Shakers' history and a copy of the music is included.

Discuss the meaning of the lyrics of the song after discussing the history of the Shakers. Have a group of students present their analysis of the illustrations and how they relate to the text of the song. After this discussion, listen to the NPR segment on *Appalachian Spring*.

London, Jeff. "Appalachian Spring." *The NPR 100.*
 URL: http://www.npr.org/ramfiles/atc/20001113.atc.06.rmm

Quotations

- Copland on *Appalachian Spring*
 I knew certain crucial things–that it had to do with the pioneer American spirit, with youth and spring, with optimism and hope. I thought about that in combination with the special quality of Martha's [Graham] own personality, her talents as a dancer, what she gave off, and the basic simplicity of her art. Nobody else seems anything like Martha, and she's unquestionably very American. There's something prim and restrained, a strong quality about her, that one tends to think of as American. (Copland, Copland since 1943, *1989, 32)*

- Copland on "Simple Gifts":
 I felt that 'Simple Gifts', which expressed the unity of the Shaker spirit, was ideal for Martha's scenario and for the kind of austere movements associated with her choreography. 'Simple Gifts' was originally meant to be used for dancing. I read that the dance would have been in a lively tempo, with single files of brethren and sisters two or three abreast proceeding with utmost precision around the meeting room. In the center of the room would be a small group singing the dance song over and over until everyone was both exhilarated and exhausted. (Copland, Copland since 1943, *1989, 32)*

- Ned Rorem, American composer, on Copland's composing style:
 Aaron stressed simplicity: Remove, remove, remove, what isn't needed…the leanness!– particularly in his instrumentation, which he himself, termed 'transparent,' and taught me the French word de'pouille! Stripped bare. (Copland, Copland since 1943, *1989, 124)*

- Copland on music's effect:
 By reflecting the time in which one lives, the creative artist gives substance and meaning to life as we live it. Life seems so transitory! It is very attractive to set down some sort of permanent statement about the way we feel, so that when it's all gone, people will be able to go to our art works to see what it was like to be alive in our time and place– twentieth-century America. (Copland, Copland since 1943, *1989, 426)*

Connections to Other Musicians in This Book

- Copland and **Leonard Bernstein** met in 1937 and were friends for the rest of their lives. **Bernstein** performed and promoted many of Copland's pieces.

- Copland used a **Stephen Foster** melody from "Camptown Races" in *Lincoln Portrait.* (Crawford, 2001, 594)

- Copland composed music for the movie versions of Steinbeck's *Of Mice and Men* and *The Red Pony.* Steinbeck wrote an introduction to **Woody Guthrie's** *Hard Hitting Songs for Hard-Hit People.* **Guthrie** wrote the song "Tom Joad" in response to Steinbeck's book, *The Grapes of Wrath.*

- **Alan Lomax** commissioned Copland to write an orchestral arrangement of the folk song "John Henry" for the CBS program for high school students. (Levin, 2000, 90)

- Copland used the fiddle tune "Bonyparte" from the **Lomaxes'** anthology *Our Singing Country* for the "Hoedown" movement of *Rodeo*. (Levin, 2000, 156)

- Copland composed *Night Thoughts (Homage to Ives)* (Levin, 2000, 112)

- Copland on **Gershwin:**

  In many ways Gershwin and I had much in common—both from Brooklyn, we had studied with Rubin Goldmark during the same time and were pianists and composers of music that incorporated indigenous American sounds . . . but until the Hollywood years in the thirties, we moved in very different circles. (Levin, 2000, 58)

Periods in American History

World War I, 1920s, Great Depression, World War II, McCarthyism, Peace movement and Vietnam war (1960s, 1970s)

Musical Highlights of Copland's Life: Teachers, Colleagues, Events

1900	Born in Brooklyn, New York
1921	Studied composition with Nadia Boulanger at the American Conservatory at Fontainebleau
1925	Wrote *Music for the Theatre*
1927	Began teaching at the New School for Social Research
1937	Met Leonard Bernstein
1938	Premier of ballet *Billy the Kid*
1939	Published book *What to Listen for in Music* Premier of movie *Of Mice and Men*, based on the book by John Steinbeck with music by Copland
1940	Wrote *John Henry* for Alan Lomax's radio show *American School of the Air: Folk-Music of America*
1942	Completed *Lincoln Portrait* Composed ballet *Rodeo*
1943	Published *Fanfare for the Common Man*
1944	Premier of *Appalachian Spring*, the ballet choreographed by Martha Graham
1945	Awarded Pulitzer Prize for ballet *Appalachian Spring*
1946	Premier of the Third Symphony Elected to membership of ASCAP
1948	Wrote *Clarinet Concerto* commissioned by Benny Goodman
1949	Release of movie *The Red Pony*, based on the book by John Steinbeck with music by Copland
1950	Premier of the song cycle *Twelve Poems of Emily Dickinson* Premier of the song cycle *Old American Songs, Set I*

1953   Appeared before the House Un-American Activities Committee
Premiere of the song cycle *Old American Songs, Set II*

1954   Premier of the opera, *The Tender Land,* inspired by *Let Us Now Praise Famous Men* by James Agee and Walker Evans

1972   Composed *Night Thoughts (Homage to Ives)* for the Van Cliburn piano competition

1990   Died in North Tarrytown, New York

COPLAND STUDENT PAGES

Inquiries

- What American themes and music are included in Copland's ballet music?

- What is the relationship between Copland's music and the literature of the times?

- What was Copland's role in the history of American music? Who were his contemporaries and collaborators? What do musicians and music historians write of Copland's place in American music history?

- How did the Depression affect classical composers and musicians? How and why did Copland's music change?

- How did the House Un-American Activities Committee investigation affect Copland? What role does the music industry have in a democratic society?

- Copland wrote music for the concert hall and the film industry. How did this dual career affect his standing as a classical composer? What were Copland's views on this?

- What jazz elements did Copland include in his music?

- How did Copland utilize folk tunes? What was happening in the folk music industry at the same time?

  Searching tips: Search American Memory collections, http://memory.loc.gov/ammem/ mdbquery.html, with search term *aaron copland* (match all of these words).

Products

- Develop a chronology for the creation of *Appalachian Spring* using the letters, sketches, and photographs in *The Aaron Copland Collection* and the NPR segment.

  Searching tips for *American Memory Collections*:

  Search Descriptive Information: *appalachian spring* (match all of these words).

  Search Full Text: *ballet graham* (match all of these words).

- Analyze the "Simple Gifts" music in Raschka's book. Compare this melody to the Copland score.

- Investigate the history of the Shaker song "Tis the Gift to be Simple" and describe why Copland and Graham used Shaker elements in the ballet *Appalachian Spring*.

- Compile a list of Copland scores that are labeled "American" and relate what they have in common musically. Compare Copland's pieces to the descriptions used in Bernstein's Young People's Concerts script entitled "What is American Music?"

- Copland composed scores for ballets and films. Write an essay describing the stories behind these productions and Copland's procedure for relating his music to the stories.

- Describe the effect of the House Un-American Activities Committee's hearings on the artistic atmosphere of the early 50s, and on Copland in particular.

- Compare Copland's pieces that have jazz elements with those of Gershwin and Bernstein.

- Compare the style of Copland's music for *The Red Pony* and *Of Mice and Men* with the literary style of Steinbeck.

- Prepare a multimedia presentation of photographs from the ballet *Appalachian Spring* and compare them to the music.

- Identify the folk songs Copland used in his pieces and compare to the originals.

RESEARCH RESOURCES

Web Sites
Biographical:

Ardoin, John. "Copland's America: Meet the Artist." *PBS Great Performances*.
  URL: http://www.pbs.org/wnet/gperf/copland/meet.html

This biographical sketch looks at Copland's life and includes quotes about his music by conductors Walter Damrosch and Leonard Bernstein.

Bernstein, Leonard. "Aaron Copland: An Intimate Sketch." *High Fidelity/Musical America.* 11 Nov. 1970. *The Aaron Copland Collection, ca. 1900–1990*.
  URL: http://memory.loc.gov/ammem/achtml/acintim.html

Leonard Bernstein relates his personal and musical experiences with Aaron Copland.

Boriskin, Michael. "Aaron Copland: Timeline of a Musical Life." *Copland House.*
  URL: http://coplandhouse.org/Timeline.htm

An extensive timeline of Copland's life.

Hampson, Thomas. "Aaron Copland, 1900–1990." *I Hear America Singing.*
  URL: http://www.thirteen.org/ihas/composer/copland.html

A profile of Copland that describes many of his compositions, including a section on their folk elements. It also includes a paragraph on the McCarthy hearings.

"Timeline for Aaron Copland." *Aaron Copland Collection, ca. 1900–1990.*
  URL: http://memory.loc.gov/ammem/achtml/actime.html

An annotated timeline of Copland's life with photographs from the Music Division of the Library of Congress.

Trudeau, Andy. "The Copland Story: An Artistic Biography." *npr online: The Copland Centennial.*
  URL: http://www.npr.org/programs/specials/copland/coplandstory.html

Trudeau's article touches on the various periods of Copland's musical output.

Historical:

Crumm, David. "150 Years of 'Simple Gifts'." *Detroit Free Press, Freep*, Nov. 11, 1998.
  URL: http://www.freep.com/fun/music/qshaker11.htm

Crumm provides a history of the song, including its appearance in Copland's Appalachian Spring *and commercials for Oldsmobile's Aurora.*

Hampson, Thomas. "The Shakers." *I Hear America Singing.*
URL: http://www.thirteen.org/ihas/icon/shakers.html

A brief history of the religious sect, the Shakers, including the origins of the Shaker hymn, "Simple Gifts," and its use by Copland.

Render, Angela. "A Foot-Stomping, Toe-Tapping Culture." *Smithsonian Journeys,* April 2001.
URL: http://www.smithsonianmag.si.edu/journeys/01/apr01/music.html

The article contains images of the original notation for "Simple Gifts" and paintings of Shakers dancing.

Musical:

The Aaron Copland Collection, ca. 1900–1990.
URL: http://memory.loc.gov/ammem/achtml/achome.html

The first release of 1,000 items from the Library of Congress's Aaron Copland Collection. It includes music sketches, correspondence, writings, and photographs and is searchable by keyword and by browsing by Musical Sketches, Writings, Correspondence, Photographs, a Title Index, and a Works List.

Bernstein, Leonard. "Young People's Concerts Scripts: What is American Music? [typescript with emendations in red, blue and black pencil (pg. 16 torn and taped)], February 1, 1958." *The Leonard Bernstein Collection, ca. 1920–1989.*
URL: http://memory.loc.gov/ammem/lbhtml/lbhome.html

Search with keywords what is american music. *(match all of these words.) Image 33 has Bernstein's description of Copland's* Third Symphony.

Copland, Aaron. "Aaron Copland Works List: Links to Related Digital Items. Appalachian Spring." *The Aaron Copland Collection, ca, 1900–1990.*
URL: http://memory.loc.gov/ammem/achtml/aclinks.html#work0030

Links to items in The Aaron Copland Collection *that relate to* Appalachian Spring.

Copland, Aaron. "Aaron Copland Works List: Links to Related Digital Items. Old American Songs. Set I." *The Aaron Copland Collection, ca, 1900–1990.*
URL: http://memory.loc.gov/ammem/achtml/aclinks.htmlwork#0041

Click on "Old American songs, set I [pencil sketch]" for the pencil sketch of the score of Old American Songs, Set I. *Image 24 contains the "The Gift to Be Simple" theme.*

Copland, Aaron. "Excerpt." *Oral History, American Music.*
URL: http://www.yale.edu/oham/frameexcerpt.html

A brief excerpt from an interview with Aaron Copland in which he describes his attempt to write "American" music.

Levang, Rex. "What Makes Copland's Music so 'American'?" *Minnesota Monthly*, Nov. 2000. *MPR Music.*
URL: http://music.mpr.org/features/0011_copland/minnmo.shtml

Levang cites the American elements in Copland's music and includes audio examples from the music.

Levin, Gail. "Visualizing Modernity and Tradition in Copland's America." *ISAM Newsletter*, Fall 2000.
URL: http://depthome.brooklyn.cuny.edu/isam/levin00.html

"This article is a revised excerpt from Gail Levin and Judith Tick's book Aaron Copland's America: A Cultural Perspective *(Watson-Guptill Publications, 2000)." Levin describes the composers and painters who influenced Copland's search for "American" elements in his music. She describes the use of Shaker design and music in the ballet* Appalachian Spring.

Lunden, Jeff. "Appalachian Spring." *The NPR 100.*
URL: http://www.npr.org/ramfiles/atc/20001113.atc.06.rmm

The audio file of NPR's All Things Considered NPR 100 *segment on Copland's* Appalachian Spring. *It describes the collaboration between Copland and choreographer Martha Graham. The ram file is on* The NPR 100 *site: http://www.npr.org/programs/specials/vote/100list.html*

Shirley, Wayne. "A Brief Introduction to the Music of Aaron Copland: Music for Dance and Film." *The Aaron Copland Collection, ca. 1900–1990.*
  URL: http://memory.loc.gov/ammem/achtml/acintro03.html
  A description of Copland's works for dance and film with links to many of the scores.

Steinberg, Michael, and David Wright and James M. Keller. "A Copland Journey." *American Mavericks Program Notes.*
  URL: http://www.americanmavericks.com/prog_notes/june_23.html

  These program notes from the Minnesota Public Radio program American Mavericks *contain information on many of Copland's compositions.*

Books

Austin, William W. "Copland, Aaron." In Vol. 4 of *The New Grove Dictionary of Music and Musicians.* Edited by Stanley Sadie. London: Macmillan Publishers; New York: Grove's Dictionaries of Music, 1995.
  Austin writes extensively about Appalachian Spring.

Copland, Aaron, and Vivian Perlis. *Copland: 1900 through 1942.* New York: St. Martin's Press, 1984.
  In this autobiography Copland describes the stories behind his compositions, his interactions with other musicians, and his conducting career. Perlis provides background information and includes interviews with contemporaries of Copland.

Copland, Aaron and Vivian Perlis. *Copland since 1943.* New York: St. Martin's Press, 1989.
  In this autobiography Copland describes the stories behind his compositions, his interactions with other musicians, and his conducting career. Perlis provides background information and includes interviews with contemporaries of Copland.

Levin, Gail, and Judith Tick. *Aaron Copland's American: A Cultural Perspective.* New York: Watson-Guptill Publications, 2000.
  Published in connection with an exhibition at the Heckscher Museum of Art in Huntington, New York for the Copland centennial, these essays cover Copland's relationship to the art of the period and his musical influences.

Pollack, Howard. *Aaron Copland: the Life and Work of an Uncommon Man.* New York: Henry Holt, 1999.
  Pollack investigates Copland's role in the history of American music and his influence on younger composers. He also provides in-depth analysis of Copland's major works.

Pollack, Howard. "Copland, Aaron." In Vol. 6 of *The New Grove Dictionary of Music and Musicians.* 2nd edition. Edited by Stanley Sadie. London: Macmillan Publishers; New York: Grove's Dictionaries, 2001.
  Pollack describes Coplands' four style periods.

CDs

Copland, Aaron. *American Songs.* Dawn Upshaw. Thomas Hampson. The Saint Paul Chamber Orchestra, Hugh Wolff. Teldec Classics International, 1994. 9031-77310-2.
  Includes Old American Songs, Down a Country Lane, Eight Poems of Emily Dickinson, *and* Billy the Kid (Selections)

Copland, Aaron. *The Ultimate Copland Album: An American Celebration.* Featuring Detroit Symphony Orchestra/Antal Dorati; English Chamber Orchestra/Carl Davis; London Sinfonietta/Elgar Howarth; Baltimore Symphony Orchestra/David Zinman. The Decca Record Co., 1999. 289 466 909-2.
  Includes Fanfare for the Common Man, Simple Gifts, Variations on a Shaker Hymn, *selections from* Billy the Kid, *and* Appalachian Spring (Ballet for Martha).

A Treasury of Library of Congress Field Recordings. Selected and Annotated by Stephen Wade. Various artists. Rounder Records Corp., 1997. 3719.
  Includes the fiddle tune "Bonyparte," played by W. H. Stepp, which Copland used in the "Hoedown" movement of Rodeo.

Chapter 20
Leonard Bernstein, 1918–1990
Conductor, Composer, Educator

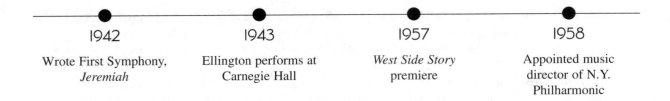

1942	1943	1957	1958
Wrote First Symphony, *Jeremiah*	Ellington performs at Carnegie Hall	*West Side Story* premiere	Appointed music director of N.Y. Philharmonic

Leonard Bernstein, with a combination of flamboyancy and casualness, changed the role and public perception of a classical music conductor. He was the first American-born conductor of a major American orchestra. His interest in an eclectic mix of music styles, including jazz and musical theater, changed the programming of classical symphony orchestra concerts. He pioneered the role of conductor-as-teacher in his television series, *Omnibus* and *Young People's Concerts*, popularizing classical music and promoting American music.

His compositions also reflected the breadth of his musical knowledge. He composed classical works for orchestra, film, and musical theater. Despite his predominant role as a classical musician, he is probably best known to the general audience for his popular musical *West Side Story*.

OBJECTIVES

Students will understand the importance and influence of a conductor in the promotion of music.

Students will understand the role of classical music in commemorating events in American history.

Students will determine Bernstein's role in the development of musical theater.

Students will identify the elements and character of American classical music.

INTRODUCING THE MUSICIAN

Video

Show one of the *Young People's Concerts* videos to introduce Bernstein as conductor and teacher. See below for the video *What Is American Music?* For descriptions and ordering information see the following web site:

> "Leonard Bernstein's Young Peoples Concerts with the New York Philharmonic." *Bernstein's Studio: Store.*
> URL: http://www.leonardbernstein.com/studio/details.asp

Scripts

Show some of the scripts for the television series *Young People's Concerts* to demonstrate Bernstein's thoughts on music and his effectiveness as an educator. Search the Title Index of *The Leonard Bernstein Collection, ca. 1920–1989* (http://memory.loc.gov/ammem/lbhtml/lbhome. html) for the *Young People's Concerts*.

Letters

Search *The Leonard Bernstein Collection, ca. 1920–1989* with the words *west side story* (match all of these words). http://memory.loc.gov/ammem/lbhtml/lbhome.html. Show the letters from Leonard Bernstein to Felicia Bernstein, August 15, 1957 and August 23, 1957.

Quotations

- Bernstein on plans for the 1958–59 New York Philharmonic season in *The New York Times Magazine*, December 22, 1957:
  The function of the orchestra has to be different—because it is in New York, the center of the music world. The programs should add up to something; they should have a theme running through them... In a way my job is an educational mission. (Secrest, 1994, 240)

- Bernstein on tonality in his book *The Infinite Variety of Music*, 1962:
  ... all forms we have ever known—plainchant, motet, fugue or sonata—have always been conceived in tonality, *that is, in the sense of a tonal magnetic center... And the moment a composer tries to 'abstract' musical tones by denying them their tonal implications, he has left the world of communication. (Secrest, 1994, 28)*

- Bernstein on the conductor's role in his TV production *Omnibus Presents: The Art of Conducting*, December 4, 1955:
  The conductor must not only make his orchestra play—he must make them want to play. He must exalt them, start their adrenaline pouring, either by pleading or demanding or raging. But however he does it, he must make them love the music as he loves it. (Bernstein Live CD cover, 2000)

- Bernstein on *West Side Story* in letter to David Diamond:
  It really does my heart good—because this show is my baby, my tragic music–comedy, whatever that is; and if it goes in New York as it has on the road, we will have proved something very big indeed, and maybe changed the face of the American musical theatre. (Bernstein Remembered, 1991, 72)

- Jon Deak, double bass player for the New York Philharmonic:
  Playing with Lenny was always a frightening but exhilarating experience. I remember the Tchaikovsky [Pathétique] *as a striking example of his coming at something totally fresh. He would say: "Wow! You know, it just came to me what that phrase meant!" And your heart would go out to him. And when you think how well Bernstein knew this symphony—I mean, I know it memorized, and he would have known it ten times better than I do—it was extraordinary. (Conversations,* 1995, 154)

Connections to Other Musicians in This Book

- Bernstein and **Copland** were friends, and Copland introduced Bernstein to musicians that could further his career. Bernstein, in turn, advised Copland on his compositions and performed many of his works.

- Bernstein conducted the program, Louis Armstrong All-Stars & The New York Philharmonic, July 14, 1956. The web site, http://www.libertyhall.com/stamp/concert.html, includes an audio clip of Bernstein introducing **Armstrong** and Armstrong responding. The page also includes a clip of "St. Louis Blues."

- Bernstein was an advocate for **Charles Ives's** music and performed his works with orchestras. He titled his series of Norton lectures for Harvard University after one of Ives's compositions, *The Unanswered Question.* (Horowitz)

- Bernstein often programmed **Gershwin's** music, especially *Rhapsody in Blue* and *An American in Paris.* The two composers were similar in their desire to be known for their classical compositions, rather than their popular ones.

Periods in American History

Great Depression, World War II, McCarthyism, Peace movement and Vietnam War (1960s and 1970s)

Musical Highlights of Bernstein's Life: Teachers, Colleagues, Events

1918	Born in Lawrence, Massachusetts
1937	First met Aaron Copland, Adolph Green, and Dimitri Mitropoulis
1940	Studied conducting under Serge Koussevitzky
1942	Completed first symphony, *Jeremiah*
1943	Appointed assistant conductor of the New York Philharmonic Debut as conductor of New York Philharmonic as substitute for Bruno Walter
1945	Appointed Music Director of the New York City Symphony Orchestra
1949	First performance of second symphony, *The Age of Anxiety* Wrote *Prelude, Fugue and Riffs* for solo clarinet and jazz ensemble
1953	First performance of the musical *Wonderful Town*
1954	Wrote the score for the film *On the Waterfront* First television appearance on *Omnibus*
1956	Premiere of *Candide*

1957   Premiere of musical *West Side Story*

1958   Appointed music director of the New York Philharmonic
First of fourteen seasons of *Young People's Concerts*

1963   First performance of Third Symphony, *Kaddish*

1969   Retired as music director of the New York Philharmonic; named Laureate Conductor

1971   *Mass: a Theater Piece for Singers, Players, and Dancers* opens at the John F. Kennedy Center for the Performing Arts

1973   Delivered six lectures, "The Unanswered Question," at Harvard University

1983   Premiere of opera *A Quiet Place*

1990   Died in New York City

BERNSTEIN STUDENT PAGES

Inquiries

- What was the significance of Bernstein's appointment as conductor of the New York Philharmonic?

- How did Bernstein, the conductor, influence the course of American music composition?

- How did Bernstein change the role of the symphony orchestra in America?

- How did Bernstein change the role of the symphony orchestra conductor?

- What was Bernstein's role as musical educator, and what effect did it have on American music appreciation?

- What role did Bernstein and the New York Philharmonic play in commemorating important American events?

- What is the difference between a musical and an opera? How do musical elements in Bernstein's *West Side Story* compare to those in an opera? What made it different than the musicals that came before it?

- What types of music did Bernstein compose? How were his classical pieces received?

- How did Bernstein's music reflect what was happening in America during the time period?

- How are Bernstein's Jewish roots reflected in his music?

- How did Bernstein's interest in many styles of music affect his compositions?

Products

- Using musical examples and Bernstein's *Young People's Concerts*, explain the musical elements in American classical music.

- Present part of one of Bernstein's television scripts along with recordings of the musical excerpts to explain a musical concept or introduce a composer.

- Compile a list of programs that the New York Philharmonic performed to commemorate important events in American history and describe why particular pieces were programmed.

- Construct a timeline of Bernstein-led performances within the context of political and historical events.

- Compare Bernstein's works: *Candide* and *West Side Story*.

- After reading about Bernstein's conducting from the viewpoints of orchestra members and critics, take a position on its effectiveness and validity.

- Investigate the works composed by Bernstein and Copland for the stage and film. Compile a chronology and description of their works to demonstrate the role they played in the history of American musical theater.

RESEARCH RESOURCES

Web Sites
Biographical:

"Biography: Leonard Bernstein." *Bernstein's Studio.*
> URL: http://www.leonardbernstein.com/lifeswork/biography/

> *An extensive biography that lists Bernstein's compositions and his accomplishments.*

Gutmann, Peter. "Leonard Bernstein: A Total Embrace of Music." *Classical Notes.*
> URL: http://www.classicalnotes.net/features/bernstein.html

> *Using information from a number of Bernstein biographies and Bernstein's own writings, Gutmann, "a deeply devoted fan," provides a lengthy synopsis of Bernstein's life.*

Hampson, Thomas. "Leonard Bernstein (1918–1990)." *I Hear America Singing.*
> URL: http://www.pbs.org/wnet/ihas/composer/bernstein.html

> *Hampson briefly describes Bernstein's life and his compositions. In one section he relates Bernstein's use of Walt Whitman's poem "To What You Said" in his song cycle* Songfest.

Hart, Peter. "Lecturer Details Leonard Bernstein's Multifaceted, Multinational Career." *University Times*, Oct. 25, 2001.
> URL: http://www.pitt.edu/utimes/issues/34/011025/09.html

> *Hart describes a lecture by Ken Meltzer, Pittsburgh Symphony community spokesperson, titled "The Career of Maestro Leonard Bernstein." In this lecture Meltzer explains why he appreciates all the facets of Bernstein's career.*

"Leonard Bernstein." *American Masters.*
> URL: http://www.pbs.org/wnet/americanmasters/database/bernstein_1.html

> *A short biography that emphasizes Bernstein's contribution in bringing classical music to a larger audience.*

"Leonard Bernstein: Biography." *Boosey & Hawkes.*
> URL: http://www.ny.boosey.com/pages/Composer/composerbiography.asp?composerid=2730

> *In addition to listing Bernstein's chronology and achievements, this article relates his influence on American composers, his awards, and festivals of his music.*

"Leonard Bernstein: Biography." *Sony Classical.*
> URL: http://www.sonyclassical.com/artists/bernstein/bio.html

> *A brief biography that includes a listing of Bernstein's compositions and significant orchestra appearances.*

"Leonard Bernstein Chronology." *The Leonard Bernstein Collection ca. 1920–1989.*
> URL: http://memory.loc.gov/ammem/lbhtml/lbbio.html

> *This chronology lists major personal and professional events in Bernstein's life.*

"Leonard Bernstein, Lover of Life, Music and People: Biography." *Unitel.*
> URL: http://www.unitel.classicmusic.com/ucatalog/conduct/bios/bernstei.htm

> *Included in this biography of Bernstein are links to videos produced by Unitel of Bernstein conducting and teaching, such as the Berlin Celebration Concert.*

"Omnibus Debut." *Bernstein's Studio.*
  URL: http://www.leonardbernstein.com/studio/element.asp?FeatID=1&AssetID=24

  A description of Bernstein's first television appearance on Omnibus *during which he dissected Beethoven's Fifth Symphony using a depiction of a part of the musical score painted on the floor.*

Historical:

Clement, Roger. "Tidings of Peace and Freedom: A Historic Performance of Beethoven's Ninth in Berlin." *Unitel.*
  URL: http://www.unitel.de/uhilites/1996/121596.htm

  This article describes the concerts conducted by Bernstein on December 23 and 25, 1989 in both formerly East Berlin and West Berlin to commemorate the destruction of the Berlin Wall.

"Tribute to John F. Kennedy, Nov. 25, 1963." *Bernstein's Studio: Events.*
  URL: http://www.leonardbernstein.com/events/news/news_page.asp?id=44

  A speech made by Bernstein at the United Jewish Appeal benefit at Madison Square Garden, New York on November 25, 1963 in which Bernstein praised John F. Kennedy for "the honor in which he held art."

Musical:

"The Bernstein Century: Three American Composers." *Bernstein's Studio.*
  URL: http://www.leonardbernstein.com/studio/element.asp?FeatID=32&AssetID=24

  This article describes three works by three American composers whom Bernstein championed: Aaron Copland, William Schuman, and Lukas Foss.

Bernstein, Leonard. "Excerpts from Bernstein's West Side Logs." *Bernstein's Studio.*
  URL: http://www.leonardbernstein.com/studio/element.asp?id=301

  Bernstein's log describes the process of creating West Side Story.

Bernstein, Leonard. "Young People's Concerts Scripts: What is American Music? [typescript with emendations in red, blue, and black pencil (pg. 16 torn and taped)], February 1, 1958." *The Leonard Bernstein Collection ca. 1920–1989.*
  URL: http://memory.loc.gov/ammem/lbhtml/lbhome.html

  This script of Bernstein's Young People's Concert *is an excellent introduction to the history of American classical music. Search the keyword phrase* what is american music *(match this exact phrase) for the typescript of this program.*

Horowitz, Joseph. "Professor Lenny." *The Leonard Bernstein Collection ca. 1920–1989.*
  URL: http://memory.loc.gov/ammem/lbhtml/lbarticle1.html

  Horowitz explores music appreciation education as it was promoted on radio, recordings and television with its apotheosis in Bernstein's television productions.

"Leonard Bernstein: Discography." *Sony Classical.*
  URL: http://www.sonyclassical.com/artists/bernstein/disc.html

  A discography of Sony recordings of Bernstein as composer or conductor.

Manoff, Tom. "West Side Story (Musical)." *The NPR 100.*
  URL: http://www.npr.org/ramfiles/atc/20000814.atc.06.rmm

  Interviews with playwright Arthur Laurents and Chita Rivera, who created the role of Anita, explore the elements that went into producing the original production of West Side Story. *The ram file is available on* The NPR 100 *web site: http://www.npr.org/programs/specials/vote/100list.html.*

"Overture to Candide, Leonard Bernstein (1918–1990)." *Evening at Pops Program Notes.*
  URL: http://www.pbs.org/wgbh/pops/programnotes/20020707_bernstein.html

  These notes describe the music of Candide *and its reception.*

Books

Bernstein Remembered. Edited by Jane Fluegel. New York: Carroll & Graf, 1991.
This book contains captioned photographs divided into five periods of Bernstein's life. An introduction by Donal Henahan, former chief music critic for The New York Times, *and a chronology provides an overview of Bernstein's life.*

Burton, Humphrey. *Leonard Bernstein.* New York: Anchor Books, Doubleday, 1994.
The chapter "Music Director at the New York Philharmonic" describes Bernstein's role as conductor and educator. "A Kaddish for a President" is about the memorial concert given after President Kennedy's death, and the subsequent premiere of Bernstein's composition Kaddish.

Conversations about Bernstein. Edited and with an Introduction by William Westbrook Burton. New York: Oxford Univ. Press, 1995.
Westbrook interviews composers, critics, musicians, and actors about Bernstein's personality and musical legacy.

Secrest, Meryle. *Leonard Bernstein: A Life.* New York: Alfred A. Knopf, 1994.
Though denied access to the Bernstein archives and to some of his family and friends, Secrest was able to interview many of Bernstein's friends and colleagues for this biography of his personal life. His musical career and compositions also play a large part in the biography.

CDs and Videos

Bernstein, Leonard. *Leonard Bernstein's Young People's Concerts with the New York Philharmonic: What Is American Music?* Broadcast date: February 1, 1958. Produced by Roger Englander. Directed by Charles S. Dubin. A Presentation of the Leonard Bernstein Society, New York. Video Music Education, 1993. SHV57431. VHS.

Bernstein Live. New York: Philharmonic-Symphony Society of New York, 2000. Compact disc. NYP2003.
Includes ten CDs and two books. Book 1 contains program notes on the music and performances, biographical notes on the performers, and English translations of texts. Book 2 contains articles on Bernstein by musicians in the New York Philharmonic who played under his leadership, a listing of all the Bernstein programs with the Philharmonic, his recordings with the Philharmonic, and a brief history of the orchestra. Recordings include Copland's Dance Symphony, *Ives's* Symphony No. 2, *and Copland's* An Outdoor Overture *with an introduction and comments by Bernstein.*

Chapter 21
Charles Ives, 1874–1954
Composer, Insurance Salesman

1899	1920	1922	1924	1939
Joplin's *Maple Leaf Rag* published	*Concord* Sonata published	*114 Songs* published	Gershwin's *Rhapsody in Blue*	*Concord* Sonata first performed

Charles Ives, the "Connecticut Yankee" of American classical music, is positioned outside the continuum of American music. He worked in the insurance industry all his life and wrote music as an avocation in isolation from other professional musicians. Trained in music at Yale University, Ives wrote music based on European classical models, but he was also greatly influenced by his band leader father. Ives's father was fascinated by the elements of sound and included Ives in his sound experiments with tone clusters, polytonality, and polyrhythms. (Swafford)

Ives used these avant garde techniques in his music and juxtaposed them with "borrowings" of melodies from earlier music. These melodies were tunes he had heard during the camp meetings and revivals prevalent during the late nineteenth century in New England. (Crawford, 2001, 513–14) Ives also admired the philosophical views of Emerson and Thoreau of the Transcendental School and applied this philosophy to his approach to composition. (Crawford, 2001, 518) Ives is an anomaly in classical music because he produced daring and innovative works in isolation from the composers of his day.

OBJECTIVES

Students will identify the sense of place and history in the music of Charles Ives.

Students will relate the literary philosophy of Transcendentalism to the music of Ives.

Students will identify and explain the compositional techniques used by Ives.

INTRODUCING THE MUSICIAN

Picture Book

Gerstein, Mordicai. *What Charlie Heard*. New York: Farrar, Straus and Giroux, 2002.

In his text and in the illustrations that are crowded with onomatopoeic sound words, Gerstein shows us what sounds from Ives's childhood became part of his later compositions.

Bernstein on Ives

Introduce Charles Ives by showing students Images 5 and 6 from Leonard Bernstein's "Thursday Evening Previews Scripts: Opening of the New York Philharmonic Season of 1958–59 [typescript with emendations in red, blue & black pencil; marked Afinal], October 2, 1958." (See below.) Ask students to guess what Ives's music will sound like, taking into consideration Bernstein's remarks.

Quotations

- Biographer Jan Swafford:

  For Ives, music is not mere sound but the underlying spirit, human and divine, which the sounds express even in the inexpert playing and singing of amateurs. (Swafford, 1998)

- Ives on Camp Meeting songs:

  I remember, when I was a boy—at the outdoor Camp Meeting services in Redding, all the farmers, their families and field hands, for miles around, would come afoot or in their farm wagons. I remember how the great waves of sound used to come through the trees… Most of them knew the words and music (theirs) by heart, and sang it that way. If they threw the poet or the composer around a bit, so much the better for the poetry and the music. There was power and exaltation in these great conclaves of sound from humanity. (Crawford, 2001, 514)

- Ives on art and its relationship to life:

  You can not set an art off in the corner and hope for it to have vitality, reality, and substance. There can be nothing "exclusive" about a substantial art. It comes directly out of the heart of experience of life and thinking about life and living life. My work in music helped my business and my work in business helped my music. (Rossiter, 1975, 159)

- Composer Aaron Copland in foreword to *Charles Ives Remembered*:

  …no one before him had ever ventured so close to setting down on paper sheer musical chaos. (Pollack, 2000, 111)

- Composer Henry Cowell on the influence of Ives's father:

  The germ of every new type of musical behavior that Charles Ives developed or organized can be found in the suggestions and experiments of his father. (Garber)

- Cowell on Ives's relationship to Transcendentalism:

  …to the Transcendentalist, music is not separate from the rest of the universe but permeates and is in turn permeated by all else that exists. For Ives, music is no more than an expression of the universe than the universe is an expression of music. (Sive, 1977, 67)

- Bernard Herrmann, conductor and composer, on Ives's musical technique:

  Ives had some original expressions. For instance, he would have a kind of simple melody and then a little complicated secondary thing that would run across it like maybe a flute doing something very fast. And he said, "That's what I call shadow counterpoint. It's a shadow that the main thing throws off." (Perlis, 1974, 161)

Connections to Other Musicians in This Book

- In 1951 **Leonard Bernstein** and the New York Philharmonic performed Ives's Second Symphony in Carnegie Hall. (Perlis, 2002, 98) He also featured Ives's music in his Thursday Evening Preview Concerts and his Young People's Concerts with the New York Philharmonic. (Bernstein)

- To develop their musical ears, Ives's father George would have his children sing **Stephen Foster's** "Old Folks at Home" in one key while he accompanied in another key. (Crawford, 2001, 503)

- Ives quoted **Foster's** "Old Folks at Home (Way Down Upon the Swanee River)" in his piece *Washington's Birthday*. (Bernstein, "Young People's Concert")

- Ives heard the **Fisk Jubilee Singers** in a concert at the Opera House in Danbury. (Swafford, 1998, 61)

- **Aaron Copland** programmed many of Ives's pieces and wrote about him in his book *Our New Music* (1941). He also wrote the forward to Vivian Perlis's *Charles Ives Remembered* (1974).

Periods in American History

The Second Great Awakening and Revivalism (late nineteenth century), World War I, 1920s, Great Depression, World War II

Musical Highlights of Ives's Life: Teachers, Colleagues, Events

1874	Born in Danbury, Connecticut
1888	Job as church organist
1892	Wrote *Variations on "America"*
1893	Ives and his Uncle Lyman attended the World's Columbian Exposition
1894	Enrolled in Yale University
1897	Wrote *Prelude and Postlude for a Thanksgiving Service*
1898	Began career in insurance
1909–1915	Wrote the *Concord* Sonata
1920	Self-published *Concord* Sonata and accompanying text *Essays before a Sonata*
1922	Self-published *114 Songs*
1927	Ives met composer and future biographer Henry Cowell
1928	Ives financially supported Cowell's magazine *New Music*
1930	Ives met composer and conductor Nicolas Slonimsky
1939	Performance by pianist John Kirkpatrick of Ives's *Concord* Sonata
1947	Earned Pulitzer Prize for Symphony no. 3
1954	Died in New York City

IVES STUDENT PAGES

Inquiries

- Why did Ives quote well-known tunes in his compositions?

- What musical styles influenced Ives's compositions?

- How did Ives's father influence his music?

- How did Ives's family history and the history of Danbury influence him?

- What is Transcendentalism, and how is it reflected in Ives's music?

- How does Ives reflect Puritanism in his music?

- What was "The Second Great Awakening" and how did it and Revivalism utilize music?

- How did Revivalism influence Ives's compositions?

- What was Ives's opinion of the classical music known at the time, and how did he reflect this in his compositions?

- What was the reaction to the *Concord* Sonata and *114 Songs*, which Ives self-published and sent to people?

- Why did Ives abandon a musical career for the insurance business?

- What other musicians did Ives know? Did they influence his compositions, and if so, how?

- How did Ives's isolation affect his music? What were the advantages and disadvantages to working in isolation?

- What were Ives's views on copyright? How did this viewpoint fit into his views on music?

- What was Ives's role in relation to new music and young American composers?

Products

- After reading Bernstein's analysis of Ives's Symphony no. 2, listen to the CD, find as many tunes as you can, and play them for the class.

- Consider the following quote from Ives in his "conductor's note" to the second movement of his Fourth Symphony:
  As the eye, in looking at a view, may focus on the sky, clouds or distant outlines, yet sense the color and form of the foreground, and then, by bringing the eye to the foreground, sense the distant outlines and color, so, in some similar way can the listener choose to arrange in his mind the relation of the rhythmic, harmonic, and other

material. *In other words, in music the ear may play a role similar to the eye in the above instance. (Crawford, 2001, 518)*
Explain how this quote relates to Ives's music and present examples from his music.

- Compare the philosophy of the Transcendental writers with that of Ives. Explain how this philosophy can be expressed in music.

- Using quotations from Thoreau's *Walden* and Emerson's *Self-Reliance,* explain how Ives's life and music reflect these philosophies.

- Describe "The Second Great Awakening" and its use of music. Explain how this music influenced Ives's compositions. Include musical examples.

- Search the *American Memory* sheet music collections and gather the sheet music for the songs quoted by Ives in his compositions. Play these pieces and compare them to the excerpts in Ives's music.

- Using Bernstein's program scripts find the pieces by Ives that have "borrowed tunes." Present these musical examples and discuss the reasons for including these tunes.

- Investigate *program music* and discuss whether this style of music is expressed in Ives's music.

- Prepare a list of the innovative compositional techniques that Ives used in his pieces and include examples from his music.

- Present an explanation of the story behind Ives's piece *From Hanover Square North, at the End of a Tragic Day, the Voice of the People Again Arose.*

RESEARCH RESOURCES

Web Sites
Biographical:

Hampson, Thomas. "Charles Edward Ives, 1874–1954." *I Hear America Singing.*
    URL: http://www.pbs.org/wnet/ihas/composer/ives.html

A short biography that delineates the influences on Ives's music and information on his 114 Songs. *The site includes Real Audio for* Circus Band *and* The Housatonic at Stockbridge.

Sudik, Nancy F. "Charles Ives: Danbury's Most Famous Composer." *Charles Ives: Father of American Music.* Housatonic Valley Tourism District.
    URL: http://www.housatonic.org/ives.html

Sudik describes the various sounds that Ives included in his music, the composers that promoted his music, and his interest in Transcendentalism.

Swafford, Jan. "Charles Edward Ives." *The Charles Ives Society, Inc.*
    URL: http://www.charlesives.org/02bio.htm

Swafford describes Ives's life in music, including the musical influence of his father, George.

Swafford, Jan. "Charles Ives." *peermusic classical.*
    URL: http://www.peermusic.com/classical/ivesessay.htm

Same essay as above.

Swafford, Jan. "Charles Ives: A Life with Music." *washingtonpost.com.*

URL: http://www.washingtonpost.com/wp-srv/style/longterm/books/chap1/ives.htm

In this first chapter of his book Swafford describes the history of Charles Ives's birthplace, Danbury, Connecticut, and some of his family history beginning with his great-grandfather, Isaac Ives.

Historical:

Hampson, Thomas. "The Great Awakening and Revivalism in America." *I Hear American Singing.*
URL: http://www.pbs.org/wnet/ihas/icon/revivalism.html

Hampson describes the camp meetings in the late nineteenth century and mentions Putnam's Campground near Danbury, Connecticut, where Charles Ives listened to the sermons and the music.

Schwartz, Steve. "Charles Ives: 'Concord' Sonata." *Classical Net.*
URL: http://www.classical.net/music/recs/reviews/r/rgy87078a.html

Schwartz defines Transcendentalism and describes Ives's Concord Sonata *and its relationship to that theory.*

Musical:

"American Memory Collections: All Collections." *American Memory: Historical Collections for the National Digital Library.*
URL: http://memory.loc.gov/ammem/mdbquery.html

Search for songs quoted in Ives's music by using the title of the song as the keyword search (match this exact phrase).

Arnowitt, Michael. "Charles Ives: The Concord Sonata." *Michael Arnowitt Home Page.*
URL: http://www.sover.net/~arnowitt/concord.htm

This description of classical pianist Arnowitt's program featuring Ives's Concord Sonata *lists the literary writings of the Transcendentalists that were the inspiration for the four movements. The authors are Ralph Waldo Emerson, Nathaniel Hawthorne, Louisa May Alcott and the Alcott family, and Henry David Thoreau.*

Bernstein, Leonard. "Thursday Evening Previews Scripts: Opening of the New York Philharmonic Season of 1958–59 [typescript with emendations in red, blue & black pencil; marked Afinal], October 2, 1958." *The Leonard Bernstein Collection, ca. 1920–1989.*
URL: http://memory.loc.gov/ammem/lbhtml/lbhome.html

Choose "Ives, Charles, 1874–1954" in the Name Index.
Bernstein's description of Ives's music, in particular his Symphony no. 2.

Bernstein, Leonard. "Young People's Concerts Scripts: Charles Ives: American Pioneer [typescript on pink paper plus 3 mimeo on pink & 2 on white, emendations in pencil], February 23, 1967." *The Leonard Bernstein Collection, ca. 1920–1989.*
URL: http://memory.loc.gov/ammem/lbhtml/lbhome.html

Choose "Ives, Charles, 1874–1954" in the Name Index.

The script from a program by Bernstein and the New York Philharmonic that included the Ives pieces: The Gong on the Hook and Ladder or Firemen's Parade on Main Street; Washington's Birthday; Circus Band March; Lincoln: The Great Commoner; *and* The Unanswered Question.

Copland, Aaron. "Charles Ives [unpublished writings]." *The Aaron Copland Collection, ca. 1900–1990.*
URL: http://memory.loc.gov/ammem/achtml/achome.html

Search with keywords charles ives. *(The third entry is a two-page document written for the* American People's Encyclopedia, *July 1964. The first two entries are the drafts.) Copland describes Ives's contributions to American music and his relationship to the New England writers of the Transcendental school of thought.*

Garber, J. Ryan. "The Influence of George Ives on His Son Charles." *Classical Music Pages Quarterly*, June 1996.

URL: http://w3.rz-berlin.mpg.de/cmp/ives_fathers_influence.html

Describes the musical elements that George Ives experimented with and examples of their use by his son Charles in his compositions.

Gutmann, Peter. "America's Greatest Composer." *Classical Notes.*
   URL: http://www.classicalnotes.net/columns/ives.html

Gutmann describes Ives's music and lists recommended recordings.

Herrmann, Bernard. "Charles Ives." *Trend: A Quarterly of the Seven Arts.* Sept.–Oct.–Nov. 1932. *The Bernard Herrmann Society.* 1997.
   URL: http://www.uib.no/herrmann/articles/archive/trend/

Herrmann, a conductor who championed Ives's works, wrote this article while Ives was still living. In it he discusses Ives's importance in American music and discusses the second piano sonata, Concord Mass., *and the Fourth Symphony.*

Key, Susan. "Maverick Icons." *American Mavericks Program Notes.*
   URL: http://www.americanmavericks.com/prog_notes/june_09.html

In her extensive analysis of Ives's Symphony no. 4, Key describes the influence of the Transcendental authors, especially in the role of nature in Ives's music.

Books

Cowell, Henry, and Sidney Cowell. *Charles Ives and His Music.* London: Oxford University Press, 1969.
Composer Henry Cowell and his wife Sidney originally wrote this book in 1955 while Ives was still living. The Cowells championed Ives's music and Ives contributed his music and financial support to their musical journal, New Music. *The Cowells analyze Ives's music, in particular* Paracelsus, Sonata No. 2, *and* Universe *Symphony.*

Crawford, Richard. "To Stretch Our Ears, The Music of Charles Ives." In *America's Musical Life: A History.* New York: W. W. Norton, 2001.
Crawford describes the musical influence of Ives's father George and analyzes Ives's music, in particular, six songs from his 114 Songs.

Perlis, Vivian. *Charles Ives Remembered: An Oral History.* Foreword by J. Peter Burkholder. Urbana: Univ. of Illinois Press, 2002.
Perlis includes fifty-eight interviews with people who knew Ives, including relatives, friends, and musicians. This paperback reprint of the original 1974 book also includes the original foreword by Aaron Copland.

Pollack, Howard. *Aaron Copland: The Life and Work of an Uncommon Man.* Urbana: Univ. of Illinois Press, 2000.
Use the index to find references to Ives and his music.

Rossiter, Frank R. *Charles Ives & His America.* New York: Liveright, 1975.
Rossiter divides his biography of Ives into two parts: Development, 1874–1921, and Recognition, 1921–1974. In addition to recounting Ives personal and musical life, Rossiter also relates Ives's "Americanness" to the culture and philosophies of the times. In the last chapter "Epilogue: An Interpretation" Rossiter compares Ives ideas with those of the Soviet composers, such as Shostakovich and Prokofiev.

Sive, Helen R. *Music's Connecticut Yankee: An Introduction to the Life and Music of Charles Ives.* New York: Atheneum, 1977.
A short, clear, and easy-to-read biography.

Swafford, Jan. *Charles Ives: A Life with Music.* New York: W. W. Norton, 1998.
Swafford combines Ives's personal biography with a study of his music in this comprehensive biography.

CDs

Ives, Charles. *Symphony No. 2.* New York Philharmonic. Leonard Bernstein. Deutsche Grammophon, 1990. 429 220–2.
Also includes the Gong on the Hook and Ladder or Firemen's Parade on Main Street, Tone Roads no. 1, Hymn: Largo Cantabile, Hallowe'en, Central Park in the Dark, *and* The Unanswered Question.

Ives, Charles. *Symphony No. 3 ("The Camp Meeting"); Orchestral Set No. 2.* Concertgebouw Orchestra. Michael Tilson Thomas, Dir. CBS Records Masterworks, 1985. MK 37823.

Appendix A
Stephen Foster Songs Analysis Guide

Title of Song:

Date of Publication:

What is the subject of the song? Who is the audience? Who is the singer?

Describe the types of words in the song. What is the mood of the song? Is there dialect? Does the song tell a story?

What is the form of the song? Is there a verse or chorus? Are they of equal length?

What types of rhythmic figures are in the song? Are they simple or complicated? Give examples.

Describe the melody. Are the phrases long or short? Give examples.

Appendix B
Spirituals Analysis Guide

Title of Song:

Composer/Lyricist:

Date:

Place of Publication:

TEXT:
What is the subject of the text? Is the composer known? Do any lines repeat? Is there a pattern?

MUSIC:
Is the rhythm simple or complicated? Are there many dotted rhythms or tied notes? Where is the strong beat? Is there syncopation? List examples of complicated rhythms. Is there evidence of *call and response*?

Does the melody move stepwise or are there large intervals between notes? Is there one note per word or do some words have many notes? List examples.

Appendix C
Civil War Songs Analysis Guide

Title of Song:

Composer:

Date and Place of Publication:

Is it a Union or Confederate song? How can you tell? Could changing a few words change it to the other side?

What is the subject of the song? Is it sympathetic toward war, or not? What words give this information?

Who is the audience for this song? Does the song have a persuasive viewpoint?

What type of song is it? What emotions does the song elicit?

Index

About the Author

Donna B. Levene has been an elementary and high school library media specialist in the Cherry Creek School District of Colorado since 1988 and is currently at Overland High School in Aurora, Colorado. In the summer of 1999 she was one of 50 educators selected to participate in the Library of Congress American Memory Fellows Program. Using the digitized resources in the American Memory collections, she and a social studies teacher developed an online lesson plan on women's suffrage. Ms. Levene has a Masters in Library Science degree from the University of Denver and a Bachelor of Fine Arts degree in Piano Performance from the University of Wisconsin–Milwaukee. She continues to study the piano repertoire and performs as a soloist and accompanist as an alumna of Delta Omicron International Music Fraternity.